FROM
TO COCAINE...

Answers to Questions

RUDOLF STEINER

*Eighteen discussions with workers at
the Goetheanum in Dornach between
19 October 1922 and 10 February 1923*

RUDOLF STEINER PRESS
LONDON

Translation revised by Matthew Barton

Rudolf Steiner Press
51 Queen Caroline Street
London W6 9QL

www.rudolfsteinerpress.com

Published by Rudolf Steiner Press 2000
Previous English edition translated by Maria St Goar and published
under the title *Health and Illness*, Volumes 1 and 2, by Anthroposophic
Press, New York 1981 and 1983

Originally published in German under the title *Über Gesundheit und
Krankheit, Grundlagen einer geisteswissenschaftlichen Sinneslehre* (volume
348 in the *Rudolf Steiner Gesamtausgabe* or Collected Works) by Rudolf
Steiner Verlag, Dornach. This authorized (abridged) translation is based
on the 4th edition, edited by Paul Gerhard Bellman and J. Waeger, and is
published by kind permission of the Rudolf Steiner Nachlassverwaltung,
Dornach. All drawings in the text are by Leonore Uhlig and are based on
Rudolf Steiner's original blackboard drawings

Translation © Rudolf Steiner Press 2000

A catalogue record for this book is available from the British Library

ISBN 1 85584 088 X

Cover by Andrew Morgan Design
Typeset by DP Photosetting, Aylesbury, Bucks.
Printed and bound in Great Britain by Cromwell Press Limited,
Trowbridge, Wilts.

Contents

Main Contents of the Discussions

Foolishness of Kant-Laplace theory. Gout. Breathing, correctly understood, throws light on birth and death. Immortal soul element must be comprehended by those active in science. All healing based on expelling earthly influences that afflict the sick person. Without a science of the spirit, mankind does away with the living Christ and retains only the cross of Christ.

9 *Discussion of 27 December 1922*
Why do we become sick? Influenza, hay fever, mental illness
Every act of drinking or eating is an act of healing. Hunger is a soul-spiritual activity that cannot be stilled. Work of the astral body in dissolving food and distributing substances to the various organs. Astral body can become stupid and deposit substances in the wrong place, contaminating the fluid organization and leading to illness. Bacilli not necessary for one person to catch flu from another. Pollen does not cause hay fever but aggravates it. The greatest medical art lies in asking the right questions. Mental illnesses not mental at all but based on improper evaporation of body fluids that mingle with oxygen and disturb the nervous system. Dementia praecox originates mainly from the wrong kind of feeding during the earliest years of childhood.

10 *Discussion of 30 December 1922*
Fever versus shock. Pregnancy
Abdomen and forebrain; heart and midbrain; lungs and hindbrain. Henbane can cause shock but, in minute dosage, can heal digestive disorders. The head and fever. Craving for different tastes and smells in early pregnancy. Materialism introduced by England's philosophers caused by constipation! Spiritual arrogance. God reveals himself through abdominal activity. Forebrain and will; midbrain and feeling; hindbrain and thinking/breathing. Influence of mother's condition of soul on developing child. A shock to the mother can cause dire results in the unborn child. Warmth spreads from the head downwards and cold spreads upwards from below; these two streams meet in abdomen, which must be cared for in right way. Ambiguity of concept of heredity. Materialism stems from the Church of the Middle Ages. Necessity to ascend from nature to spirit.

11   *Discussion of 5 January 1923*
     ## The brain and thinking
     Fire at the Goetheanum and hatred towards the anthroposophical movement. Authority of science. Nonsense that the brain thinks. The burying-beetle, wasps and other insects do not owe their intelligence to having a large brain. Newly hatched maggots are already clever. Suppression of facts by nineteenth-century scientists. What works as intelligence through the human head is at work everywhere. Wasps and paper. Thanks to his brain, man can utilize for his own benefit the intelligence contained in all things. The claim that intelligence is produced by the brain is as foolish as claiming that water from a pond is produced by its container. Soul-spiritual element of man that collects the intelligence. The spleen as regulator. Anthroposophy slandered out of a spirit of pure falsehood.

12   *Discussion of 8 January 1923*
     ## The effects of alcohol
     Hangover produced by waste products in the head. 'Curing' the hangover by morning drinking merely drives it into the rest of the body. Delirium tremens. Blood-letting. Alcohol pre-eminently attacks the blood. Ruinous process only begins when alcohol attacks the bone marrow, which produces red and white corpuscles. Marked difference between men and women as regards their blood. Red corpuscles more important for the woman and white for the man. Effects of alcohol on human reproductive capacity. Man's drinking harms the child's nervous system, the woman's drinking harms the child's inner organs. Embryo harmed from two different sides when both parents drink. Effect on human development of minute amounts of substances. Corroded jaws of workmen who produced phosphorus matches. By gradually penetrating the bone marrow, alcohol ruins the blood and harms the offspring and future descendants. Long-term negative effect manifests in many generations. Effects of prohibition. Alcohol benign compared to effect of cocaine addiction on human reproductive forces. Enlightening explanations bring people to refrain from alcohol without infringing human freedom. Laws work only on the intellect, real insights work on feeling.

13   *Discussion of 10 January 1923*
      The power of intelligence as the effect of the sun.
      Beaver lodges and wasps' nests
      Construction of dams and lodges using front paws and sharp teeth.
      Cleverness of beavers when they congregate is brought about first
      by winter and second by night. Correct thinking comes from
      allowing facts to guide one. Wasps hatched in spring are sterile and
      work all summer long constructing cells. In autumn male and
      female wasps emerge from eggs laid in the summer. This shows
      how the sex life of animals is connected with the year's course.
      Sun's light and heat destroy reproductive tendencies in the wasp.
      Along with sunlight and warmth the beaver gathers intelligence
      during the summer in its single burrow. This it can use to build its
      villages together with other beavers in the autumn. Beavers' tails
      their most ingenious aspect for they store their accumulated intel-
      ligence in them, thus forming the communal brain of the beaver
      colony. The wasps' nests, as well as the beavers' constructions, built
      by the cleverness that flows to earth from the sun. People conceived
      in spring and born the following winter tend to acquire forces of
      intelligence more easily than those born at other times. Beer less
      harmful for the reproductive organs than wine and hard liquor,
      because the sun's effects then work as an internal poison.

14   *Discussion of 13 January 1923*
      The effects of nicotine. Vegetarian and meat diets. On
      taking absinthe. Twin births
      Effect of nicotine on blood circulation, making it go faster. Blood
      demands too much oxygen, resulting in shortness of breath.
      Anxiety — thickening of heart — illness of kidneys. Power of thought
      undermined. People with weak blood circulation can benefit from
      smoking. Osteoclasts in the bones find fertile ground when nicotine
      is introduced into the body. If an ox were to consume meat directly,
      it would go mad. Meat eaters less gentle than plant eaters. A
      vegetarian uses forces that are left unused in meat-eaters. The
      English and sugar consumption. Kosher cooking follows ancient
      Mosaic dietary laws — prohibition of pork that aggravates diabetes.
      Taking the baths at Karlsbad purges the system of waste products.
      Absinthe more damaging than ordinary alcohol because it ruins
      sleep. The effects of phases of the moon on twin births. Triplets and
      quadruplets.

A haemophiliac man can marry a woman who is not and their children will be without haemophilia. A daughter, however, can pass on the disease to her children even though she does not have it herself. Haemophilia thus passes to descendants by way of the female line. Importance of administering a lead remedy in pregnancy to counteract haemophilia. Ether active in fluid element, the soul in the air element. Effect of absinthe prevents the soul from working on the body's organs in the right way. Male absinthe drinkers produce children who are weaklings, female drinkers children susceptible to disease. Days of the week named after the planets. Glaciers in Europe. Influences from the stars when it snows in winter help us to mould ourselves in the right way. Absinthe drinking prevents this. Barbarian invasions renewed whole of western civilization when Roman culture declined. Tendency to hold on to declining Latin language. Bees completely given up to the influence of the planet Venus; they live in an atmosphere pervaded by love. The benefits of eating honey.

18   *Discussion of 10 February 1923*
The relationship between the planets and the metals and their healing effects

Mercury as a cure for syphilis. In ancient times the planets were looked upon quite differently. Copper as a remedy for typhoid-like illnesses aggravated by Venus. Eye ailments linked to Jupiter counteracted by tin. Bone diseases — Saturn — lead. Mars and iron. Moon and silver. Knowledge founded on ancient observations. A modern chemist can make nothing of the writings of Basilius Valentinus who knew of the ancient cosmic connections. Suppression of this knowledge by the Church. Metals extracted from plants especially effective in healing. Modern books on botany lack the most important facts for medical men — they do not mention what metals are dissolved in the blossoms or roots. Lack of a healing instinct in modern people. Abdominal illnesses are best healed by the blossoms and leaves of plants, the head by plant roots. An entire plant is contained within man. The human being is connected with the natural history of the whole earth.

Publisher's Foreword

The truly remarkable lectures — or, more accurately, question and answer sessions — contained in this book, form part of a series (published in eight volumes in the original German)* dating from August 1922 to September 1924. This series features talks given to people involved in various kinds of building work on Rudolf Steiner's architectural masterpieces, the first and second Goetheanums in Dornach, Switzerland. (The destruction by fire of the first Goetheanum necessitated the building of a replacement.) A vivid description of the different types of workers present, as well as the context and atmosphere of these talks, is given by a witness in the Appendix to the first volume of this English series, *From Elephants to Einstein* (1998).

The sessions arose out of explanatory tours of the Goetheanum which one of Steiner's pupils, Dr Roman Boos, had offered. When this came to an end, and the workers still wished to know more about the 'temple' they were involved with and the philosophy behind it, Dr Steiner agreed to take part in question and answer sessions himself. These took place during the working day, after the mid-morning break. Apart from the workmen, only a few other people were present: those working in the building office, and some of Steiner's closest colleagues. The subject-matter of the talks was chosen by the workers at the encouragement of Rudolf Steiner, who took their questions and usually gave immediate answers.

---

* 347–354 in the collected works of Rudolf Steiner, published by Rudolf Steiner Verlag, Dornach, Switzerland. For information on English translations, see the list on page xv.

After Rudolf Steiner's death, some of the lectures — on the subject of bees — were published. However, as Marie Steiner writes in her original Preface to the German edition: 'Gradually more and more people felt a wish to study these lectures.' It was therefore decided to publish them in full. However, Marie Steiner's words about the nature of the lectures remain relevant to the present publication:

> They had, however, been intended for a particular group of people and Rudolf Steiner spoke off the cuff, in accord with the given situation and the mood of the workmen at the time. There was no intention to publish at the time. But the very way in which he spoke had a freshness and directness that one would not wish to destroy, taking away the special atmosphere that arose in the souls of those who asked the questions and him who gave the answers. It would be a pity to take away the special colour of it by pedantically rearranging the sentences. We are therefore taking the risk of leaving them as far as possible untouched. Perhaps it will not always be in the accustomed literary style, but on the other hand it has directness and vitality.

In this spirit, the translator has been asked also to preserve as much of the original style, or flavour, as possible. This might necessitate that readers study a passage again, trying to bring to mind the live situation in which the talks were given, before the whole can be fully appreciated.

S G

Rudolf Steiner's Lectures to Workers at the Goetheanum

GA (*Gesamtausgabe*) number

347 *The Human Being in Body, Soul and Spirit* (New York/London: Anthroposophic Press/Rudolf Steiner Press 1989). Revised translation forthcoming, Rudolf Steiner Press

348 *From Comets to Cocaine, Answers to Questions* (London: Rudolf Steiner Press 2000)

349 *From Limestone to Lucifer, Answers to Questions* (London: Rudolf Steiner Press 1999)

350 *From Mammoths to Mediums, Answers to Questions* (London: Rudolf Steiner Press 2000)

351 Nine of the 15 lectures in the German edition are published in *Bees, Nine lectures on the Nature of Bees* (New York: Anthroposophic Press 1998)

352 *From Elephants to Einstein, Answers to Questions* (London: Rudolf Steiner Press 1998)

353 *From Beetroot to Buddhism, Answers to Questions* (London: Rudolf Steiner Press 1999)

354 *The Evolution of the Earth and Man and the Influence of the Stars* (New York/London: Anthroposophic Press/Rudolf Steiner Press 1987). Revised translation forthcoming, Rudolf Steiner Press

The world situation. Causes of illness

Dr Steiner: Good morning, gentlemen! Have any of you thought of something you would like to ask me?

Question: Concerning the political situation, is Britain sincere in its dealings with Germany, or is it actually conspiring with France to destroy her? On the one side stand the French trying to suppress Germany with reparations, and on the other stand the big capitalists. It is the same with Russia. We know that Germany has made a trade agreement with her, but now we learn that France, too, has made one with Russia. Was this done to sabotage the German agreement? Are you perhaps in a position to make a few remarks on these and other German affairs?

Dr Steiner: Well, gentlemen, perhaps this is the reason why lately we have been more inclined to speak about scientific matters than to discuss political problems. It is much wiser to do so for the simple reason that all these affairs you have touched upon lead to absolutely nothing. In reality, nothing at all can come of them. Just look at the present situation. Basically, none of the protagonists know where they're heading; everything they do is done from fear, is really a product of fear.

Other things are much more important than all these matters that are based, for example, on the fact that England does not know what it ought to be doing at the moment. England cannot turn her back on France because in England the opinion prevails that promises must be kept. It is the general attitude over there that a person is obliged to keep his promises. But to what extent this notion is sincere — well, that's something that has nothing much to do with actual circumstances. Sincerity pertains only to individual human beings. In regard to public life the most we can say is that a kind of basic principle of 'fair play' is acknowledged, that promises must be kept. One must play the game by the rules of fair play. Therefore England quite naturally takes the position that she cannot desert the old Entente, yet this stand contradicts the whole purpose of the war, which was to shift industrial production towards the West and to suppress the economies of Eastern and Central Europe, to turn these areas into markets. This was, in fact, the war's original intention. The economy of Central Europe — and the same would have eventually held true of Eastern Europe as well — was much too prosperous to suit people in the West; they simply didn't want things that way.

Now in England this view exists side by side with another. If Germany is totally suppressed, a needed export market is lost. On the other hand, the French, above all else, feel their lack of money and purchasing power. Their only objective is to squeeze profits out of Germany by hook or by crook. You can understand now that the English are falling between two stools and, as a result, don't accomplish much of anything. They swing back and forth. If they think that Germany has been hurt a bit too much, then a little something is done here or there to brighten the general mood again.

In the affairs of the Middle East, England and France are right now in sharp confrontation. England must push back the Turks because she wants to dominate the world. Granted, the English are is protecting the Christians, but how sincere their motives are something we needn't consider. At the moment, France is not interested in that cause. First and foremost the French want an influx of money, and for this reason they support the Turks. In the Middle East, then, these two powers are squared off. Basically, world politics everywhere are in a state of chaos today.

Added to all this is something else especially evident in England just now. With this we come to the really important issue, and many people should realize its importance. Everything that is publically aired and debated is actually of very little importance. What Lloyd George or anybody else says matters not in the least; it is all at odds with the facts. Of course, it isn't done consciously; people imagine they are talking about the issues, but in fact they are bypassing them. Another matter, however, is of much greater significance. In England, Lloyd George is the centre of a controversy. Should he or should he not remain in office? Now, why is the position of such a man, who can express himself most eloquently in public, so precarious? Quite simply, he no longer has strong party support; his backing is minimal. Yet, what would happen if Lloyd George were replaced? The minister taking his position would himself soon be ousted. Lloyd George has to be retained solely because he has no qualified successors. The crux of the matter is that no new people of real ability are coming along, and so we must settle for individuals whose past performances are a matter of public knowledge, because people can no longer discern whether or not candidates are competent and have a real grasp of the issues.

Not even the Social Democratic Party can find capable people any more. It just continues to support the old guard and shuts the door against aspiring younger members. Because everywhere people cannot recognize human ability, grey-beards, who have lost the faculty to comprehend the present situation, are being kept in office. This is why nothing is accomplished anywhere! So today it doesn't matter what party a person joins; what matters is that we bring about an environment from which individuals arise who have insight into existing conditions and whose words and actions are based only on facts. People's awareness for what is required diminishes daily. Comments like, 'Well, it would be better if the English did this, the French that, and the Germans and the Turks thus and so,' are so much idle chatter. Whatever is done merely from the standpoint of the past cannot succeed.

Take an issue of the last few days. You'll agree that Germany has suffered greatly from speculation in foreign currency. Even schoolboys have bought foreign money and have 'made deals' in foreign exchange. Somebody with 50 marks one day could buy foreign currency and have 75 the next. Huge sums of money could be made from speculation. So what does the German government do? As you know, it passed an emergency law controlling speculation in foreign currency. Now, let's assume that the government agencies are so clever that they themselves can succeed in speculation. I don't believe they are, but let's assume so. In the next few weeks there would then be less private trading in foreign currencies in Germany. It is no exaggeration that boys 13 and 14 years old were trading in foreign money. What would happen if all this were stopped for a few weeks? A huge gap would arise between the price of necessities like groceries and the amount of money people could afford to spend on them. For example, in Germany today one cigarette costs seven marks. Well, people will pay that amount. Why? Because of the speculation in foreign money. You know that an old man today can't afford seven marks for a cigarette, but young people who have made all kinds of money speculating can. Now, if this source of income were cut off, soon no one would be able to buy a good cigarette. This is just one aspect of the matter; another is that wages would have to be lowered in the cigarette industry. Then you would have the discrepancy of consumer goods being kept at their former prices and consumers unable to afford them. A new crisis would arise, and this is, in fact, just around the corner.

Everything is done on the spur of the moment, which

ensures that one crisis follows another — and all this because people see only what is closest at hand. No results can be achieved in this manner. The only way to get out of the present chaotic situation is to have competent people in office again. To achieve anything we must have people who know what they're doing, but present conditions tell us that nowhere are capable persons being trained or educated. So we must see to it that we start educating people again in a way that makes them capable. Things won't progress by the clichés and vacuities people utter; all this is worthless. Just look at any newspaper. You may even happen to like one because it represents your party, but regardless of their political persuasions the facts they publish are worthless and lead to nothing. For this reason it's almost a waste of time to occupy oneself with world politics; the field is barren. The only thing that needs to be considered is that once again education should produce competent people. Competence is what we should aim for because today nobody knows anything.

Those powers confronting the Europeans know the most. The Turks, for example, know exactly what they want, as do the Japanese. They want to further their own cultures, solely their own. Strangely enough, Europeans are indifferent about theirs. You can see now why one is reticent to talk about politics. It's like going to a party and discovering that everyone is indulging in platitudes — you lose interest in joining in. That's pretty much the situation in politics these days.

Not long ago Lloyd George delivered a speech. If you want to give a figurative description of it and you said it resembled a pile of chaff in which a few grains of wheat yet remained, then this comparison would not be quite accurate. You should say, rather, that there was no substance to it at all, that every last grain had been flailed out. Only then would we have a true picture of the speech Lloyd George gave a few days ago. Yet, I can say without a moment's hesitation that it was the most significant address delivered by a statesman in recent weeks. You see, even though his speech was vapid, he did have his fist where his mouth was. He did not actually do so, but one can imagine him pounding the table every so often. That's one thing he can do. His words are empty, but there is something in his fist.

It's the same everywhere. I've stopped reading the speeches of Wirth, because the few lines that appear on the front page of the Basel newspaper tell me enough. It's quite clear that his whole speech amounts to nothing. It's all so much hot air, and it's pointless to become elated or depressed about any of it. The thing is, anyone who is really sincere in his regard for humanity must say to himself that everything hinges on our finding competent people who can understand something of the world's problems and who can think, truly think.

For if one considers the remarks of Lloyd George—and perhaps he is actually the most capable of all these politicians—one discovers that he has *never had an original thought*. He can hold on to his position just *because* he has no thoughts. Thus, he can vacillate in one or the other direction and what he says is really trite. Were he ever to utter a thought, were the Union Party, the Conservative Party and the Labour Party to discover where they all stood with him, he would, of course, be thrown out of office. His whole skill consists in speaking in such a way that the others can't discern how they fare with him. If somebody's speech is continually inane, no one knows what to make of it. His great asset is his lack of thoughts, one he can only make use of because he himself does not know where he stands.

These are the conditions today, but this wasn't the case a few years ago. Two or three years ago one always had to say, 'Something must be done before it's too late.' But now it is too late. Nothing can be suggested because we've missed the boat; it's simply too late. The most I can say is that things will improve only when qualified, competent people again enter public life. Germany and Russia can sign as many treaties as they want but nothing will come of them. It isn't a question of signing treaties but of unfolding a healthy economic life.

The Stinnes conglomerate is a good example. Do you think for a moment that Mr Stinnes could accomplish anything within the German labour force? Of course not; that's impossible. Stinnes is an industrialist who has advanced through skilful manipulation of foreign currency. But that is all he knows, how to advance himself, nothing else. Many people today have noticed that the government is getting nowhere, that all its treaties have had no effect on the economy. Since Stinnes acts independently of the government, the results are probably better, some say, but in any event his ideas are based solely on the manipulation of his interests in Germany and France. This is their only basis. Look at the Stinnes agreements and you'll see what heavy financing they would require. What Stinnes intends to do must be financed somehow. Things are at such a pass, however, that to finance such ventures would just about deplete all one's resources, would mean felling all Austria's forests.

Naturally, a person can *talk* about all the things he would like to do when in reality none of them can succeed. As soon as he tries to carry one out, it won't work. People have seen that government treaties lead nowhere, no economic growth results from them. Stinnes's ventures are independent of government help so it is hoped that they will produce results. But it won't work. It doesn't matter that he naturally works arm in arm with other big capitalists. His plans cannot be realized because even he will not be able to finance them. Hence Stinnes offers no solution.

Journalists are fascinated by the columns of figures he

manipulates, and you see, gentlemen, when they write their editorials or feature sections, they are under no obligation; they can say whatever they please. You probably haven't saved them, but if you compare the articles written in 1912 with those written today in the same paper, you will discover a curious thing. After all, newspaper articles are ephemeral, no one gives them a second thought, and so journalists can make them as 'interesting' as they like. Anyone who feels responsible for his statements, however, and does not fabricate articles at random knows that all of them are nothing but rubbish. This is the situation everywhere. Because people have no original ideas things have become desperate. Above all else we need original thoughts, new ideas; without these everything will go to ruin.

In Germany today it takes 215 marks to buy a toothbrush. But what are 215 marks? Not even one franc! This sounds cheap to us here, but where does a German get 215 marks? Other consumer goods are proportionately more expensive. Today no one can afford an umbrella, but it can't be helped. When I was in Vienna I once went by taxi because I was in a hurry and it happened to be a holiday. The distance was half a mile, no more. The fare, gentlemen, was 3,600 kronas! Today it would be ten times that. The same ride would cost 36,000 kronas. This is obviously absurd, but other things are equally so, even if people don't know it. For what is done to remedy this situation? If a short taxi ride costs 36,000 kronas, notes worth 500,000 kronas will be printed, and if it costs 360,000 kronas, notes worth one million will be issued. But such measures have no effect on economic life. Nothing is altered except that those who have a little money in their pockets today have nothing tomorrow, and those who speculate cleverly have double their former amount. But speculation with currency accomplishes nothing as far as the foreign currency exchange market is concerned. It merely enables some people to make money without thought or effort, and when work comes to a halt in the world, hampered by usurious speculation, then things will have indeed reached breaking point. So it accomplishes nothing at all. People simply have to realize that capable persons with insight into the affairs of the world must again take things in hand; there is no other way forward.

To accomplish this we must start with the right kind of education. Today people must begin to learn to understand the world in school. The other day I was reading a textbook that recommended a certain problem in arithmetic, and when I describe it you'll say, 'So what?' But the arithmetic problem posed in this textbook is something of utmost importance. It goes like this:

One person is $85\frac{2}{12}$ years old
Another is $\quad 18\frac{7}{12}$ years old
Another is $\quad 36\frac{4}{12}$ years old
Another is $\quad 33\frac{5}{12}$ years old

What is the total number of years of these four persons?

The children are asked to add all this together; this is what the textbook recommends. Of course, they will do so and arrive at the total of $173\frac{6}{12}$ years. Now I ask you, gentlemen, what bearing has this sum on reality? When would you ever need to figure out something like this? For the problem to have any meaning at all, it would have to be posed so that the first person happened to die just when the second was born, and the third died when the last was born. How many years elapsed from the birth of the first person to the death of the last? The former problem is unrealistic; no one will ever have to figure it out in actuality. Giving children problems like this amounts to giving them the most abstract arithmetic imaginable. Children are required to apply their good sense to working out things that are quite unreal.

the person who dreamed up this problem knew no more than that things could be added up. Now let's consider this case. Someone was born on a certain date, went to school until he was $14\frac{1}{2}$ years old and then served as an apprentice for $5\frac{1}{2}$ years. Following that, he worked under various masters for 3 years and then got married. Four years later he had a son, and when the son was 22, the father died. By adding up the years we arrive at the man's age, which is 49. This is something concrete, something real. Children are led out into real life when they are given problems like this and this applies to all situations. Otherwise, they sit for an hour over something that never occurs in actuality, but no one is shocked by this. If you point this out to people, they reply, 'It doesn't matter how children learn arithmetic.' They don't think it's terribly important. But it happens to be of prime importance, for the people who read rubbish in textbooks as children will eventually spout it as adults; they'll talk nonsense, nothing but nonsense.

From all this you can understand the need for a renewal in education. The educational method I have spoken of bases everything on reality; from the very beginning it leads the human being into reality. This is what actually counts, and this is also why conditions will invariably worsen if people do things as they have in the past. You can start as many newspapers as you like, but if they are written in the same tired spirit, the same chaos will remain. This is why it is so important today for us to occupy ourselves with matters that will turn people into thinking human beings. For this to happen, however, we must see to it that teachers and textbooks do not present arithmetic problems like the one cited but only those that apply to life. Unfortunately, children are also learning languages, science and social studies in that unrealistic way. Everything is divorced from reality.

I've told you that in England it is customary to give those who receive a Master of Arts degree a medieval gown. This had meaning a few hundred years ago and was a reality. Today, it's different. Today someone can be a consultant to the government or something else and it means absolutely nothing. Things are just the same in those countries that underwent revolutions. You must realize that a complete change in education is called for; everything depends on that.

Does anybody else have a question that concerns you?

Question: It is claimed that the appendix may be removed without harm to the patient. We know that frequently this and other organs are taken out in operations. Earlier, we discussed the significance of the internal organs, and I would like to know what effect it has on a person if he is missing any.

Dr Steiner: I can only answer this question after we have considered something else first, which I shall gladly do now.

Additional question: In recent lectures we have discussed the influence of the planets on man; I am interested in hearing more about this.

Dr Steiner: What I have to say now will have a bearing on it. I shall answer these questions today and see how far we get. But first I would like to tell you a story to demonstrate the kind of knowledge we will be pursuing from now on.

In the early 'nineties of the last century, about 30 or 31 years ago, an official North American trading and transport company held a convention. Invited to this meeting was a prominent financier named William Windom. By the standards of those gathered there he was a brilliant man, a person whom one immediately recognized as an authority. He was expected to give an address at this convention, and indeed he did so.

Windom began his speech by saying, 'We need to reform

our whole trade and transport system, for as they are today they contain something unhealthy.' He then went on to explain what money is; in his fairly short speech he touched on the significance of money. He said, 'Well, gentlemen, I have now analysed national economic matters for you. But the point is that one realizes that the whole thing does not work. However much the currency circulates due to commerce and passes from hand to hand, that does not determine what in fact makes national industry sound. What does make an industry sound are the moral concepts that people have. Unless moral concepts also flow through commerce, and money circulates in such a way that moral concepts are tied in with it, we get no further.' That is what he said.

Windom said that immoral concepts in commercial and industrial life is like having poison in the human bloodstream. If immoral concepts accompany the circulation of money in transportation and industry, it is as if poison were to contaminate the blood in the arteries. Just as a person becomes ill from poison in his system, so does the economic body become unhealthy when poison—that is, immoral concepts—runs through its network.

Now it struck his listeners that Mr Windom became a bit grey as he spoke of arteries in the context of economic life. They were surprised that someone who had previously spoken only of matters pertaining to economy and finance, who had in fact begun his speech on these subjects, should suddenly use this rather apt analogy and even elaborate on it. He described in detail how poison penetrates the blood and referred to moral concepts. This was indeed a change of subject, and after uttering the words, 'Immoral concepts go like poison through the arteries of industrial commerce,' he collapsed. He had a stroke and died on the spot.

Here you have an example of the phenomenon I have often mentioned and from which we may learn a great deal.

It is quite obvious what happened here. The speech certainly did not kill him because he was not even excited at the time. He would have had a stroke even if he had been doing something completely different; the conditions for it were simply present in his system. By no means was the stroke brought on by the speech, although it conceivably hastened it by an hour. In any event, his system had been predisposed to a stroke for a long time, and he would have had it anywhere else as well.

The other point to be observed here is that he suddenly left his topic and began to describe his own inner condition. This he did quite logically and within the boundaries of his talk. Imagine, the man stands before his audience and speaks to them about something thoroughly economic; suddenly the course of this thought changes as he turns rather grey. He keeps to the theme of his address, but what he describes now is his own condition before death. This is what he turned to; his speech took this direction on account of his own inner condition. Much can be learned from this, which also happens in other, less drastic forms.

Let us suppose a speaker loses his train of thought. This is something I have witnessed more than once. The speaker usually faces his audience confidently at first, but having lost his train of thought he makes a slight movement and glances downward—to where he has placed his top hat, which his speech is under! After he has found the thread of his thought again he can resume talking. Something like that can happen. I once saw a mayor, who got stuck after the first ten words, pick up his hat and bravely proceed to read the speech right off. The mayor could read, but if he had continued to talk without his notes, if he had spoken impromptu, well, nothing but twaddle would have come out. He could read; otherwise, his speech would have amounted to nothing.

How did William Windom fare? The conditions for the

imminent stroke were in his system, and if we consider man's whole constitution, it makes little difference whether we are in the situation of William Windom or of the mayor. The mayor could read, as we saw, and so could the man who suffered the stroke. But *where* did William Windom read? He read what was happening in his own body; he simply read from what was going on inside him. From this you may see that what spiritual science has discovered is correct. Whenever we talk we are actually always reading something that is going on within us. Naturally, what we say is based upon our external experiences, but that mingles with what goes on in our bodies. Our utterances are actually read off from our inner processes, which of course do not always have such sad consequences for us as a stroke. Every time you say something, even if it's only five words, you read it from within your body. If you jot something down, five days later you can read it in your notebook; and if you commit it to memory, then it becomes part of the script within you and you can read it from within. It is the same process as reading from a book. The act of reading is the same whether done from without or within; only the direction in which we look is different. It doesn't matter if you have noted 'five nails, seven hooks' on paper or in your brain. If you have noted it in a book you can read it off from the page where it was recorded; if you have made a mental note of it, a brain cell imprinted with 'five' has linked itself with others carrying the messages 'seven', 'nails' and 'hooks'. A whole loop has come into being in your brain, and, without being aware of it, you look at these loops within yourself and read off the mental notations. This is what we are led to realize from examining such an extreme case as William Windom's.

I have mentioned another example that we may briefly recall now. This incident concerns Karl Ludwig Schleich, a well-known doctor, and was reported by him. A man came rushing up to him and said, 'I've just pricked myself with this pen; look, there is still ink in it. You must amputate my right arm or I'll die of blood poisoning!'

Schleich, whom I knew well — he died just recently — told me this himself. He said to the man, 'What's the matter with you? As a surgeon I cannot take the responsibility of amputating your arm! The ink just needs to be sucked out. It's really nothing, and it would be nonsensical to cut off your arm!'

The person replied, 'If you don't I will die! You absolutely must take off my arm.'

Dr Schleich said to him, 'I won't do it; I can't cut off an arm for no reason whatsoever.'

'Well,' said the patient, 'then I will die.'

When Schleich let him go, the man rushed to a second doctor to ask him to amputate. Naturally, he also refused the request, and the fellow kept running around the whole evening saying, as he had to Dr Schleich, that he would die in the night.

Schleich was quite concerned about the man. Of course, there were no grounds for amputating his arm, but the first thing the following morning Schleich asked after him. He had easily sucked the ink out of the man's small wound, since pricking yourself with a pen is a minor matter. But when Schleich arrived at the man's house the next morning he found him dead; he had indeed died! Now, what did Schleich say? He said that the man had died of auto-suggestion, that he had talked himself into dying and that his own thoughts had killed him. It's true that in a case like this, one speaks of auto-suggestion, but I told Schleich that even though all kinds of things happen through auto-suggestion it cannot account for a death like this. To say so is nonsense. Schleich did not believe me.

What really happened? Only one who fully understands the human being can discover what really occurred in this case. The doctors performed an autopsy and found no trace of blood poisoning. There was no sign of anything amiss, and so they were satisfied with the conclusion that death had been caused by auto-suggestion. But here, too, the real cause was a stroke that would have been difficult to diagnose and, as you can imagine, had been building up for several days. The conditions for the stroke had been mounting in the delicate organs for days. The man dimly saw this happening within himself, just as Windom sensed that poison was penetrating his arteries moments before he was stricken. One can carry on for a long time without any apparent change on the surface, while within the conditions of death are maturing. The man in question somehow sensed this, became nervous and pricked his hand. He would not have done so otherwise. Up until this moment he was not aware of what was occurring within him and what was going to happen, but when he pricked himself, he said what he could not have said before, 'I shall die from the pen prick!' Nobody says, 'I feel death approaching me' if he feels perfectly healthy otherwise, but now he could ascribe his imminent death to the pen prick, even though it was the wrong cause. There was no auto-suggestion here; the man would have died the following night in any event. But he became nervous, and when he pricked his hand with a pen, the thought of imminent death arose in him, but transferred to a completely erroneous cause. He consulted doctors, but even Ludwig Schleich, who was a brilliant man, did not believe him. He thought that this was just a case of auto-suggestion and was convinced that the man had talked himself into dying. But this is nonsense. In fact, the cause of death already existed and the pen prick was but the result of apprehension.

From this you may see that much is happening within ourselves, and if these matters are not properly studied we simply cannot understand them. Our starting-point must be the origin of man. We must know in what form he existed when the ichthyosauri, the plesiosauri and the megatheri swam about in a thick fluid on what was then the earth. We cannot discover the interconnections of things without reference to and study of the human being.

There are many other aspects to be considered as well. At what age do most people die? We know that infants die most often within the first few months after birth. Afterwards, the mortality rate slowly decreases. Children have their childhood illnesses up to the time of their change of teeth; and if people were more sensible, children would suffer fewest illnesses during their school years (7 onwards). Some illnesses which do occur then can even be caused by poor posture while sitting. Even so, the fewest illnesses occur between the ages of 7 and 14. Then it starts up again. There is a great difference, however, between the diseases of infancy and those of puberty.

If we look at the illnesses that children die from during the earliest periods of life, we always find a quite definite form of blood disorder. The blood becomes infected. The child has a delicate constitution at that age and can die before the cause can be established. In fact, the child would develop jaundice. When an adult has an infection of the blood, the condition progresses to the stage of jaundice, which generally can be cured quickly. The infant, however, dies before reaching this stage.

Many children get diarrhoea, which cannot be cured by the means one uses with adults. External remedies such as enemas or compresses must be used, but it's worthless to give a child medication. Children also get rashes and blisters that spring up mainly on the tongue, and all the other childhood diseases that sprout up from within—scarlet fever, measles and the like—as though the whole internal constitution were 'blooming'. Adults can also get these illnesses, of course, but they belong essentially to childhood.

They predominate during the early ages and then decline after the child gets his second teeth. These illnesses, which call for a careful diet and preferably external treatment, do not occur in this form after the second teeth. It is difficult to discover what causes infected blood in a child. It arises from deep within the system. Convulsions, so-called childhood spasms, also frequently afflict children.

The illnesses that human beings contract during puberty are completely different. You need only consider the complaints of young girls. They develop anaemia, a problem caused by the body not properly nourishing the blood. When a child has an infection of the blood, something else within the constitution contaminates the bloodstream; when a girl has anaemia, the blood itself becomes ill. It is one problem if something within the system is infecting the blood and quite another if the blood becomes diseased. It is quite a different problem if the blood becomes sluggish, as it may, for example, in a boy or girl, a condition that then leads to haemorrhoids.

Thus it is that in two periods of his life man is particularly prone to illness: up to the age of 7 and between the ages of 14 and 21. In the intervening period he is predisposed to health. It is important to understand that the human being is not at all times equally prone to illness, that the times vary and that the illnesses have a completely different character at these various times. A study of this can lead us ever deeper into an understanding of the human organization, and in this way we can begin to understand the functions of the inner organs.

You see, on the one hand you have the case of Mr William Windom, who suddenly starts to speak of his organs as death approaches; on the other, you have the appearance of diseases in early childhood and the 'teens, which tell us that different processes occur during the successive stages of life. We must learn to decipher what occurs in man; we must learn to read these processes. When a child gets rashes or red patches on the body, for example, we must understand what is happening internally. Only when we have learned to read his inner processes can we arrive at a real knowledge of man.

If you merely put a dead human being on the dissecting table and only examine an individual organ, the removal of which causes no special effect, you won't discover anything pertinent. A diseased spleen, for example, can be surgically removed, and the operation can benefit the patient. He will be in better health for a period of time than if the spleen had remained in his body in its diseased condition. If you simply look at a spleen that has been surgically removed, you won't see what distinguishes it from, say, the stomach. Yet, if the whole stomach is removed, the patient has a difficult time. This is risky and in the long run someone with an artificial stomach cannot expect to have good health. There are organs that simply cannot be taken out: both lungs, for instance, and least of all, the brain. If a certain spot in the brain is hit with a mere needle, the person will die immediately. The elephant also has this spot in his brain. If you make a puncture there and hit it precisely — it need not even be cut out — this huge beast will be instantly killed. You may remove its spleen, however, and the animal will live on for many years. Thus, you see, it makes a difference which organ is removed from the body — a spleen, an appendix or something else.

To grasp this fact we must thoroughly study the human being. Remember what I have said about these little brain creatures, these cells representing memory that I have sketched here. They are still soft and alive in the small child and only gradually harden. Only when a child reaches his 7th year and has gone through the change of teeth have they hardened sufficiently. Then, at the onset of puberty, other cells called leucocytes start to move about more freely in the blood. They go through the whole bloodstream and become more active at puberty. Before that time they move about sluggishly. There are two periods in our lives when conditions arise that make us prone to illness. The first occurs from infancy to age 7, when the organism — or actually, the soul within the physical organism — must exert itself to mould and harden the brain cells. The second falls at puberty, when the soul must take pains to give mobility to the leucocytes, those little creatures contained in the blood.

To use an analogy, if you are building a house you must use mortar that will properly harden; otherwise, you will not succeed. So it is with the brain cells; they must harden sufficiently. When they do not, children become victims of this or that disease. We shall go further into the causes of these various illnesses next time. After puberty one is dealing with millions upon millions of white blood corpuscles. Until then, they are sluggish, and if they were a herd, it would take a great many shepherds to get them going. If this goading impulse is absent, anaemia results. So we see it depends on these aspects that in the early years of childhood and again at puberty certain illnesses may appear.

If the human being is studied like this, we can gradually grasp all the interconnections. Indeed, we cannot accomplish anything in the social realm either unless we know these facts of natural science.

Illnesses at different periods of life

Gentlemen, at our last session I started to answer your question about the inner organs of man. Of course, this subject must be seen from a broad perspective, and with regard to its deeper, underlying aspects. We saw how William Windom, who died while delivering a speech, expressed his own inner condition by reading it off, as it were, from his body. After citing another case, we found in examining certain facts about the course of human life that the mortality rate is highest in infancy, that human beings die most frequently in their early years. In the period from birth up to the change of teeth at age 7, the mortality rate is at its peak, though it diminishes with the 3rd, 4th and 5th years.

The human being is healthiest from the time of his change of teeth to puberty. This is indeed so, and if we ourselves are careful to prevent the causes of ill health, such as bad posture, which can lead to curvatures of the spine, and foul air, which can afflict the internal organs, we can count on children to be healthiest during their school years. The illnesses that do befall them then are for the most part due to external causes. Not until the teens does the danger again arise of illness caused by the inner constitution.

These illnesses, however, are quite different from those of early childhood.

I have mentioned that infants are highly susceptible to infections of the blood. It can become so bad that symptoms of jaundice appear. In children, irregular digestion frequently results in diarrhoea. They also get thrush — those little white pustules in various places — and another, completely different kind of illness, so-called infantile convulsions. A childhood disease that is particularly prevalent these days is infantile paralysis, which can also affect adults. It is extremely damaging; the children cannot move their legs and become quite paralysed. This disease is increasing rapidly. Perhaps you have read that schools have had to be closed in the Thüringen region because of an epidemic there.

Thus, we can see that childhood illnesses have a distinctive character; they are quite different from the diseases man gets in later life. Scarlet fever and measles are specifically childhood illnesses, though adults too can contract the latter. But we must now ask ourselves why young children are particularly susceptible to all these illnesses.

We can explain this susceptibility only if we know how forces work in the human body. When we examine the human embryo in the first, second or third months of pregnancy, we see that it is utterly different from what the human being later becomes. In the first and second months the child is all head; the other organs are only appendages to the head. What later turn into limbs, hands and feet are little stumps, and the actual lung and abdominal regions are not yet functioning.

You see, if you take the human embryo [a sketch is drawn here, Fig. 1] it looks like this. It is enclosed in a kind of sack, to which are attached blood vessels from the body of the mother. These blood vessels penetrate throughout the embryo, which the mother supplies with blood and nourishment. The other matter is supplementary and is later discarded. In comparison to the rest of the body the embryo's head is huge. See [*pointing to the drawing*], this is the head; the rest consists of appendages not yet functioning. This part will later become the heart and digestive system. The blood circulation is provided from outside, from the mother. These little stumps will develop into

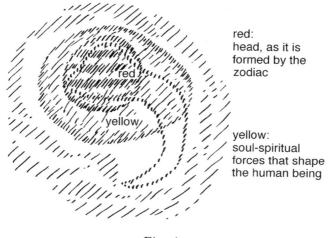

red:
head, as it is
formed by the
zodiac

yellow:
soul-spiritual
forces that shape
the human being

Fig. 1

hands and feet. So we can say that the embryo is all head. Its other organs are insignificant because the mother's system provides all the nourishment and air. Hence, during the first few months, the embryo consists primarily of a head.

People are surprised that mental illnesses are hereditary. In fact, mental illnesses are always based on physical ailments; they arise from a malfunctioning of the body. Neither the spirit nor the soul can fall ill. Though mental illnesses are always rooted in physical problems, people wonder how they can occur through heredity, which indeed they can do. If a parent, particularly the mother, suffers from tuberculosis or another disease like arteriosclerosis, which admittedly occurs rarely in younger persons, the children do not necessarily become afflicted with these illnesses but instead can suffer from mental deficiencies. People are surprised about this, but need it puzzle us, gentlemen? Whatever the child can inherit must be inherited first of all from its head. Therefore, if the mother is consumptive, one need not be surprised that her condition is not passed on to the lungs of the unborn child, which, after all, are not even functioning yet. The condition is rather carried over into the head and comes to expression in the brain. Thus, nobody should be surprised that the disease inherited is quite different from that of the parent. Venereal disease, for example, can appear in children as an eye disease. It is no wonder, for when the child's head is developing, its eyes are exposed to what afflicts the parents; its eyes are in an environment that's venereally diseased! So it is not at all surprising.

When the child is born, everyone knows that the most completely formed part of it is its head. In the succeeding years it is the rest of the body that grows the most; the head has much less growing to do than the other organs. This fact tells us how, in reality, the inner organs of man function. Materialistic science cannot form an accurate conception of this because it fails to realize that all growth proceeds from the head. In the child everything is regulated from the head. We can see this most clearly in the embryo, which is nothing more than a head. But even after birth all inner processes are regulated from this part of the body. The digestion, the blood circulation and all other activities in human organization are directed by the head.

Suppose that a child is born whose blood circulation is too slow. For some reason, through some hereditary factor, it can happen that the child's blood circulation is too slow. Let us imagine this case. [See Fig. 2.] Here is the child's heart, and here its arteries; through both the blood is travelling too slowly. The heart is being formed from the head, but even when the head functions perfectly, the circulation can still be too slow. Thus, even though the heart is properly developed, the blood doesn't flow into it correctly. This is often the case in earliest infancy. The head is perfectly developed, but the blood flows too slowly into the heart. Poor circulation may result simply from keeping the child

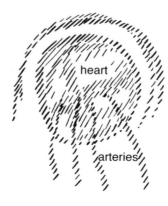

Fig. 2

in stifling air. It cannot breathe properly, and its circulation slows down. The blood circulation may slacken also if the baby is not properly nourished. Then its blood cannot thoroughly penetrate the body. The head may be in excellent shape and try to form the heart aright, but the blood circulation remains sluggish. What happens in such instances is that, because the blood is not circulating well enough, certain substances that normally would be pushed down from the heart into the kidneys and expelled remain in the body; they stay in the blood. When these substances that should have been discharged stay in the system, the blood becomes infected.

In the 7th, 8th or 9th years, this danger is not so acute as it is in the earliest years of childhood. You see, the fact that a child has its second set of teeth shows that its body is sufficiently strong; if it were not, the teeth would not come in properly. Why? Well, you must understand that what is contained in a tooth comes out of the whole body. The second teeth emerge from within the whole system; they are the product not just of something in the jaw but of the whole body. This is true only of the second teeth, however, for the first teeth, the so-called milk teeth, are completely different. They are the result of heredity, of the fact that the child's mother and father have teeth. Only after the milk teeth are expelled in the course of the first seven years does the child get its own teeth. The body must make the second teeth for itself.

Actually, a child 9 or 10 years old already has its second body. It has already completely discarded the one it had inherited, and comes into possession of its own body only around the age of 7. During these first seven years it demonstrates that it was born with enough resistance to tolerate air and nourishment. After it has built up its body and produced its second teeth, the danger of falling ill is no longer so acute. The danger is most acute in earliest infancy while it is learning to cope for itself in breathing, eating — that is everything that once was done for it within the protection of the mother's womb. In these early years the head is actually in good shape; only with age does it become less perfect. In old age the head doesn't work as well as it did in infancy. It must think and occupy itself with its surroundings and so something often goes awry. But the infant does not yet need to learn anything, go to school or possess skills. The head works only on the child's own body, and in most cases it does this quite well. During these tender years, however, when the human being is just becoming used to the world, the rest of the body is quite vulnerable. Modern science also has described these matters but not quite as I have, for what I tell you is exact. Popular science does not really comprehend the whole process and cannot explain why the human being is most vulnerable in its earliest years. It cannot come to terms with this fact because it explains away the soul and spirit.

In reality, soul-spiritual elements are united with the child, mainly with the head, while it is still in the mother's womb and after birth. The forces that work on the child

from within the head are invisible soul-s
Should any of you think that this is mere
opinion, you would be committing a sim
following. Suppose one man says, 'Here is a piece ...
and the other says, 'Fine! I'll shoe my horse with it.' The first
man then says, 'No, it would be stupid to shoe your horse
with this. It's a magnet, and it has a hidden force. Magnets
are used for quite other things than for shoeing horses!' The
one man thinks the piece of iron should be used for a
horseshoe, while the other knows that it is a magnet containing an invisible force. Well, the person who says, in
accordance with materialistic science, 'The head is nothing
but a bit of bones and brains,' is just like the fellow who says
of the magnet, 'This is a horseshoe.' Indeed, it is not a
horseshoe, nor is the head of the infant just flesh and bone.
Within it invisible forces are working like a sculptor to build
up the whole organism. The human form is among those
things the child keeps as an inheritance, but the forces
which, during the first seven years, tirelessly build up this
form from the head are brought into the world not from the
parents but from quite another source.

Suppose we received these forces from our parents. Well,
gentlemen, if a parent is a genius, does that make the child a
genius as well? Or if a child is a genius, does that mean the
parents were also highly gifted? Not at all! Goethe, for
example, was certainly a genius, but his father was a
dreadful philistine, and his mother was a kind and pleasant
woman who could tell a good story but surely was no
genius. Goethe's son was rather stupid; he was no genius
either. Whatever pertains to the soul and spirit is not hereditary; it is brought into this world from quite other realms
and then is united with the part that is inherited. Aside from
the time he spends in his mother's womb, man lives before
birth as a being of soul and spirit.

The only reason people reject this idea today is that all

through the Middle Ages the Catholic Church forbade anyone to ascribe to man a life of soul and spirit before birth. It asserted that the soul was created at birth by the kind of God which the Catholic Church assumed to exist. So throughout the Middle Ages, the Catholic Church forbade the concept of pre-existence, as it was called, meaning 'existence before, prior to birth'. Modern materialistic science has merely followed suit and then congratulated itself on its cleverness. Now people think they are extraordinarily clever to hold this opinion; unfortunately, they fail to realize how they were conditioned to do so.

In truth, man not only inherits a physical existence from his parents and forebears but also brings into the world a soul-spiritual element that works within him. If one does not acknowledge that the soul-spiritual aspect is present before birth, one cannot see that the same soul and spirit remain after death; at most, one can believe it. Knowledge of the immortality of the soul is dependent on knowledge of its existence before birth. If one maintains that the soul came into being with the creation of the body, then, of course, a divine creator would equally be happy to let the soul disappear upon the body's dissolution. If, however, it is the soul that builds up the body in the first place, then it certainly remains unaffected when the body dies.

Thus, the existence of the human soul follows readily from all the aspects that one can correctly observe. Indeed, how could the soul die, since it is the soul itself that builds up the physical body! One would have to enter quite other spheres to discover whether or not the soul can perish. In future lectures we shall consider this question and find that it cannot die in these realms either. It certainly cannot die with the body because it is the soul which builds this body up.

We have now become acquainted with illnesses that originate because the soul-spiritual element working out of the head meets a body that is malfunctioning. But the blood circulation can also be too slow. Stagnation sets in and the blood then suppurates. Still, something entirely different can happen, too. The infant may be too weak to absorb nourishment through its intestines into its blood. Because the body is too weak, nourishment does not pass through the villi and the child becomes afflicted with diarrhoea. What should have been absorbed so as to remain longer in the body is expelled. Because the food was not properly digested, diarrhoea results, and the substance is discharged unchanged. This is connected with something else. Obviously, a child can get diarrhoea in different degrees, and it may even get summer cholera. Whatever the degree, however, it is only the first stage. If the child cannot digest its food for a considerable length of time, its inner organs cannot be built up properly. The head constantly wants to work on them, but the inner organs cannot be correctly constructed because the necessary substances are lacking. Say you were working on a statue and ran out of clay but continued to make empty-handed motions in the air. In a like manner the head starts to move and fidget around when the child lacks the substance from which its organs can be built. It wants to form the heart or stomach but can only aimlessly fidget about because the substances the head should have received have been eliminated, causing diarrhoea.

The educated but materialistic scientist faces a complete puzzle here. He examines the child, discovers diarrhoea and prescribes some medication to stop it. As a result, food will merely accumulate in the intestines because it cannot be absorbed, and the child will get nothing more than a swollen stomach. If one were to examine the organism further, one would discover that the heart is malformed, that it is an empty pouch, or that the lungs are empty sacks. They want to be formed but lack the necessary substances.

The forces originating from the head that penetrate into the lungs, which may now be empty sacks, need something to grasp and work with. I can grasp this chair and shake it or, without having taken hold of it, I can merely fidget about and make empty gestures like an idiot. But what happens when the head forces fidget about in the lungs? Convulsions occur. A rational explanation of convulsions must acknowledge that the head forces are fidgeting around and find nothing to take hold of. Diarrhoea may be explained materialistically but convulsions can no longer be accounted for along such lines.

All this demonstrates that in the infant soul-spiritual processes are at their height of activity. Later, this activity subsides. Up to the child's sixth or seventh years, however, these spiritual forces are so active that they can separate minute amounts of matter from food, from which the second teeth are then formed. Imagine having to do that yourself! You would have to be clever enough to distinguish the magnesium salts and carbonates contained in the food. Even if you could do that you would first have to analyse the teeth chemically and learn from them themselves. The teeth made artificially today are not living teeth; no one really knows how teeth are produced. Yet minute portions of the nourishment the child receives up to its seventh year are separated out to make the second teeth. Furthermore, to correctly separate the various substances you would need to know not only the chemical composition of food and teeth but also about the stomach's activity. What happens to the minute particles secreted in the second or third years? How do you retain them long enough in the bloodstream so that, at just the right time, during the sixth and seventh years, they will penetrate the jaws to build up the teeth? All this that must be accomplished is done unconsciously by the child's soul and spirit. No one here would feel insulted if I said that you cannot produce or make one hair grow on your head. But a child can. It drives the proper substances to the spot where the hair takes root and then offers them to the light, for hair grows under the influence of light. All this occurs in the child, but modern science is unwilling to consider these aspects. It leaves people in the dark by refusing to acknowledge that soul-spiritual forces working within the organism originate not from the parents, but from the spiritual world.

Let us return to this matter of hair. Man normally grows hair only on certain parts of his body, but once, ages ago, he was covered completely with a shaggy growth of hair. Why did he lose it? I will not give you a theory, which anyone can dream up, but merely point out some facts. Consider another creature, the pig. When pigs are free in nature, they are covered with hair, but domesticated pigs lose it. In their natural habitat wild boars grow thick coats of fur; when they are domesticated and in surroundings not originally their own, they lose it. Man, like the domesticated animals, did not originally live under today's conditions. But there was a time when, under the influence of light and warmth, he grew hair all over his body, and we may witness this fact today in an embryo a few months old. During the first months of pregnancy the whole embryo, which is almost all head, is covered with hair. Later, the hair disappears. I have already explained how plants in their first stage of growth utilize light and warmth from the previous year. Likewise, the child has hair on account of the light and warmth emanating from the mother. Only later is it lost. So a consideration of hair, too, can show us how forces of soul and spirit work on the body.

I have said that the human being is most healthy during the school years, between the ages of 7 and 14. Why is this so? Only those children who can develop those strong forces that produce the second teeth survive. During that period, the child unfolds vigorous forces, but they must first be acquired in the earliest years through radical adaptation. Everything that the head accomplishes within the organism is most pronounced during those early years. Though the child is unaware of its activity, the head must really exert itself and be a great artist. It has to overcome the body's constant resistance all by itself because it gets no support in its continual and taxing efforts during the first seven years. This tremendous strain causes all those illnesses I have told you about.

Let us now suppose that the circulation of the blood is malfunctioning, not on account of its absorbing too little nourishment, but because it absorbs too much. This can also happen. Indeed, parents who think it is best to stuff their baby with food may not be as wise as the organism. They can hardly be reproached for this practice, though, because it is usually quite difficult to tell when the child has had enough. Children know their limits, as a rule, through their own inherent wisdom and instinct. If the mother produces too much milk, however, and it is fed to the child, its instinct will become uncertain through eating too much. Now, if too much food is absorbed by the system, the head cannot keep up; it cannot handle too large an amount and will try to eliminate the surplus. The food has already been absorbed into the blood through the intestines, however, so the head cannot eliminate the surplus in the normal way. What does it do then? It discharges the superfluous substances through the skin. Measles and scarlet fever are the result.

These illnesses differ completely from diarrhoea and convulsions. A child gets the latter because it does not receive enough food and its forces fidget around aimlessly within the body. When too much food is absorbed, however, it must somehow be eliminated, occasionally even through the lungs. Diphtheria and pneumonia are the body's defence measures used to rid itself of substances it cannot otherwise eliminate through the skin. When one understands the human being and the processes that occur in the body, one finds it quite natural that an infant is susceptible to these illnesses.

A child can be afflicted with yet other diseases. Take the case of a child who is too weak to produce his second teeth. His milk teeth were inherited and required no effort from his system. Now, it can happen that the forces unable to produce the new teeth are diverted into the lungs. The lungs become inflamed and the child gets pneumonia. You see, the human body is extremely complicated, and when a child falls ill with pneumonia the doctor should examine the condition not only of the lungs but also of the kidneys, stomach, etc. When an illness arises, one must always examine the whole body and not just the part immediately affected.

When a child has reached the age of 7, however, its breathing processes have become sufficiently developed to function without the intervention of the head. In the infant the head must constantly regulate the breathing. It must not only build up the teeth but also care for the organs of breathing. When the head has been relieved of these tasks at age 7 or 8, the child is now in a position to breathe properly. It is of utmost importance to realize that with the second teeth the child can bring order into its breathing, and can receive its second lungs and bronchi, as it were, which have by now been built up. The child no longer breathes with a weak inherited organism but with the new one that has been built up. Now it is in quite a different situation; now it has support. It is one thing if the child has inherited from, say, a weak mother and father, a breathing apparatus that must be directed from a head that is too weak, and it is quite another thing if it has properly built up a second apparatus suited to its needs. A head that is too weak simply cannot build up the lungs properly. Thus, because from age 7 to 14 the organs of breathing are in such fine shape, the individual is then at his healthiest. The positive aspect of these years is that the breathing process is at its best. With the onset of puberty, however, some of the nourishment is now diverted to this development. In the younger child substances are not yet absorbed through the later processes of puberty; but now digestion must take a completely new form. The reason is easily understood, for something completely new has come into play and food is diverted in a new direction. From the age of puberty onwards the new form of breathing that has come about means that the digestive organs must readjust, so that the right counter-pressure is exerted from the stomach and intestines — since some of the former overall pressure has been diverted. The proper counter-pressure must now come about. No wonder that anaemia and other illnesses afflict girls of this age since the organism must take time to adjust.

From age 7 to 14 the child enjoys its greatest protection from illness. In earlier years the head must make a tremendous effort to work into the rest of the organism and it must adjust to this task. Then, during the school years, the child is at its healthiest. The second breathing system is unhindered and can freely distribute the oxygen to the benefit of both the brain and the digestion. As I have mentioned before, things can be upset only through outside causes — activities in school and the like.

But now the child reaches puberty. Look at a boy. Up to this point he has perfected his body and is as healthy as a human being can be. He has successfully renewed his organism and everything has gone smoothly. But with the onset of puberty his metabolism begins to affect his whole body. The processes of digestion begin to work upward into his breathing system and, as a result, his voice changes. At the age when he must again reform his organism, the metabolic system becomes influential. This is expressed in a deepening of the voice. He must make new exertions and again illnesses threaten.

You see, only when we observe the human being in this manner are we able to answer the question one of you gentlemen posed last time. Otherwise, we cannot even think about it, let alone learn anything. But knowing now that it is the head that works the most during the first seven years, what conclusion may we reach? You must understand that, while the head is developed in the mother's organism, it is not merely formed by conception and substance but by the whole universe. The mother's substances represent only the foundation on which the form occurs. The head is a representation, an image of the universe. Its roundness indicates the working of the whole universe, and it is no idle fancy that the starry heavens work upon the skull. It is as true as this fact that I've mentioned to you before. Suppose we have a compass; the magnetic needle always points north, not just anywhere. Now, no one thinks that the needle *contains* the forces that determine its position. Everyone agrees that it is the magnetic forces of the earth, and that the needle takes its direction from these earthly forces. Everyone comprehends that. Yet people falsely think that human embryonic development is caused by conception. It would be just as clever to think that the direction pointed to by the magnetic needle was determined by its own forces.

The human head represents the whole cosmos, and this is what has worked upon it. In addition, these forces bestowed by the universe continue to work within the child through its head. To build up the lungs, for example, the head must receive the right forces from the universe. To perfect the kidneys, forces must be received from far-off regions, from Jupiter, for instance. This is no idle fancy. It can be investigated just as other, physical matters can be investigated. Thus, when a child is born, it carries within its head all the forces of the universe.

Of course, it is nonsense to say that the moon, sun or Jupiter have an influence on an organ, or to cast a horoscope thinking the planet Jupiter, for example, is dominant. The head is formed from the whole universe, and the forces that work on the human being during the first seven years have been given to the head from the cosmos. During the next seven years, man becomes increasingly accustomed to the earth's atmosphere, so that whereas before he was influenced by the stars, he is now influenced by the air.

After this period the substances of digestion and the metabolic system play such an important part that they can even affect the voice. What does this mean? It is all a result of what we absorb through digestion from the earth. I have already explained this process to you: how, for example, substances from the earth must first be made lifeless within the intestines. This becomes man's main task when he reaches puberty. At that time he becomes dependent on the earth. As males we owe our voices first of all to the air, but the deepening results from the action of earthly substances. We can be born on earth because originally we were beings of the stars. After birth we let the forces we have brought with us from the starry worlds echo within our organisms. Then we become beings of the air. Only at puberty are we assigned to the earth to become its beings. Only then do we become attached to those things that fetter us to this planet. Thus, you see the course of man's descent to the earth from the cosmos.

Often materialists blindly fantasize about human development. They do not realize that man gradually accustoms himself to the earth and then, in old age, grows away from it. For what happens in old age? The forces we possess in advanced age we also possessed in youth. They hardened the bones while the other parts stayed pliable. But in old age the forces contained in the bones pass into the rest of the body, and the initial result is arteriosclerosis. The arteries harden, and the brain can calcify. Actually, the brain must always contain a minute amount of what arises through calcification. The child would be dull if its brain lacked these minute traces of calcium secreted by the pineal gland. The soul could not act; it would not have the substances in which to work. But if later in old age too much calcium is secreted and calcification occurs, this hinders the soul and stops it taking hold. This can result in paralysis or apoplexy or some other kinds of stroke. One can also become senile, since one can no longer take hold of and use the brain. Calcification in other parts of the body has the same effect, denying one access to the region of earthly forces. Thus we can see how man, up to the end of puberty, grows into the forces of the earth and how, later, when the secreted deposits become increasingly resistant and the soul's activity is impeded, he grows away from the earth again.

So you see that it is, in fact, possible to discover what man has received and brought down from the universe. But one must not fall for superstitions — such as that a certain star is influencing the lung of, let's say, a 35-year-old man. What *is* true, though, is that the lung has indeed been built up by the forces that initially descended from the stars into the head of the infant.

By examining such things scientifically, one arrives at a real science of the spirit. A spiritual science exists, and it can be studied just like any other science. We can belittle ancient times as much as we like, but in those days people did know something. Granted, we cannot bring back the past; what was right for people then is not so for us today. But if once again we have people who understand the world and man, people who know that the human head is not produced in the mother's womb as merely a kind of physical ball, then we shall also have better politicians. You see, gentlemen, a person who knows nothing of these matters and of the nature of the human being cannot be a good politician simply because he will not know what people need. It is absolutely essential that once more there be people who really know something about the world. This is what we must strive for.

Schools must again teach people something of value. Today, much importance is placed on learning the skills required for making machines. Nothing can be said against this from the standpoint of spiritual science because it is quite worth while. But the skills needed to live together and understand one another are neglected. An abstract social science, ignorant of man's needs, was invented and this is taught instead. Above all, one must study man as we have done here, but unhappily what I told you is not taught. Look back on your own school days! Where is something like this taught today? That is what our age lacks. Teaching people the things they learn today is about as good for them as feeding them stones instead of bread. Maybe the stomach of a goose can take stones but that of a human being cannot! To do so would ruin the digestive system, and when you teach people what is being taught today, you actually ruin their heads. You know that the arm becomes weak if it is unused, and the head also becomes weak if it is not used in the right way. While the head is developing in the mother, it receives forces from the stars. If it is later told nothing about them, if it entertains no thoughts of them, it grows weak, just as muscles do when they are not exercised. If the child learns nothing of the real world, it remains weak. The worst thing about conditions today is that people have weak heads and do not understand anything about one another. They separate themselves according to social standing and do not speak to those of other classes. This is like training a person to become an athlete while neglecting his biceps. If, in educating people, I leave their heads weak, they will not know the very thing that matters most. This is how things stand.

When children have finished building up their organisms with inherent, unconscious wisdom and have received their second teeth, it is of utmost importance to impart to them something that they have previously employed unconsciously. Then do they become proper human beings, people who can direct their thoughts properly and conceive of spiritual science in the right way. Once social thinking is ruined, nothing rational can be achieved. But if we make use of a genuine science of the spirit, much can be improved in that respect.

The formation of the human ear. Eagle, lion, bull, man

A question was asked about the design that appeared on the cover of the Austrian journal *Anthroposophy*, showing the heads of an eagle, a lion, a bull and a man.

Dr Steiner: Gentlemen, I think we should first bring to a conclusion our descriptions of the human being, and then next time consider the aspects of man that these four symbols — the eagle, lion, bull and man — represent. Before we can say anything about them we must build a foundation, and this is something I shall try to do before the end of today's lecture. These four creatures, including man, spring from an ancient knowledge of the human being. They cannot be explained as the ancient Egyptians, for instance, would have done, but today they must be explained differently. One must interpret them correctly, of course, but nowadays one must begin from slightly different suppositions.

I would like now to direct your attention again to the way the human being evolves from his embryonic stage. I would like you to look once more at the very first stage, the earliest period. Conception has occurred, and the embryo is developing in the mother's womb. At first, it is just one microscopic cell containing proteinaceous substance and a nucleus. This single cell, the fertilized egg, actually marks the beginning of man's physical life.

Let us look then at the processes that immediately follow. What does this tiny egg, placed within the body of the mother, do? It divides. The one cell becomes two, and each of these cells divides in turn, thus creating more and more cells like the first. Eventually, our whole body is made up of such cells. They do not remain completely round but assume all manner of shapes and forms.

We must now take into account something I have mentioned before, which is the fact that the whole universe acts upon this minute cell in the mother's body. Nowadays, of course, such matters generally cannot be met with the necessary understanding, but it is nonetheless true that the whole cosmos works upon this cell. It is not at all the same if the ovum divides when, say, the moon stands in front of, or at a distance from, the sun. The whole starry heavens shed an influence on this cell, whose interior forms itself accordingly.

I have said before that during the first few months only the head of the unborn child is developed. [*A drawing is made.*] The head is already formed to this extent, and the rest of the body is really only an appendage. There are tiny little stubs, the hands, and other small protrusions, the legs. As it develops, the human being will transform its little appendages into hands, arms and feet.

How does this come about? How does it occur? The reason lies in the fact that in the earlier embryonic stages the influence of the starry heavens is greater. As the embryo develops and grows during those months in the mother's womb, it becomes increasingly subject to the gravity of the earth. When the world of the stars acts upon man, the emphasis is always on the head. It is gravity that, in time, draws out the other parts. The farther back we go, examining the second or first months of pregnancy, the more do we find these cells exposed to the influence of the stars. As more and more cells appear and millions gradually develop, they become increasingly subject to the forces of the earth.

Here is convincing evidence that the human body is magnificently organized. I would like to make this evident by considering one of the sense organs. I could just as easily take the example of the eye, but today I shall speak about the ear. You see, one of these cells develops into the ear. The ear is set into one of the cavities of the skull bones, and if you examine it properly, you will find that it is quite a remarkable structure. I shall explain the ear so that you can get some idea of it. You will see how such a cell moulds itself while it is still partially under the influence of the stars and partially under the influence of the earth. The ear is formed in such a marvellous way so that man can actually make use of it. [See Fig. 3.]

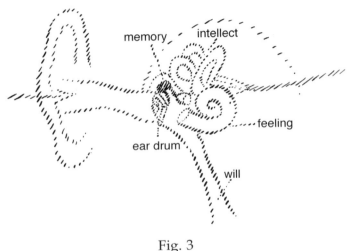

Fig. 3

Let us proceed from the outside inward. To begin with, each of you can take hold of your auricle, the outer ear. We have sketched it as seen from the side. It consists of gristle and is covered with skin. It is designed to receive the maximum amount of sound. If we had only a hole there, the ear would capture much less sound. You can feel the passage into your ear; it goes into the interior of the so-called tympanic cavity, the interior of the head's bony system. This passage or canal is closed off inside by the ear-drum, the tympanic membrane. There is really a thin, delicate, tiny skin attached to this canal, which might be likened to that of a drumhead. The ear, then, is closed off on the inside by the ear-drum.

I'll continue by drawing the cavity that one observes in a skeleton. Here are the skull bones; here are the bones going to the jaw. Inside is a cavity into which this canal leads that is closed off by the ear-drum. Behind the outer ear, the auricle, you have a hollow space, which I shall now tell you about. Not only does this canal, this outer passage that you can put your little finger into, lead into the head cavity, but another canal also leads into this cavity from the mouth. In other words, two passages lead into this cavity: one from the exterior that extends inwards to the ear-drum, and one from the mouth that enters behind the ear-drum, which is called the Eustachian tube, though the name does not matter.

Now we come to a strange-looking thing—a veritable snail shell, the cochlea. It consists of two parts. Here is a membrane, and here is a space, the vestibule. Over here is another space, the tympanic cavity. The whole thing is filled with fluid, a living fluid, which I have described to you in another lecture. So within all this fluid is something made of skin that looks like a snail shell. Inside this snail shell, called the cochlea, are myriad little fibres that make up the basilar membrane. This is quite interesting. If you could penetrate the ear-drum and look beyond it, you would find this soft snail shell, which is covered on the inside with minute, protruding hairlike fringes.

What, actually, is inside the cochlea? When one approaches the question truly scientifically, one notices that this is really a small piece of intestine that has somehow been placed within the ear. Just as we have the intestines within our abdomen, so do we have a tiny piece of intestine-like structure within our ear. The ear's configuration, then, is such that it contains a little intestine, just as in another part of the body we have a larger intestine. The cochlear duct, which is surrounded by a living fluid called the endolymph, is filled with another called the perilymph. All this is extremely interesting. The cochlea is closed off here by a tiny membrane shaped like an oval window, and here, again, by another little membrane that looks like a round window. Just as we can beat on a drum and make it vibrate, so do the sound waves, coming in from both sides, set into motion this little membrane, the oval window.

The oval window is a membrane set in the middle of the cochlea, and it closes off the inside of the little snail shell, which is filled with the slightly thicker fluid, the peri-lymph. The fluid on the outside is thinner. Below the oval window is another little membrane called the round win-dow. Here we now approach something marvellous. Two tiny delicate bones sit on the membrane of the oval win-dow. They look like a stirrup and are called the stapes. People also refer to them as the stirrup. So the stirrup sits on the little membrane, protruding in such a way as to resemble an upper and a lower arm on the membrane. Picture such an upper and lower arm of the stirrup and then here, strangely enough, another independent bone, the incus or anvil. The first two bones of the stirrup are connected by a joint; the incus is independent. These tiny bones are all in the ear, and since materialistic science looks at everything superficially, it calls the bone that sits directly on the ear-drum, the hammer, this other bit of bone in the middle, the anvil, and this other, the stirrup — or malleus, incus and stapes.

Ordinary science, however, doesn't really know what these bones are. What is found here in the two arms of the stirrup is only a little different from an arm bent at the elbow. See, an elbow joint is the same as this joint of the stirrup above the membrane. And there is a kind of hand, on which sits an independent bone. We don't have such a bone in our hand, but it is comparable to our kneecap. So we can rightfully say that this is also like a leg, a foot; then that would be the thigh, that the knee [*sketching*], there the foot stands on the membrane, and there is the kneecap.

You see, it is most interesting that in the cavity of the ear we have first a kind of intestine and then a real hand, arm or foot. What is the purpose of all this? Well, imagine that a sound strikes the ear-drum and everything in there begins to vibrate. Without being aware of it, the person is determining within the ear what kind of vibration it is. Now think of this, which you may have experienced at some time. You are standing somewhere on a street when something explodes behind you. You feel the explosion inwardly and may feel sick to your stomach from the shock. But this delicate shock that vibrates through the cochlea's 'intestine' is felt by the fluid within, which conveys the vibrations that are imparted by the 'touching' of the ear-drum with a 'hand', as it were.

Now I would like to point out something else to you. What is the purpose of this Eustachian tube leading from the mouth to the inner ear? If sounds simply passed into the ear from the auricle, we would not need it, but to comprehend another's speech we must first have learned to speak ourselves. When we listen to someone else and wish to comprehend him, the sounds we have learned to speak pass through the Eustachian tube. When another person is speaking to us, the sounds come in through the auricle and make the fluid vibrate. Because the air passes into the ear from the outside, and since we know how to set this air in motion with our own speech, we can understand the other person. In the ear, the element of our own speech that we are accustomed to meets the element of what the other person says; there the two meet.

You see, when I say 'house', I am accustomed to having certain vibrations occur in my Eustachian tube; when I say, 'powder', I experience other vibrations. I am familiar with these vibrations. When I hear the word 'house', the vibration comes from outside, and because I am used to identifying this vibration when I say the word myself, and since my comprehension and the vibration from outside encounter each other in the ear, I am able to recognize its meaning. The tube that leads from the mouth into the ear was there when I learned to speak as a child. Thus, we learn to understand other people at the same time as we learn to talk. These matters are most interesting.

Now, things are really like this. Imagine that nothing but what I have just sketched here existed in the ear. Then you could at least understand another person's words and also listen to a piece of music, but you would not be able to remember what you had heard. You would have no memory for speech and sound if the ear had nothing more than these parts. There is another amazing structure in the ear that enables you to retain what you have heard. These are three hollow arches, which look like this [*sketching*]. The second is vertical to the first, and the third vertical to the second. Thus, they are vertical to each other in three dimensions. These so-called semicircular canals are hollow and are also filled with a living, delicate fluid. The remarkable thing about it is that infinitely small crystals are constantly forming from this living fluid. If you hear the word 'house', for example, or the tone C, tiny crystals are formed in there as a result. If you hear a different word — 'man', for instance — slightly different crystals are formed. In these three little canals, microscopically small crystals take shape, and these minute crystals enable us not only to understand but also to retain in our memory what we have comprehended. For what does the human being do unconsciously?

Imagine that you have heard someone say, 'Five francs.' You want to remember what has been said, so with a pencil you write it into your notebook. What you have written with lead in your notebook has nothing to do with five francs except as a means of remembering them. Likewise, what one hears is inscribed into these delicate canals with the minute crystals that do, in fact, resemble letters, and a subconscious intelligence in us reads them whenever we need to recall something. So, indeed, we can say that the memory for tone and sound is located within these three semicircular canals. Here where this arm is located is comprehension, intelligence. Here, within the cochlea is a portion of man's feeling. We feel the sounds in this part of the labyrinth, in the fluid within the little snail shell; there we feel the sounds. When we speak and produce the sounds ourselves, our will passes through the Eustachian tube. The whole configuration of the human soul is contained in the ear. In the Eustachian tube lives the will; here in the cochlea is feeling; intelligence is in the auditory ossicles, those little bones that look like an arm or leg; memory resides in the semicircular canals. So that man can become aware of the complete process, a nerve passes from here [*drawing*] through this cavity and spreads out everywhere, penetrates everywhere. Through this auditory nerve, all these processes are brought to consciousness in our brain.

You see, gentlemen, this is something quite remarkable. Here in our skull we have a cavity. One enters the inner ear cavity by passing from the auricle through the auditory canal and ear-drum. In this cavity is contained everything I have described. First, we stretch out the 'hand' and touch the incoming tones to comprehend them. Then we transfer this sensation to the living fluid of the cochlea, where we feel the tone. We penetrate the Eustachian tube with our will, and because of the tiny crystal letters formed in the semicircular canals, we can recall what has been said or sung, or whatever else has come to us as sound.

So we can say that within the ear we bear something like a little human being. The human being has will, comprehension, feeling and memory. In this small cavity we really carry a tiny man around with us. We actually consist of many such minute human beings. The large human being is in fact the sum of many little human beings. Later, I'll show you that the eye is also such a miniature person. The nose, too, is a little human being. All these 'little beings' that make up the total human being are held together by the nervous system.

These miniature 'people' are created while man is still an embryo in the mother's womb. All that is being formed and developed there is still under the influence of the stars. After all, these marvellous configurations — the canals that produce the crystals, the little auditory bones — cannot be moulded by the gravity and forces of the earth. They are organized in the womb of the mother by forces that descend from the stars. The cochlea and Eustachian tube are parts that belong to man as a being of earth and are developed later. They are shaped by the forces that originate from the earth, from the gravity that gives us our form and that enables the child to stand upright long after it is born.

You see, if initially one knows how the whole human being originates from one small cell, and how one cell is transformed into an eye while another becomes an ear and a third the nose, one understands how man is gradually built up. Actually, there are ten groups of cells that transform themselves, not just one, but we may still imagine there to be one cell in the beginning. So, at first, just one cell exists. This produces a second, which by being placed in a slightly different position comes under a different influence and develops into the ear. Another develops into the nose, a third into the eye, and so on. But by no means does all of this proceed from influence of the earth. The forces of the earth can mould only those parts that are mostly round — in the abdomen, for example, it organizes the intestinal system. Everything else is formed by the influence of the stars.

We know of these matters today because we have microscopes. After all, the auditory bones are minute. Remarkably enough, these things were also known by people of ancient times, though the source of their knowledge was completely different from that of today. For example, 3,000 years ago the ancient Egyptians were also occupied with a knowledge of man's organization and knew in their way just how remarkable the inner functions of the human ear are. They said to themselves that man has ears, eyes and other organs belonging to the head. If we wish to explain them, we must ask how the ear, for instance, was moulded so differently from the other organs. The ancients said that those organs that are part of the head developed primarily from what comes down to the earth from above. They said, 'High up in the air the eagle develops and matures. One must look up into that region if one wishes to observe the forces that form the organs in the human head.' So these ancient people drew an eagle in place of the head when they were depicting the human being.

When we observe the heart or lungs, we find that they look completely different from the ear or eye. When we look at the lungs, we cannot turn to the stars, nor can we do so in the case of the heart. The force of the stars works strongly in the heart, but we cannot deduce the heart's configuration solely from the stars. The ancient Egyptians knew this; they knew that these organs could not be as closely linked to the stars as those of the head. They pondered these aspects and asked themselves which animal's constitution emphasized the organs similar to the human heart and lungs. The eagle particularly develops those organs that man has in his head. The ancients thought that the animal that primarily develops the heart, that is all heart and therefore the most courageous, is the lion. So they named the part of man that contains the heart and lungs 'lion'. For the head, they said 'eagle', and for the middle realm, 'lion'.

They realized that man's intestines were organs of a different kind again. You see, the lion has quite short intestines; their development is curtailed. The minute 'intestine' in the human ear is formed most delicately, but man's abdominal intestines are by no means shaped so finely. In observing the intestines, you can compare their formation only with the nature of those animals that are mainly influenced by their intestinal system. The lion is under the influence of the heart, and the eagle is under the sway of the upper forces. When you observe cows after they have been grazing, you can sense how they and their kind are completely governed by their intestines. When they are digesting, they experience great well-being, so the ancients called the part of man that constitutes the digestive system 'bull'. That gives us the three members of human nature: eagle — head; lion — breast; bull — abdomen.

Of course, the ancients knew when they studied the head that it was not an actual eagle, nor the middle realm a lion, nor the lower part a bull. They knew that, and they said that if there were no other influence, we would all go about with something like an eagle for our head above, a lion in our chest region and a bull down below; we would all walk around like that. But something else comes into play that transforms what is above and moulds it into a human head, and likewise with the other parts. This agent is man himself; man combines these three aspects.

It is most remarkable how these ancient people expressed, in such symbols, certain truths that we acknowledge again

Fig. 4

today. Of course, they could form these images easier than we because, though we modern people may learn many things, the thoughts we normally acquire in school do not touch our hearts too deeply. It was quite different in the case of these ancient people. They were seized by the feeling emanating from thoughts and therefore dreamed of them. These people dreamed true dreams. The whole human being appeared as an image to them, and from his forehead they saw an eagle looking out, from the heart, a lion, and from the abdomen, a bull. They combined this into the beautiful image of the whole human being. One can truly say that long ago people composed their concept of the human being from the elements of man, bull, eagle and lion.

This outlook continued in the description of the Gospels. People frequently proceeded from this point of view. They said that in the Gospel of Matthew the humanity of Jesus is truly described; hence, its author was called 'man'. Then take the case of John, said the ancients, who depict Jesus as if He hovered or flew over the earth. John actually describes what happens in the region of the head; he is the 'eagle'. When one examines the Gospel of Mark, one will find that he presents Jesus as a fighter, the valiant one; hence, the 'lion'. Mark writes like one who represents primarily those organs of man situated in the chest. How does Luke write? Luke is presented as a physician, as a man whose main goal is therapeutic, and the healing element can be recognized in his Gospel. Healing is accomplished by bringing remedial forces into the digestive organs. Consequently, Luke describes Jesus as the one who brings a healing element into the lower nature of man. Luke, then, is the 'bull'. So one can picture the four Gospels like this: Matthew — man; Mark — lion; Luke — bull; John — eagle.

As for the journal whose cover depicts the four figures that you asked about, its purpose is to present something of value that can be communicated from one human spirit to another. So the true human being should be depicted in it. In rendering this drawing, the eagle is represented above, then the lion and bull, with man encompassing them all. This was done to show that the journal represents a serious concern with man. This is its aim. Not much of the human element is present in the bulk of what newspapers print these days. This drawing was intended to draw attention to the fact that this newspaper or journal could afford man the opportunity to express himself fully. What he says must not be stupid: the eagle. He must not be a coward: the lion. Nor should he lose himself in fanciful flights of thought but rather stand firmly on earth and be practical: the bull. The final result should be 'man', and it should speak to man. This is what one would like to see happen, that everything passed on from man to man be conducted on a human level.

Well, I did have time after all to get to your question after looking at those subjects I started with. I hope my answer was comprehensible. Were you interested in the description of the ear? One should know these things; one should be familiar with what is contained in the various organs that one carries around within the body.

Question: Is there time to say something about the 'lotus flowers' that are sometimes mentioned?

Dr Steiner: I'll get to that when I describe the individual organs to you.

The thyroid gland and hormones, Steinach's tests. Mental and physical rejuvenation treatments

Dr Steiner: Gentlemen, someone has handed in a written question concerning the thyroid gland.

Question: The thyroid gland can become enlarged and when it does a goitre is formed. Since goitres may exert pressure on the windpipe and thus cause a problem, operations have been performed on this gland, whose function is unknown. Soon after surgery, however, a strange phenomenon was observed. Persons whose whole thyroid gland had been removed exhibited both physical and mental changes. Growth stopped, limbs became enlarged and perspiration ceased. There also was evidence of some mental retardation. When the cause for this was realized, people sought to remedy the defects by feeding the unfortunate patients thyroid glands taken from freshly slaughtered calves or wethers. The result was astonishing. All negative effects subsided. But these results were short-lived, and within a few weeks the trend was reversed again. The patient's stomach also rebelled. Then sections of thyroid glands were introduced into the throat. Again, the results were amazing, but signs of deterioration reappeared. Injections made with preparations from thyroid glands were not much more successful. An English firm has achieved surprising results with certain tablets even in cases of cretinism. A short interruption in their use, however, reverses the process of recovery. What is to be expected with the continued use of these tablets?

Dr Steiner: Gentlemen, if you take into consideration what we have already discussed here, you will be able to understand this matter fairly well. You see, until about 70 years ago, until about the middle of the nineteenth century, no particular significance was attached to the thyroid gland, which is located here in the front of the neck. It was thought to be like the appendix or some other organ that had had a function in man's ancestors but was no longer needed. In short, no special importance was attributed to this gland. Then it was noted that its degeneration, with the formation of a goitre, had a specific effect even on mental faculties. Its purpose and pathological enlargements were studied in cretins, that is, retarded and mentally deficient people. One can observe that in certain geographic regions persons afflicted with goitres are also retarded. It is known throughout Europe that in Halberstadt the retarded population has goitres so large that in some cases they extend over the shoulders.

Now, it was thought at first that if pathological enlargement of the thyroid had such a pronounced influence on the mental faculties, surgical removal was indicated. This is how they think today. A great preference is shown for surgery because significant progress was made in surgical methods in the nineteenth century; this has become the most important aspect of medicine, that most deserving of recognition. So the first thought is to remove those organs that apparently have no significance. This is the procedure followed in the case of the appendix. It is surgically removed if it shows any pathological symptoms.

This manner of thinking ignores something I have repeatedly emphasized here. You will recall that when you observe man in his totality, you often note that something is present in certain processes of the child that has effects much later on, even in advanced age. Ordinary medical opinions are concerned only with what is needed at any one particular moment. Therefore, steps are taken that seem most beneficial at the given moment, but no attention is paid to the future course of events. It is difficult to make an overall judgement about these matters because, if a patient is not operated on when he exhibits symptoms of appendicitis, for example, he may immediately die. Then, of course, the doctor is held responsible. The point is to investigate other than surgical means to solve these problems. You are familiar, perhaps, with the fad these days of letting youngsters go about as much as possible with bare feet and legs, even up to the knees. Well, this habit contributes to the degeneration of the appendix! Of course, once the appendix has become inflamed, it must be removed, but when you see matters in a larger context, you know how to prevent such problems from arising in the first place.

Now, it is correct that the thyroid gland has great significance and important implications for the whole human organism. As I have said, people have been aware of this since the last half of the nineteenth century. They know that a malfunctioning thyroid does not support normal mental activities. Everything referred to in the question actually occurred. If a portion of the gland was allowed to remain, the patient did, indeed, make some improvement. He was relieved of the enlargement and his mentality was not adversely affected. But when the whole thyroid was removed and nothing of the gland remained, the patient became more retarded than before. Naturally, it was learned from this that even a diseased thyroid gland has significance for the expression of man's faculties of soul and spirit.

The secretion of the thyroid has been administered to patients in a number of ways. Incidentally, the fluid contained in a gland is called a secretion. Injections of thyroid substance could result in an increase of thyroid fluid in the body, but this method led to no lasting improvement. The organization of the body did not seem to respond favourably to what was being administered. So far, the best results have been obtained by administering thyroid fluid in the form of tablets, which are absorbed by the digestive system. Introducing the substance of the thyroid into the stomach and hence into the bloodstream permeates the body with the secretion of this gland. This remedy proves that the body needs such a secretion. It shows, too, that when the thyroid is functioning properly its secretion passes into the blood in minute amounts and penetrates the entire body. If the thyroid secretion is introduced into the stomach rather than directly into the body, it also finds its way into the bloodstream. But you understand, of course, that administering thyroid by way of the stomach is effective only as long as it comes to circulate in the blood. If the tablets are discontinued, the amount of thyroid in the blood will decrease. So persons who receive thyroid substance in this manner must take it continually. Then it does remain effective.

It can be said that this does, indeed, offer concrete proof for materialism because we see that we only need to administer certain substances to man in order to increase his mental faculties. The same is true when the substance is manufactured within the body, as is the case with thyroid secretion. By thoroughly checking all the experiments made in this area, however, we discover something else.

Thyroid glands are quite large, as you may know, and are located in the front of the neck. Within them are many small glands, to the right and left, that are no bigger than the head of a pin. They secrete a substance that is produced also in other parts of the body. Similar, but not identical, substances are secreted by small glands in various parts of the body. Though it differs from the substance produced in the small glands of the thyroid, such a substance, for instance, is secreted in the adrenal glands. Tiny glands like these are found in other parts of the body as well. In other words, the body contains traces of substances secreted in various parts of its organization. These substances are called hormones. Such a hormone that permeates the body in minute amounts is also contained in the tiny glands within the thyroid.

You may picture it this way. If you take a fish out of its watery environment, it will die because it cannot exist in air. Likewise, these hormonal glands, which resemble minute living organisms, can survive only within the thyroid, the real purpose of which is to provide a place where they can function. When the thyroid is surgically removed, the body is deprived of the hormones it produces. If these minute glands are removed with the thyroid, the prognosis is negative, but if enough of the thyroid containing them remains, then things don't look so bad. Enough must be left to permit some of these small glands to continue to function. When the entire thyroid gland is cut out, the hormone-producing glands are also removed and that is harmful. Less radical surgery that doesn't remove them all is successful. Preferably, then, just parts of the thyroid should be removed; the hormonal glands should be allowed to remain. But, if the secretion from the missing amount of thyroid substance containing these glands is replaced with tablets, so that the blood receives what it needs from them and also from passing through the remaining glands, the patient's general state of health may be expected to improve. The matter is really rather complicated, and much depends on how the thyroid secretion is produced.

When an experiment is performed on a wether in which only part of the thyroid is removed, leaving behind the part containing the hormonal glands, then it is found that the secretion does not have the medicinal value for human beings it would have had if the entire gland had been removed. When the entire gland is taken, however, the hormone produced by the hormonal glands combines with the thyroid secretion, permeating the blood of the thyroid, and an effective extract can be obtained. But, if only parts of the wether's thyroid is removed, leaving the hormonal glands behind, the thyroid extract will be less effective; then, such tablets will not work as well. So you see that not everything depends on the thyroid gland as such. Its purpose is only to nourish the minute hormonal glands, which, as you can imagine, were not discovered for a long time. Being so small, how could they have been noticed?

From all this you can understand that man's well-being simply requires certain substances. You need only recall that his mental faculties are altered also when he drinks wine, for instance. Cheerfulness is engendered by drinking wine but, later, things are likely to change. The next day his mood is usually quite the opposite of cheerfulness! So it is with this substance that is contained in the hormonal glands and that is required in minute amounts throughout man's body. He makes use of this substance, and animals need it, too. Much can be accomplished by working with such substances in the organism.

Well, in recent times, this has led to a more attentive examination of these delicate substances. What is the basis of the efficacy of such substances as those secreted by the hormonal glands? Gentlemen, you can understand this only when you realize that the body is constantly subject to processes of deterioration. It is a peculiarity of the organism that harmful substances are forever being formed in it. The substances secreted by the hormonal glands neutralize the destructive effect of these poisons that form in the body. It is a most interesting phenomenon that the processes of life consist in man's constantly poisoning himself, and then continuously counteracting the effects of the poisons by means of these little glands placed within his system. Take the case of the adrenal glands. If those little hormonal glands work properly, man appears the way you all look.

But when they malfunction, his complexion turns brown, a yellowish brown. Such an affliction is called Addison's disease, because a Dr Addison was the first to observe it. We once had such a patient who was a member of our society and who was looking for a cure here. This brown discolouration and darkening of the skin is caused by certain harmful substances in the body that are not neutralized by those substances normally produced in the adrenal glands. Likewise, mental retardation is caused by a lack of the substances normally produced in the hormonal glands of the thyroid.

When administered in tablets, hormones that act as antidotes are transmitted to the body, and their effects have led doctors to pay closer attention to this entire sphere of problems. It is interesting that this question also arises in connection with Steinach's theory. Since this theory is somewhat related to our topic, it will be worthwhile to consider them together. Steinach's theory is just about ten years old now. About ten years ago, a professor in Vienna sent a report of his experiments to the Academy of Sciences. Now known as Steinach's theory, the report is based on the fact that the body is continually permeated with hormones, the products of minutely small glands. It is interesting that the body seems to be constantly out to poison itself through its organs, but tiny glands located everywhere in the system produce antidotes. Starting at the neck, we have the hormonal glands of the thyroid, which enable us to speak rather than to stammer, and to connect thoughts with our speech. The hormones produced in the adrenal glands prevent us from turning dark. Also, hormonal glands of the reproductive organs emit small amounts of delicate fluid. These glands, of the gonads, are found in animals and humans, both male and female. They are only slightly developed in the child, but when he or she reaches puberty in the 14th or 15th year, they become fully developed. In the case of the male, the gonads or testes are located in the scrotum. They contain small hormonal glands whose secretion penetrates the whole blood circulation in minute dispersion.

Steinach's experiments have demonstrated that this particular hormone has the characteristic of suppressing the ageing process. Scientists have been concerned with ageing for a long time and, long before Steinach's theory became known, a physician-scientist in Paris named Metschnikoff published some interesting things about the phenomena of old age. His point of departure was that the body continually poisons itself. He emphasized the fact that poisons are constantly accumulating in the intestines and that man ages from the effect of the microscopically small animal- or plant-like creatures that produce them.

Now, Steinach concluded that the ageing process, this quite natural and normal process of deterioration, can be counteracted. He conducted his experiments mainly with rats; the most important tests were with rats. In cases like these, it must be said that experiments with animals are not completely applicable to humans. Not everything that occurs in animals, especially in rats, can be applied unreservedly to man. After all, the organism of the animal is different from that of man, and I must say, even if one has a low opinion of the size of the human being when compared, for example, with the vastness of the universe, yet a difference does exist between the physical organism of a human and a rat.

Most of the scientific results were obtained, as I have said, through experimentation on rats, which are particularly suitable for such tests. You see, the normal life span of the rat is about two and a half years, and before it dies it exhibits quite pronounced signs of ageing. Rats are quite agile and aggressive creatures, and when they age they turn dull and listless. They lose their fur in some spots and become bald; in other spots, their fur turns bristly and ragged. Also, they lose their appetite. Their age is shown particularly in that, when males are locked together in a cage, they don't fight but keep to themselves, and when an aging male rat is placed with a female, it shows no interest in her.

Of course, one has to be careful with such experiments because rats are susceptible to all kinds of disease. They easily become tubercular and frequently become infested with tapeworms or other intestinal parasites. Also, rats are subject to infectious diseases. Therefore, if a rat exhibits the symptoms I have described, it must be determined whether they are caused by such diseases or are truly signs of old age. So to conduct such experiments with rats one must start with quite a number and constantly examine them for intestinal parasites. Those with coarse fur or loss of hair due to illness must be eliminated. Eventually, you will be left with a few rats that are truly old.

Steinach experimented primarily with male rats. The ageing males that were listless and had bald spots, that had lost hair and were no longer interested in the females, were treated in the following manner. When not breeding, the gonad of the male rat is found above the scrotum. This gland constantly discharges fluid into tiny canals. It can be pictured like this [*drawing*]. Minute canals lead from the gonad into the spermatic cord, from which the semen is discharged. The hormone of the gonad passes through this canal and is mixed with the seminal fluid, which becomes permeated with the hormone. When the animal is young, this gland produces the hormone that passes through these canals, or vasa deferentia. From them, it enters the spermatic cord, so that the semen ejaculated by the male that impregnates the female contains this hormone. It is also diffused throughout the body. The principal part of the hormone flows into the spermatic cord, while the rest is distributed in minute amounts throughout the rat's organism by the blood.

Let us now take the case of a rat that is getting old and feeble. The feebleness and slackness of the body is indicated in that it can no longer control its excretory functions, having lost control over them. You may have heard that this also happens to people who are executed. This is what happens when the body becomes slack. When the organism ages, too much of this hormone flows into the spermatic cord, and too little is retained in the body. The body then contains the toxic substances of advanced age because the gonadal hormone is lacking and therefore not effective as an antidote. This explains why the rat's organism ages in the first place. It ages because various toxic substances produced in the body come to permeate it.

When a child reaches puberty much of the hormonal substance passes into the body. This is not the main point, however. Because the organism is young and vigorous, it can retain the hormone it receives and allow the surplus to be discharged.

Now, when the rat grows old, too much of the hormone is discharged. So Steinach tied off the tiny canal with a small thread, thus closing the passage from the gonad to the spermatic cord. Since the hormone now could not leave the gonad, it entered the body through the blood. You understand how that worked, don't you? When you shut off a pipe, the fluid backs up. He closed it off here [*indicating drawing*], made a ligature, as it is called, and thus caused all of the hormone to penetrate the body. The rat became lively again and even grew new hair. When it was put with females, it showed sexual desire and attacked them, though it could no longer impregnate them because the operation had rendered it sterile. This was really what happened.

You see, it is actually quite simple. The ageing body lets too much hormone escape, but because of ligation it is retained and the ageing process is reversed, even if only temporarily. It is quite interesting to observe how these male rats become agile and youthful again after the ligature is made in the spot I have indicated. These ligatures can be made in a variety of ways. The way I have just drawn it is a method that is rather complicated because an operation must be performed to reach this spot. First, an incision must be made on the outside, then the thread must be inserted around the canal to tie it off. Experiments have been performed in other ways, too. For example, the testicles, particularly in the case of humans, were destroyed with X-rays, thereby holding back the gonadal hormone. In short, all of these tests are based on somehow retaining the hormone in the organism. You see here the similarity with the thyroid gland. There too, it is a question of getting the hormone into the blood. It is the same with the gonadal hormone, except here it is done by closing this canal when a person has become incontinent in old age.

Steinach has successfully continued these experiments over the past ten years and today it can indeed be asserted that what was proven to occur in rats applies also to a certain extent in humans. Such experiments have been made on humans and similar results obtained by using ligatures or by introducing the hormones of a young person directly into the gonads. This has been done with injections or by injecting directly into the testicles the seminal fluid of a young animal. In other words, all kinds of ways have been tried to reintroduce this hormone into the body. Results have indeed been attained, and although they have been generally somewhat exaggerated, they cannot be denied. Experiments were, in fact, performed not only on rats but also on old people who had become feeble; they then regained some youthfulness. Of course, the effect doesn't last too long. The human body can live only a certain number of years and it is not at all certain yet whether the life span can be lengthened by these means. A man can be somewhat rejuvenated but, at present, one cannot lengthen his life. It is feasible, however, that the life span, too, will eventually be lengthened this way.

You understand, though, that all these matters also have their negative aspects. It is true, is it not, that some people are poor sleepers? If one treats young people who do not sleep well with sleeping pills of opium or morphine, they will certainly sleep better, no doubt about it. One can't argue against it, but the fact is that if sleeping pills and related chemical medication is administered repeatedly to young people, it will, after a while, weaken the body. It will have an increasing need for the medication and will come to be unable to live without it, thus becoming addicted to it. Then, in later life, one will have to deal with a person who is not in full possession of his health. So it is much better to try to cure insomnia by psychological means, combating it in a more inward way. If the patient is encouraged to think and concentrate on one word, he will gradually gain the strength from within to fall asleep. This method is much better because, this way, man does not weaken himself. The effects of sleeping pills are uncontested; it is indisputable that a person sleeps better with them, but it should really be considered from another aspect. One should try to induce sleep from an inward, mental direction. Of course, this method is more difficult and is related somewhat to education. If children are raised correctly, they can easily be induced to get the right amount of sleep every night. Then later in life people needn't be given sleeping pills if they have been treated properly in school.

These rejuvenation methods can really be compared to taking sleeping pills. Yes, gentlemen, the following is of particular interest. I have told you that Metschnikoff had already dealt with the symptoms of old age; as yet, Steinach's experiments were unknown. You may be surprised to learn that a thoroughly materialistic doctor recommended that his patients read things like Goethe's *Faust*! Really, they were told to read books like *Faust*; this was supposed to rejuvenate them.

There is much truth in this recommendation. If in old age one has an interest that completely occupies one's soul and spirit, something that inspires and enthuses one, this will make one youthful. The meaning of 'inspiration' is that something spiritual enters the mind. Otherwise, the term used would not be 'inspiration' but something like 'materialization'. When addressing the public, even materialists do not say, 'Let us be full of materialization!' Though they deny the spirit they nevertheless say, 'Let us be inspired and full of enthusiasm!' Being filled with enthusiasm is indeed a source of rejuvenation. Of course, one cannot prove this in rats! It is a source of rejuvenation in humans, however, and if observations in life were made in this direction, one would discover that, depending upon a person's health and stamina, whatever rejuvenation could be brought about would be attained much more easily if he could be allowed sufficient time to engage in some mental activity. Mental or spiritual activity has the peculiar effect of holding together and keeping strong the glandular walls. If a man is interested only in superficial matters all his life, his glands and vascular walls tend to become slack more quickly than if he has an interest in spiritual and mental activities. If he has been educated correctly as a child, and then given enough time to permeate himself rightly with spirit, he will not need such ligatures because he will maintain his strength on his own and his body will retain what it requires.

It is a different matter with the thyroid gland. Here, medical means must quite often be resorted to because it is extremely complicated to improve it with, well, spiritual means. Yet, here, too, results will be attained and have, in fact, already been achieved. If a patient repeats certain sayings day after day in a songlike speech, carefully prescribed in a definite way, the size of the thyroid gland will decrease.

So it must be said that hormone therapy is just as effective as medications are for insomnia. It would be better, however, if humans would at last begin to think about accomplishing things in other than just materialistic ways and would finally consider giving civilization the opportunity to afford everyone a chance for a certain degree of spiritual activity. Then these medical interventions wouldn't be valued quite so highly, because it would be recognized that one becomes feeble in old age in the first place because of the negative aspects of our civilization. All these operations on humans that give them a few months of rejuvenation in old age basically serve only to equalize what has already been damaged. From the medical standpoint it is a brilliant, remarkable accomplishment, but when it is viewed in a larger cultural context, one sees its darker side as well.

Of course, we must consider something else, too. I said earlier that administering sleeping pills to younger persons actually weakens them. If rejuvenation treatments are resorted to in elderly persons who are shrivelled up and can barely grope about, it is naturally a source of great happiness for them to be able to act a bit lively once more. At their age one doesn't have to be quite so concerned that such a rejuvenation treatment could be harmful to them later on!

Our materialistic world conception is attaining remarkable results today, but when they are seen in a larger cultural context, they take on a different appearance. This is why I always stress that people should be concerned with protecting children in school, and also in later years, to prevent them from getting premature symptoms of old age. This problem is not confined to a certain segment of society. Nowadays people hardly 30 run around with terribly bald heads, particularly those who belong to the so-called affluent professions. Premature baldness is caused by our unnatural forms of higher education. It would be much wiser to educate people in such a way that the body itself would be capable of holding everything together for as long as it retains its life forces.

This is what I can tell you about these matters. It is always interesting to view such things from the two or more angles which they always have. Anything else concerning this I shall talk about another time.

The eye. Hair colour

Dr Steiner: Well, gentlemen, perhaps one of you has a question you would like to ask me today.

Question: I would like to know why people with blond hair are becoming increasingly scarce. Formerly, there were many fair-haired people in the region where I was born, but now there are far fewer. Why is this so?

Dr Steiner: Your question fits quite well into our discussions, and I can consider it after I describe the human eye for you, as I promised to do earlier. We have already studied the ear; now we shall look at the eye. You may have noticed that blond hair is closely linked with blue eyes; as a rule, blonds have blue eyes. Your question relates to this matter, which you will understand fully when we examine the eye.

Eyes have great significance for the human being. It might be assumed that people born blind do not benefit at all from their eyes; nevertheless, they are still part of them, and they have the function not only of seeing but also of influencing the entire nervous system, inasmuch as this originates in the brain. The eyes are still there in one who is born blind even though they cannot see. They are placed in the socket but something is wrong internally, especially with the optic nerve. In addition, the muscles that control eye movements exist also in a blind person, and actually continuously influence the nervous system. Thus, the eye is, indeed, one of the most important organs of our body.

The eye, which is really like a miniature world, is placed in a cavity formed by the skull bones. You might say that it is something like a tiny world. The optic nerve fills out the retina and terminates in the brain, which I shall outline here [*sketching*]. So, if this is the eye seen in profile and sitting in the eye-socket, then here on the right is a canal through which the optic nerve passes. The eyeball lies buried in fatty tissue and is surrounded by bony walls. Attached to it are six ocular muscles that extend back into the bony walls of the socket. These bones are directly behind the upper jaw-bone.

In the anterior part of the eye is a completely transparent, clear tissue through which light passes. That the tissue looks black is an illusion. In reality, you see through the eye to its rear wall; you are looking through the transparent skin all the way to the back of the eye. The round blackness you see is the pupil, which looks black because the back of the eyeball is that colour. It is like looking through the window of a dark room; if you think the window itself is black, you are mistaken. The interior of the eye is completely transparent. This tissue is tough and opaque here and transparent in front. Within it and towards the rear is another layer of tissue possessing a network of fine, delicate blood vessels, which thicken here. Around the pupil is the iris, which in some people is blue and in others grey, green, brown or black.

Between the iris and the transparent tissue is a transparent fluid. Where you see the round blackness is the transparent skin, the cornea; behind that is the anterior chamber. It consists of living fluid and is shaped somewhat like a little glass lens. The actual lens of the eye is located here, where these delicate blood vessels come together and where the iris is formed. This structure, called the crystalline lens, also contains a living fluid. Its outer cover is transparent, permitting you to see the blackness behind it. Unlike a glass lens, it is mobile; it moves especially when you need to focus on something nearby. In that event, it is shaped like this [*sketching*], thick in the middle. When you need to look into the distance, it is bent like this, thin in the middle.

Next to the iris are delicate little muscles, which we tense to make the lens thicker when looking at something close up, or relax to make the lens thinner. A person's habits also affect the lenses. If you often use your eyes for close work, like reading or writing, gradually the lenses become permanently thick in the middle, and you become near-sighted. If you are a hunter, however, frequently looking into the distance, then the lenses become thin in the middle and you will become far-sighted. Another thing to consider is that in youth the tiny muscles located in and around the iris are still strong and elastic, and we can accommodate to our field of vision. In old age they become slack. This explains why many people become far-sighted with age, but this problem can be corrected. If a person's lenses are too thick in the middle, glasses are prescribed with lenses that are concave. These will compensate for the thickness of the eye's lenses. Some people even have a twofold problem, needing one set of glasses for clear distance vision and another set for close up. If the lenses of the eyes are too thin, the glasses will have convex lenses. Their thickness is added to the lens of the eye and compensates for the defect. You could say that we are able to see because we can correct the defect of the lens. The lens in our eye is like that of our glasses: near- and far-sighted. But the lens in our glasses stays the same, while that in the eye is living and can adjust and accommodate itself.

Behind the lens is also something like a living fluid. It, too, is completely transparent, permitting light to pass through everywhere. This gelatinous and crystalline substance completely fills the interior of the eyeball. So here in front is something like transparent 'hard water', the aqueous humour; next comes the transparent lens, and then comes the vitreous humour, which is also transparent. The optic nerve enters the eye here, and reaches approximately to here.

This optic nerve is extremely complicated. I have drawn it as if the main nerve fibre simply divides here, but there's more to it than this. There are actually four layers of nerves surrounding the vitreous humour. This is the outer layer of the nerve [*sketching*], which acts like a strong mirror. When light enters the eye and hits the layers of the retina, it is reflected everywhere. It does not go into this [*probably referring to the nerve canal*] but stays in the eye. The outer layer acts like the wall of a mirror and reflects the light. A second layer of nerves intensifies this reflecting capacity. As we have said, the nerve that lines our eyeball consists of four layers. The outermost layer and the second outer layer reflect back all the light into the interior sphere. Thus, within the vitreous humour we have actually only reflected light. A third layer of nerves consists of the same substance that makes up the grey matter of our brain. The outer parts of our brain are grey matter, not white. Another 'skin' constitutes the fourth layer. You see, the vitreous humour is placed within a complicated 'sack'. This enables all the light that penetrates into the interior of the eyeball through the pupil to be reflected within the vitreous humour and to remain there.

What we have in our eye is something that looks like a complicated physical apparatus. What is it for? Well, imagine that a person is standing somewhere. When you look at him, an inverted picture is produced in your eye because of the lens and vitreous humour. So, if a person stands there [*sketching*], you have a small image of him in your eye, but owing to this apparatus, it is an image that stands on its head. The eye is just like a camera in this respect; it is much like a photographic apparatus in which the object photographed appears in an image upside down. That also happens in the eye; since it is a mirroring device, when light enters, it is reflected. Thus, in the eye we have the image of a little person. Even with all our modern sophisticated machinery, something like the human eye can certainly not be manufactured. We must admit that it is altogether extraordinary and marvellous.

Now, picture to yourselves the starry heaven; form an image of the light-filled sphere around the earth, and then reduce this picture until it is quite small. What you then have is the interior of the human eye. The human eye is actually a world in miniature, and the reflections in the eye resemble myriad surrounding stars. You see, these outer walls do not reflect evenly. There are many tiny bodies, which, like miniature stars, radiate light towards the centre. If we were as small as the image of the human being in the eye and could examine it from inside, its interior would seem infinitely large. Our impression would be the same as when on earth we look up to the glittering stars at night. It is indeed so. It is interesting that the eye is like a miniature world and that the tiny human image produced in the eye by reflections would have the same feeling, if it were conscious, that we have at night under a starry sky. It is really quite interesting!

Well, I said, 'if that image possessed consciousness.' But if we did not possess our eyes, we would not be able to view the starry night. We see the night sky and its brilliant stars only because we have eyes; if we close them, we do not see the stars. Nor could we see the starry firmament if the eye did not already contain within it a miniature world. We say to ourselves that this miniature universe really signifies a big world. This is something that must be clearly understood.

Imagine that someone shows you a small photograph of himself or another person. You will realize that even though it is small it was taken of a regular-sized man. You are not encountering the actual person in this picture, and likewise in the eye; in reality you have only this miniature starry sky within you when you look up at the heavens. You then say to yourself, 'What I have here before me is the "photograph" of the immense starry sky.' You do this all the time. You have within your eye the little starry sky and then you tell yourself, 'This is the photograph of the great starry sky.' You actually always picture the real starry sky from the miniature firmament in your eye; you conceive of the universe by means of this picture within. What you really experience is the infinitesimal firmament in its miniature form within the eye.

Now you might say, 'Yes, but this would be true only if we possessed just one eye like the cyclops, whereas we have two eyes.' Well, why do we have two? Try this. Look at something with only one eye. It will appear to be painted on a backdrop. We do not have two images of an object, which we see in proportion and in the right dimensions only because we possess two eyes. Seeing with both eyes is like grabbing your right hand with your left. We are conscious of ourselves because from childhood we have been used to saying 'I' to ourselves. The little word 'I' would not be in the language if our right side were not aware of our left. We would not be conscious of ourselves. We become so accustomed to the most important things that we take them for granted. A hidebound philistine would say, 'The question of why one says "I" to oneself does not interest me. It goes without saying that one says "I" to oneself!' Well, he is a narrow-minded and prosaic person. He does not realize that most subtle matters are based on the most complicated processes. He does not know that, as a child, he became used to an awareness of himself based, for example, on touching his left hand with his right, and thus grew accustomed to saying 'I' to himself.

This fact can be traced in human culture. If we go back to ancient times, to the days of the Old Testament for instance, we find priests who — excuse me for voicing such a heretical opinion — often knew much more than the priests nowadays and who said, 'We want to teach man self-awareness.' So they taught people to fold their hands. This is the origin of folding your hands in prayer. Man touched one hand with the other in order to find the strong ego within him and to develop his will. Things like this are not said today because they are not understood. Priests today simply tell members of the congregation to fold their hands in prayer; they do not give the meaning of this gesture because they themselves do not know it any more.

When we see with our two eyes, we feel that what is there in the light is in fact spatial. If we had only one eye, everything would appear as if painted on the firmament. Our two eyes enable us to see things in three dimensions and to experience ourselves as standing within the centre of the world. In a good or bad sense, every person considers himself to be the centre of the world. Therefore, it is of great importance that we have two eyes.

Now, since it is so important for man to use his eyes for seeing, we overlook something else about them. We are not so ignorant in the case of the ear. I believe I have mentioned already that when we hear we also speak; that is, we ourselves produce what we hear. We can understand a spoken language only because of the Eustachian tube, which runs from the mouth into the ear. You surely know that children born deaf cannot speak either, and that people who are not taught to speak a language cannot understand it. Special means must be used to gain an understanding of what has been heard.

At first glance it does indeed appear that seeing is the only purpose of the eye, but a child learns not only to see with its eyes but also to speak with them, even if we don't pay much attention to this. The language of the eyes is not as suitable for everyday use as is the language directed to the ears, but with it you can discover whether a person is telling a lie or the truth. If you are the least bit sensitive, you can discover in the way he looks at you whether or not he is telling you the truth. The eyes do speak, and the child learns to speak with them just as it does with its mouth.

In speech the larynx, with its function of uttering sounds, is separated from the ear, and thus there are two separate aspects. In the case of the eye, there are muscles right within the organ and also around it. It is the muscles that make the eye into a kind of visible organ of speech. Whether we look somebody straight in the eye, or have a shifty look, depends on the muscles that surround the eyeball. It is as if the ear were contained within the larynx, as in fishes. In man the ear is separated from the larynx, but in fishes they are joined to form one organ. The act of speaking is separated from hearing, but with the eye it is as if the larynx with its muscles surrounded the ear. The eye is situated within its speech organ as if the ear were placed within the larynx. In humans it is like this [sketching]. Here we have the larynx, the voice box, which goes down through the windpipe into the lungs and up into the palate. It enables us to speak. From the mouth we have a connection with the ear.

Now imagine that the larynx is not like it is in humans but that it spreads out much wider. Then we would have the broad larynx that Lucifer possesses in my wooden statue. The larynx is so large that the head fits in between, and it reaches up on both sides to surround the ear. With this organ we would both speak and hear. With the eye we do just that; we speak through the muscles that surround the eyeball, and through the eye we simultaneously see. So in some respects the eye is conceived like the ear, but in other respects it is, of course, quite different. This, then, is the purpose of the muscles I have drawn here.

We can say that we speak of what we know, and we consider those who say things of which they know nothing to be more or less fools. We say of such people that they are talking to themselves, shooting their mouths off. As a rule, however, sensible and rational people express what they know. We do not speak consciously with the eye, however, for we would have to be shrewd fellows, indeed, if we could consciously speak the language of the eyes. This process is unconscious and accompanies our other behavior. The people in southern Italy, for example, still speak of an 'evil eye'. They still know that a person who has a certain look about him is false. They talk of an evil eye because they sense that the eye expresses the whole nature of a man without his being aware of it. This superstition in southern Italy goes so far that some hang little charms or religious medals around their necks as protection from it.

So you see how marvellously the eye is formed. A person who studies the eye in this way simply cannot say that there is nothing of the soul in it. It is simply stupid and philistine to say that the eye has no element of the soul. People say that light penetrates through the pupil into the eye, passes through the lens into the vitreous humour, produces an image here on the retina, and then is transmitted into the brain. Modern science stops right there; or it might perhaps go as far as to say that the light in the brain is used to produce thoughts. This description gives rise to all sorts of nonsensical statements that lead to nothing.

In reality, the light does not reach the brain. I have explained how it is reflected in the eyeball as in a mirror. The light remains in the eye, and it is important to know that it stays there. The interior of the eyeball is like the illuminated starry expanse. The light remains within the eye and does not penetrate directly into the brain. If the light did enter the brain, we would not be able to see anything at all. We can see because it does not do so. Just imagine, gentlemen, that you are standing here in this room all by yourselves; there are no chairs, nothing but the walls.

The room is completely illuminated within, but you see nothing. You know only that it is illuminated, but you can see no objects of any kind. If the brain were only filled with light, we would see nothing because it is not solely on account of light that we see. Everywhere the light is kept in the eye and illumines its interior. What does this mean? Well, imagine that we have a little box. I stand with my back to it; I have not seen it before. I must reach behind myself to be able to know that it is there. Likewise, when the eye is illuminated from within, I must first feel the light to know that it is there. I must first feel the light, and this is done with the soul. In other words, the apparatus of the eye produces something we can feel. The soul passes through the muscles and feels or senses the little person I have mentioned within the eye.

Every organ within the human being shows us that the soul observes, feels or senses what is within. If we examine everything carefully, we discover the soul and the spirit everywhere, especially in the eye. After a while, we can get the feeling that we are sitting in front of a peephole here. When I look at you, you appear within, but I *form the conception* that the image within is the person outside. This is how the eye works. Just imagine that it is a little peephole through which the soul forms the idea that what it observes is the vast world. We simply must recognize the soul's existence when we actually examine the matter.

Now, I said that here is the choroid [*referring to his sketch of the eyeball*]. It contains tiny blood vessels and lies under the optic nerve and its network. The optic nerve does not reach all the way to the front of the eyeball but the choroid, with its muscles, does. It extends to the lens and actually holds it in place. Here, as I have mentioned, is the iris surrounding the black pupil, which is nothing but an aperture. The iris is quite complicated. I will draw it a little larger, as seen from the side. So here is the iris, attached to the ciliary muscle.

The choroid and lens sit within, held in place by the iris. Seen from the front, the iris has a front wall and a back wall. On the back wall are little coloured granules, which are microscopically small sacks. In everyone they are filled with a blue substance, and this is what one sees in blue-eyed people. In their case, the front layer is transparent, so you see the back layer of the iris, which is filled with this blue substance. In a blue-eyed person you are really seeing the back wall of the iris; the front part is transparent. Brown-eyed people have the same blue substance in the back layer of their iris, but they possess also brown granules in front of it. These cover up the blue ones so that all you see are the brown. A black-eyed person has black granules. You see not the blue but the little black sacks. It is the iris that causes a person's eyes to be blue, brown or black. The iris is always blue at the back, and in blue-eyed persons it possesses no coloured substance at all in front; in brown-eyed and black-eyed people, it contains coloured granules in front that obscure the blue granules at the back. Why is that? Well, you see, these tiny little sacks are constantly being filled with blood and then emptied. The blood penetrates the tiny granules in minute amounts. In a blue-eyed person, they are constantly being filled with and emptied of a little blood. The same thing happens with brown- and black-eyed persons. The blood enters, deposits blue or black coloured substance, then leaves again and takes the coloured substance with it. This is a continual process.

Now, some people have a strong force in their blood that drives the substances from food all the way into the eyes. This gives them brown or black granules. Those with black granules are people whose organisms can drive the blood most strongly into the eyes; the substances from nourishment easily reach into the eyes. This is less the case with brown-eyed people. Their eyes are not so well-nourished, and a blue-eyed person's organism does not drive the nourishing substances far enough into the eyes to fill the front part of the iris with them. It remains transparent and all we can see is the back part. Thus, a person is blue-eyed because of the way all the substances circulate through his organism. If you observe such a blue-eyed person, you can say that he has less driving force in his circulation than one who is black-eyed.

Consider the Scandinavians. Much of their nourishment must be utilized in fighting off the surrounding cold. A Nordic man does not have enough energy left to drive the nourishment all the way into the eyes; his energy is needed to ward off the cold. Hence, he is blue-eyed. A man who is born in a warm, tropical climate has in his blood the driving force to push the nourishing substances into his eyes. In the temperate zones it is an individual matter whether a man possesses more or less inner energy.

This also affects the colour of hair. A person with strong forces drives food substances all the way into his hair, making it brown or black. A person with less driving force does not push these substances all the way into the hair, and thus it remains light. So we see that blue eyes and blond hair are related. The one who drives the food substances forcefully through his body gets dark hair and eyes; the one who does it less vigorously gets light hair and eyes. This can be understood from what I have told you.

When you take into consideration the most important aspects, you can find meaning for everything. The earth on which we live was young when it brought forth those giant megatheri and ichthyosauri that I have described for you. The earth was once young. Now it is past its prime; it is growing older and some day will perish from old age, though not in the way described by materialists. We are already faced with some of the signs of the earth's old age. Therefore, the entire human race has been weakened in regard to the driving force that moves food substances through the body. So what part of the population is going to be the first to disappear from the earth? Dark people can last longer, for they possess greater driving force; blonds have less and become extinct sooner. The earth is indeed already into its old age. The gentleman who asked the question pointed out that there are fewer blonds around than in his youth. Because the earth has less vitality, only the black and brown peoples attain sufficient driving force; blonds and blue-eyed people are already marked for extinction because they can no longer drive nourishment with the necessary force through their bodies.

In the age when those giant beasts existed — the ichthyo-sauri, plesiosauri and megatheri — cows certainly did not yet exist, cows from whom milk is taken for human consumption. Of course, neither did human beings exist then who would have required such milk. But just yesterday I read a statement by somebody who is really afraid of progress. He thinks people who express ideas today that should be formulated only after many centuries have passed ought to be persecuted, because, he says, the time is not ripe for their utterances. Gentlemen, it seems to me that if this had been the case in the period when cows were supposed to come into existence, no creature would have had the courage to become a cow! It is like saying, 'What is taught today as anthroposophy should emerge only after many centuries.' Well, then it wouldn't appear at all, just as no cows would have come into being. In effect, it is like saying, 'I would rather remain an old primeval hog than transform myself into a cow!'

The situation on earth is such that we must have the courage to change and to ascend from those periods when mankind knew things instinctively, to one in which everything is known consciously. This is why I present everything to you here in such a way that you can comprehend fully what is really going on and know in what direction the wind is blowing. When you read a book nowadays, or when you hear about what goes on in the great wide world, you cannot actually get to the bottom of what makes everything tick. But people don't know that. You can understand a phenomenon like the gradual extinction of blonds if you comprehend how nourishing substances penetrate into both the eyes and hair, the colouring of which is closely related.

If you go to Milan, you will find that the head of the lion there is depicted in such a way that its mane, that is, the largest accumulation of hair the lion possesses, looks like rays of light. This rendering is based on an ancient wisdom in which it was known that both the eyes and hair are related to light and its rays.

Hair is indeed like plants, which are placed in the ground and whose growth is subject to light. If light is unable to draw nourishing substances all the way into the hair, it remains blond. If a person is more closely tied to matter, the food substances penetrate the hair completely and counteract the light; then he gets black hair. Sages of old were still aware of this, just as were people even a few centuries ago. Thus, they did not depict the lion's mane as being curly but instead they gave it a radiating, straight form, as if the sun had shone its beams right into the lion's head. It is most interesting to observe such things.

6. *Discussion of 16 December 1922*

The nose, smell and taste

As you recall, gentlemen, last time we talked about the eye, and we were particularly impressed with its marvellous configuration. Even in regard to its external form, the eye reproduces a whole world. When we become acquainted with the interior of the eye, the way we did last time, we discover that there is indeed a miniature world within. That I have explained to you, and thus we have become familiar with two senses of man — sight and hearing.

Now, in connection with other questions you have recently posed, we shall see that a particularly fascinating and interesting human sense is that of smell. This sense appears to be of minor importance in man but, as you know, it is of great significance in the dog. You could say that all the intelligence of the dog is, in fact, transferred to the sense of smell. You need only consider how much the animal can accomplish by smell. A dog recognizes people by smell long after it has last been with them. Anyone who observes dogs knows that they recognize and identify somebody with whom they have been acquainted, not by the sense of sight, but by that of smell. If you have heard recently how dogs can become excellent detectives and search for lawbreakers or for people in general, you will say to yourselves that here the sense of smell accomplishes rare things that naturally appear simple but are in actuality not so simple at all. You need only consider these matters to realize that they are not so simple.

'Well,' you may say casually, 'the dog merely follows the scent.' Yes, gentlemen, that is true, the dog does indeed follow the scent. But think about it. Police dogs are used to follow, say, first the track of thief X and then the track of thief Y, one right after the other. The two scents are completely different from each other; if they were alike the dog could naturally never be able to follow them. Imagine now that you had to point out the difference between these tracks that the dogs distinguish by smell; you would discover no significant difference. The dog, however, does detect differences. The point is not that the dog follows the tracks back and forth in general but that it is capable of distinguishing between the various traces of scent. That, indeed, indicates intelligence.

There is yet another extremely important consideration. Civilized people use their sense of smell for foods and other external things, but it doesn't inform them of much else. In contrast, primitive tribes in Africa can smell out their enemies at far range, just as a dog can detect a scent. They are warned of their foes by smell. Thus, the intelligence that is found in such great measure in the dog is also found to a certain degree among primitive people. The member of a primitive tribe in Africa can tell long before he has seen his adversary that he is approaching; he distinguishes him from other people with his nose. Imagine how delicate one's sense of discernment in the nose must be if one can know that an enemy is nearby by means of it. Also, Africans know how to utter a certain warning sound that Europeans cannot make at all. It is a clicking sound, somewhat like the cracking of a whip.

It can be said that the more civilized a man becomes, the more diminished is the importance of his sense of smell. We can use this sense as an indicator of whether we are dealing with a less 'civilized' species like the canine family—and they are an uncivilized species—or one more civilized. If we were to follow up on this, we would probably make some priceless discoveries about pigs, which, of course, have an exceptionally strong sense of smell.

There is something else in regard to this that will interest you. The elephant is reputed to be one of the most intelligent animals, and it certainly is; the elephant is a highly intelligent animal. Well, what feature is particularly well developed in the elephant? Look at the area above the teeth in the dog and the pig, the area that in man forms itself into the nose. When you picture an especially strong and pronounced development of this part, you arrive at the elephant's trunk. The elephant possesses what is nose in us to a particularly pronounced degree, and therefore it is the most intelligent animal. The extreme intelligence of the elephant does not depend on the size of the brain but on its extension straight into the nose.

All these facts challenge us to ask how matters stand in respect to the human nose, an organ that civilized man today does not really know too much about. Of course, he is familiar with its anatomy and structure, but basically he does not know much more than the fact that it sits in the middle of his face. Yet the nose, with its continuation into the brain, is actually a most interesting organ. If you will recall my descriptions of the ear and the eye, you will say to yourselves that they are complicated. The nose, however, is not so complicated, but it is quite ingenious.

Seen from the front, the nose has a wall in the middle, the septum. This can be felt when you hold your nose. The septum divides the nose into a left and a right side, and to the left and the right are the actual parts of this organ. From the front it looks like this [*sketching*, Fig. 5]. The cribriform plate is located in the skull bone up where the nose sits between the eyes. It is like a little sieve. In other words, it is a bone with many holes. It is intricate but in my drawing I shall simplify it. On the exterior, the nose has skin like the skin on the rest of the body; inside, it is completely lined and filled out with a mucous membrane. This is everywhere in the nose, a fact that you can readily confirm. This

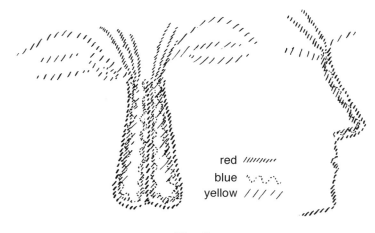

red ////////
blue ·.·.·.·.
yellow /// //

Fig. 5

membrane secretes mucus; if you did not have it, you would not have to blow your nose. So, inside the nose is a membrane that secretes mucus, but the matter is more complicated. You will have noticed that children who cry secrete a lot of nasal mucus. A canal in the upper part of the nose leads to the tear glands, which are located on both sides in the interior. There the secretion, the tears, enters the nose and mixes with the nasal mucus. Thus the nose has a kind of 'fluidic connection' with the eyes. The secretion of the eyes flows into the mucous membrane and combines with the secretion of the nose. This connection shows us again that no organ in the body is isolated. The eyes are not only for seeing; they can also cry, and what they then discharge mixes with what is primarily secreted in the membrane of the nose.

The olfactory nerve, the actual nerve used for smelling, passes through the cribriform plate, which is located at the root of the nose. This nerve has two fibres that pass from the brain through the sievelike bone and spread out within the nose. The mucous membrane, which we can touch with our finger, is interlaced by the olfactory nerve, which reaches into the brain. We can easily discern that because the nose is constructed quite simply.

Now we come to something that can reveal much to one who thinks sensibly. You see, a thorough examination will show that no one has eyes of equally strong vision, and when we examine the two hands we readily discover that they are not of equal strength. The organs of the human being are never completely equal in strength on both the left and right side. So it is also with the nose. Generally, we simply do not smell as well with the left nostril as with the right, but it is the same here as it is with the hand; some individuals are better at smelling with the left nostril than with the right, just as some people are left-handed. As you know, some people in the world are screwed together the wrong way. I am not referring to those people whose heads are screwed on wrong* but to those whose hearts are screwed on the wrong way. In the average person, the heart is located slightly off-centre to the left, as are the rest of the internal organs. Now, in a person whose heart is 'screwed on the wrong way', as it were, whose heart is off-centre a bit to the right, the stomach is also pushed over slightly to the right. But this phenomenon is much less noticeable than when one is 'not quite right' in the head. The fact only becomes apparent when a person has fallen ill or has been dissected. Autopsies first led to the dis-covery that there are such odd people whose hearts and stomachs are shifted to the right. Of course, since not everyone who is a bit odd in the head is dissected after death, one often doesn't even know that there are many

---

*(A play on words. In German, a 'Querkopf' is a person who is odd. Rudolf Steiner then uses the term 'Querherz' to indicate the anatomical oddity of the heart.)

more such 'odd people' than is normally assumed, whose hearts are off-centre to the right.

A truly effective pedagogy, however, must take this into consideration. When dealing with a child who does not have its heart in the right place, speaking strictly anatomically, this must be taken into account; otherwise, it can have awkward consequences for the youngster. Because man is not just a physical apparatus, he does not necessarily have to be educated in such a way that abnormalities like this have to become an obstacle. Taking such aspects into consideration is what truly makes pedagogy an art.

A Professor Benedikt has examined the brains of many criminals. In Austria this was frowned upon because the people there are Catholics and they see to it that such things are not done. Benedikt was a professor in Vienna. He got in touch with officials in Hungary, where at one time there were more Calvinists, and he was given permission to transport the heads of executed criminals to Vienna. Several things then happened to him. There was a really ruthless killer who had I don't know how many murders on his conscience but who also had religious faith. He was a devout Catholic. When a rumour broke out that the brains of criminals were being sent to Professor Benedikt in Vienna, this criminal who was a cold-blooded murderer protested. He did not want his head sent to the professor because he didn't know where he would look for it to piece it together with the rest of his body when the dead arise on Judgment Day. Even though he was a hardened criminal, he did believe in Judgment Day.

So what did Professor Benedikt find in the brains of criminals? In the back of our heads we have a 'little brain', the cerebellum, which I shall speak about later on. It is covered by a lobe of the 'large brain', the cerebrum. It looks like a small tree [*drawing*]. On top it is covered by the cerebrum and the occipital lobe. Now, Professor Benedikt discovered that in people who have never committed murder or a theft—and there are such people—the occipital lobe extends down to here [*drawing*], whereas in those who had been murderers or other criminals the lobe did not extend so far; it did not cover the cerebellum below.

A malformation like that is naturally congenital; a person is born with it. And, gentlemen, there are a great many people born with an occipital lobe that is too small to properly cover the cerebellum! It can be made up for by education, however. Nobody has to become a killer because he has a shorter occipital lobe; he becomes a criminal only if he is not properly educated. From this you can see that if the body is not correctly developed one can compensate for it with the forces of the soul. Therefore it is nonsense to say that a person cannot help becoming a criminal—which is what the otherwise brilliant professor stated—because as an embryo he was incorrectly positioned in the mother's womb and thus did not properly develop the occipital lobe. He might be quite well educated by accepted standards, but he is not properly educated in regard to such an abnormality. Of course, he cannot help the inadequacies of education, but society can help it; society must see to it that the matter is handled correctly in education. I mention this so you may realize the great significance of the whole organization of man.

Let us return again to the subject of the dog. We must admit that in the dog the nose is especially well developed. Now, gentlemen, what do we actually smell? What does a dog really smell? If you take a bit of substance like this piece of chalk, you will not smell it. You will be able to smell it only if the substance is set on fire, and the ingredients evaporate to be received into the nose as vapour. You cannot even smell liquid substances unless they first evaporate. We smell only what has first evaporated. Also, there must be air around us with which the vapours from substances can mix. Only when substances have become vaporous can we smell them; we cannot smell anything else. Of course, we do smell an apple or a lily, but it is nonsense to say that we smell the solid lily. We smell the *fragrance* arising from the lily. When the vapour-like scent of the lily wafts in our direction, then the nerve in the nose is able to experience it.

What a primitive tribesman smells of his enemy are his evaporations. You can conclude from this that a man's presence makes itself felt much farther than his hands can reach. If we were primitive people and one of us were down in Arlesheim, he would know if an adversary of his were up here among us. This would mean that his foe would make his being felt all the way down to Arlesheim! [Arlesheim is about $1\frac{1}{2}$ miles from Dornach.] Indeed, all of you extend to Arlesheim by virtue of what evaporates from you. On account of a man's perspirations, something of himself extends a good distance around himself, and through that he is present to a greater degree than through what one can see externally.

Now, the dog does something interesting that man cannot do. All of you are quite familiar with it. If somewhere you meet a dog you know well that is equally well-acquainted with you, the animal will wag its tail because it is glad to see you. Yes, gentlemen, why does it wag its tail? Because it experiences joy? A man cannot wag his tail when he is happy, because he does not have one any more. In this regard man has become stunted, in so far as he has no way to immediately lend expression to his joy. The dog, however, smells the person and wags its tail. On account of the scent, the dog's whole body reaches a state of excitement that is expressed by the tail muscles receiving the experience of gladness. In this respect man has reached the stage where he lacks such an organ with which he could express his joy in this way.

We see that while man is more cultivated than dogs, he lacks the ability to drive the sensation of smell down his spinal cord. The dog can do this; the scent enters its nose and is transmitted down the spinal cord, and then the dog wags its tail. What enters its nose as scent travels down the spinal cord. The end of the spine is the tail, and so it wags it [Fig. 6]. Man cannot do that and I shall tell you why he cannot. Man also possesses a spinal cord, but he cannot transmit a scent through it. Now, I shall draw the whole head of the human being in profile [Fig. 7]. The spinal cord continues down on the left. In the case of the dog it becomes the tail, which the animal can wag. Man, however, turns the force of his spinal cord in the other direction. Indeed, he has the capacity to change many things around, something that the animals cannot do. Thus animals walk on all fours, or if they do not, as in the case of some monkeys, it is all the worse for them. They are actually organized to walk on all fours. But the human being raises himself up. At first man too walks on all fours, but then he stands erect. The force through which he accomplishes this, and that passes through the spinal cord, is the same force that pushes the whole brain forward. It is actually quite interesting to see a dog wag its tail. If a human being compares himself to the dog, he can exclaim, 'Isn't that something; it can wag its tail, and I cannot!'

Fig. 6

Fig. 7

The whole force that is contained in this wagging tail, however, has been dammed back by man, and it has pushed the brain forwards. In the dog it grows backwards, not forwards. The force that the dog possesses in its tail we turn around and lead into the brain. You can picture to yourselves how this really works by realizing that at the end of the spine, where we have the so-called tail bone, is the coccyx, which consists of several atrophied vertebrae. In the dog they are well formed and developed; in us they are a fused and completely stunted protrusion that we can no longer wag. It ends here and is covered by skin. Now, we are able to turn this whole 'wagging ability' around, and if in fact the top of the skull were not up here, upon smelling a pleasant odour we could wag with our brain, as it were. If our skull bones did not hold it together, we would actually wag with our forebrain when we are glad to see somebody.

You see, this is what marks the human organization; it reverses the function found in animals. This tail wagging ability is still developed but it is reversed. In reality, we too wag something, and some people have a sensitivity for perceiving it. Isn't it true that court officials fawn and cringe in the royal presence? Of course, theirs is not a wagging like that of a dog, but some people still get the feeling that they are really wagging their tails. This is because their wagging is on the soul level and indeed looks like tail wagging. If one has acquired clairvoyance — something that is easily misunderstood but that merely consists of being able to see some things better than others — then, gentlemen, one does not just have the feeling that a courtier is wagging his tail in front of a personage of high rank; one actually sees it. He does not wag something in the back, but he does indeed wag something in the front. Of course, the solid substances within the brain are held together by the skull bones, but what is developed there in the form of delicate substantiality, as warmth, wags when a courtier is standing before royalty. It fluctuates. Now it is warm, now a little cooler, warmer, cooler. Someone with a delicate sensitivity for this fluctuating warmth, who is standing in the presence of courtiers surrounding Lords, sees something that looks like a fool's cap wagging back and forth in front. It is correct to say that the etheric body, the more delicate organization of man, is wagging in front. It is absolutely true that the etheric body wags.

In the dog or the elephant all this is utilized to form the spinal cord. What remains stunted in both these animals is reversed and pushed forwards in man. How is that? In the brain two things meet: the 'wagging organ', which has been pushed forwards and is present in this form only in man, and the olfactory nerve, which is also present in man. In the case of the dog, the olfactory nerve enlarges considerably because nothing counteracts it; what would restrain it is wagging in the back. The human being turns this around. The whole 'wagging force' comes forward to the nose, and thus the olfactory nerve is made as small as possible; as it penetrates into the brain it is compressed from all sides by what comes to meet it there. You see, man has within the head an organ that, on the one hand, forces back his faculty of smell but, on the other, makes him into a human being. This organ results from the forces that are pushed up and forwards.

In the case of the dog and the elephant, much of the olfactory nerve is located in the forward part of the brain; a large olfactory nerve is present there. In man, this nerve is somewhat stunted. The nerves that were pushed upwards from below spread out instead. As a result, this spot — where in the dog sensations of smell spread out much further — is located the noblest part of the brain in the human being. There, located in the forward part of the brain, is the sense for compassion, the sense for understanding other human beings, and that is something noble. What the dog expends in its tail-wagging, man transforms into something noble. There, in the forward part of the brain, just at the spot where the lowly nose would otherwise transmit its olfactory nerve, man possesses an extraordinarily noble organ.

I have mentioned that we do not smell equally well with the left and the right nostrils. Now, try to recall someone who is in the habit of making pronounced gestures. What does he do when he is pondering something? I am sure you have seen it. He reaches up with his finger or his hand and touches his nose; his index finger comes to rest directly over the septum, the inner wall dividing the nasal passages. For right here, behind the nose and within the brain, the capacity for discrimination has its physical expression.

The septum of the dog enables it not only to follow a lead precisely but also to distinguish carefully with the left and the right nostrils how the scents appear to either one or the other. The dog always has in its right nostril the scent of what it is pursuing at the moment, while in the left it has the scents of everything it has already pursued. The dog therefore becomes increasingly skilful in pursuit, just as we human beings become more and more intelligent when we learn more and commit facts to our memory. The dog has a particularly good memory for scents, and that is why he becomes such a keen tracker.

A trace of that still exists in human life. Man's sense of smell has become dulled, but Mozart, for example, was sometimes inspired with his best melodies when he smelled a flower in a garden. When he pondered the reason for this, he realized that it happened because he had already smelled this flower somewhere else and that he had especially liked it. Mozart would never have gone so far as to say, 'Well, I was once in this beautiful garden in such and such a place, and there was this flower with a wonderful fragrance that pleased me immensely; now, here is the fragrance again, and it makes me almost want to, well — wag my tail.' Mozart would not have said that, but a beautiful melody entered his mind when he smelled this flower the second time. You can tell from this how closely linked are the senses of smell and memory.

This is caused not by what we human beings absorb as scents but rather by what we push forwards in the brain and against it. Our power of discrimination is developed there. If a person can think especially logically, if he has the proper thought relationships, then we can say that he has pushed his brain forwards against his olfactory nerve, that he has actually adjusted the brain to what otherwise would have also been the olfactory nerve. We can say, too, that the more intelligent a man is, the more he has overcome the dog nature in himself. If a person were born with a doglike capability to smell especially well, and he was educated to learn to distinguish things other than smells, he would become an unusually clever person because he would be able to discriminate among these other things by virtue of what he had pushed up against the olfactory nerve.

Cleverness, the power of discrimination, is basically the result of man's overcoming his sense of smell. The elephant and the dog have their intelligence in their noses; in other words, it is quite outside themselves. Man has this cleverness inside himself, and that is what distinguishes him. Hence it is not enough just to check and see whether the human being possesses the same organs as the animals. Certainly, both dog and man have a nose, but what matters is how each nose is organized. You can see from this that something is at work in man that is not active in the dog, and if you perceive this you gradually work yourself up from the physical level to the soul level. In the dog the nose and the bushy end of the spine, which is only covered by skin permeated with bony matter, have no inclination to grow towards each other. This tendency originates only from the soul, which the dog does not have in the way a human being does. So, then, I have described the nose and everything that belongs to it in such a way that you see its continuation into the brain and find that man's intelligence is connected with this organ.

There is another sense that is quite similar to the sense of smell but in other respects is totally different: the sense of taste. It is so closely related that people in the region where I was born never say 'smell'; the word is not used there at all. They say instead, 'It tastes good,' or 'It tastes bad,' when they smell something. Where I was born they do not talk of smelling but only of tasting. [Someone in the audience calls out, 'Here, too, in Switzerland!'] Yes, also here in Switzerland you don't talk of smelling; smelling and tasting appear so closely related to people that they don't distinguish between the two.

If we now investigate the sense of taste, we will find that here there is something strange. Again, it is somewhat like it was with the sense of smell. So, if you take the cavity of the mouth, here in the back is the so-called soft palate, in the front is the hard palate, and there are the teeth with the gums. If you examine all this you will find something strange. Just as a nerve runs down into the nose, so here, too, nerves run from the brain down into the mouth. But these nerves do not penetrate into the gums, nor do they extend into the hard palate in front. They reach only into the soft palate in the back, and they go only into the back part of the tongue, not its front part. So if you see how the nerves are distributed that lead to the sense of taste, you will find only a few in front, practically none. [Fig. 8] The tip of the tongue is not really an organ of taste but rather one of touch. Only the back part of the tongue and the soft palate can taste. The mouth is soft in the back and hard in the front; only the soft parts are capable of tasting. The gums also have no sensation of taste.

Fig. 8

The peculiar thing is that these nerves that convey the sense of taste in man are also connected primarily with everything that makes up the intestinal organization. It is indeed true that first and foremost a food must taste good, although its chemical composition is also important. In his taste man has a regulator for the intake of his food. We should study much more carefully what a small child likes or does not like rather than examine the chemical ingredients of its food. If the child always rejects a food, we shall find that something is amiss with its lower abdominal organs, and then one must intervene there.

I have already sketched the 'tail-wagging ability' that is reversed in man and that in the dog extends all the way down its back. If we now move forwards from the tail, we reach the abdomen, the intestines, and to these the taste nerves correspond. It is like this: when a dog abandons itself to smelling, it wags its tail, which signifies that it drives everything through its entire body. The effects of what it smells pass all the way through to the end, to the very tip end of the tail. The tip of the nose is the farthest in front, and the tail is the farthest behind. What is connected with smelling in the dog passes through the entire length of its body, but what it tastes does not; it remains in the abdominal area and does not go as far. We can see from this that the more something related to the nerves is located within the organism, the less far-reaching is its effect in the body. This will teach us to understand even better than we know already that the whole form of man depends on his nerves. Man is formed according to his nerves. In the case of the dog, its tail is formed in accordance with the nose. What do its intestines relate to? They are formed according to the nerves of the muzzle. The nerves are situated on one end, and they bring about the form on the other end. This is something that you must take as a basis for further consideration. You will gain much from realizing that the dog owes its whole tail-wagging ability to its nose, and that when it feels good in the abdominal area this is due to the nerves of the mouth. We shall learn more about this later.

It is extraordinarily interesting how the nerves are related to form. This is why I said the other day that even a blind person benefits from his eyes; even though the eyes are useless for sight, their nerves still help shape the body. The way a person appears is caused by the nerves of his head and in part by the nerves of his eyes, as well as by many other nerves. Therefore, if we want to understand why the human being differs in form from the dog, we have to think of the nose! The nose plays an important part in the shape of a dog, but in the human being it is overcome and somewhat subdued in its functions. In the dog, the nose occupies a higher rung on the ladder; it is the head-master, so to speak. In man, the function of the nose is forced back. The eye and the ear are certainly more important for the human form than is the nose.

Spiritual-scientific foundations for a true physiology

Gentlemen, this time let us finish answering a question raised the other day.

By virtue of his skin, man is an entire sense organ. The skin of the human being is something extraordinarily complicated and truly marvellous. When we trace it from the outside inwards, we find first a transparent and horny layer called the epidermis. It is transparent only in us white Europeans; in Africans, Indonesians and Malayans it is saturated with coloured granules and thus tinged with colour. It is called 'horny' because it consists of the same substance, arranged a little differently, from which the horns of animals and our nails and hair are fashioned. Our nails actually grow out of the uppermost layer of the skin. Under this layer lies the dermis, which consists of an upper and a lower layer. So we are in fact covered and enclothed with a three-layered skin: the outer epidermis, the middle layer of the dermis and the lower part of the dermis.

The lowest layer of the dermis nourishes the whole skin; it stores the nourishing substances for the skin. The middle layer is filled with all kinds of things, but in particular it is filled with muscle fibres. Everywhere in this layer are myriad tiny onion-like things, one next to the other; we have thousands upon thousands in our skin. We can call them 'onions' because the distinguishing feature of an onion is its many peels, and these little corpuscles have such 'onion peels'; the onion skin is on the surface, and the other, thinner part is on the inside. They were discovered by the Italian Pacini and are therefore called 'Pacinian corpuscles'.

Around these microscopic corpuscles are from 20 to 60 such peels, so you can imagine how small they are [Fig. 9]. Man is constituted in such a way that he has these microscopic little bulbs over the whole surface of his body. The largest number is found—in snakes as well as in people—on the tip of the tongue. Yes, it is almost comical, but most are found on the tip of the tongue! There are many on the tips of the fingers, on the palms of the hands and on other parts of the body, but most are on the tip of the tongue. For example, there are seven times more such little nerve bulbs on the tip of the tongue than there are on the fingertips.

Fig. 9

A nerve fibre originates from each of these corpuscles and finds its way into the brain via the spinal marrow. All these nerve fibres radiate from the brain, and everywhere in the body they form such nerve bulbs on its surface. So these nerve fibres in the brain go everywhere and eventually form the onions within the skin or dermis. It is interesting to realize that just as real onions grow in the ground and form onion blossoms above, so do these onions grow in the human body. There [pointing to his sketch, Fig. 10] are the onions and the stem within. In those nerves of the tongue the stem is rather short, but in other nerves it is sometimes quite long. The nerve fibres going from the feet into the brain through the spinal marrow are extremely long. Everything that we have as onions in our skin actually has

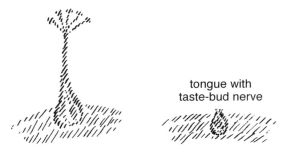

tongue with
taste-bud nerve

Fig. 10

blossoms within our skull. You may imagine, then, that in regard to his skin man is a kind of soil; it is strangely formed, but it still is a kind of soil. On the surface is the epidermis, in which various crystal substances are deposited. Below are the solid masses of the body, and above is the layer of 'humus'. Going from outside inwards, beneath the hard horny layer of the epidermis lies the dermis, which is the soil. From it grow all these onions that have blossoms in the brain. Their stems pass up into the brain and have blossoms there.

Well, gentlemen, in us older fellows things are such that only during sleep can we properly trace this network, but in a child it is still much in evidence. The child has a lively nerve bulb activity in the nerves as long as its intellect is unawakened; that is, throughout its first year, and just as the sun shines over the blossoms of the onions, so shines the light into the child that as yet does not translate with the intellect what it receives with its eyesight. This is indeed like the sun shedding its rays inside the head and opening up all the onion blossoms. In the nerves of the skin we carry a whole plant kingdom around within us. Later, however, when we enter school this lively growing comes to an end, and then we use the forces from the nerves for thinking. We draw these forces out and use them for thinking. This is

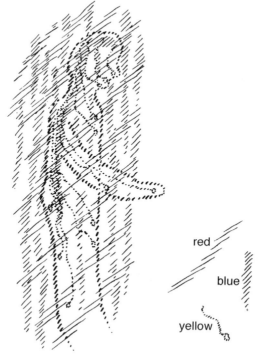

Fig. 11

extremely interesting. Ordinarily, it is assumed that the nerves do the thinking, but the nerves do not think. We can employ the nerves for thinking only by stealing their light, so to speak. The human soul steals the light from the nerves, and it uses what it has taken away for thinking. It is really so. When we truly ponder the matter, we finally recognize at every point the independently active soul.

We have such inwardly growing bulbs in common with all animals. Even the lowest life-forms, which have slimy, primitive shapes, possess sensory nerves that end in a kind of onion on the surface. The higher we ascend towards man, the more are certain of these nerve bulbs transformed in a specific manner. The nerves of the taste buds, for example, are such transformed skin nerves.

Now, we possess these sensory bulbs at the tip of the tongue and that is why it is so sensitive. We taste on the back of the tongue and on the soft palate where such little bulbs are dispersed. Actually, they sit there in a little groove and within these grooves a bulb penetrates into the nerves and pushes into the dermis as a nerve corpuscle. First, a tiny groove forms behind the tongue, and then a bulb pushes itself into this groove. The root of the bulb penetrates all the way to the surface of the tongue. On the base of the tongue are a tremendous number of tiny grooves, and in each little groove a 'bulb' grows up from below. This accounts for our experience of taste.

We can be aware of everything with the sense of touch, or these bulbs located on our body's surface. Now, you know that what one feels one does not remember so well. I know with my feeling that a chair is hard because I feel its hardness with a certain number of nerve bulbs that constantly change, but my memory is not strained by this sensation. With the sense of taste it makes a little, though unconscious effort. Gourmets, however, always know beforehand what is good, not afterwards when they have already tasted it, and that is why they order it.

So the nerve corpuscles pass through the spinal marrow directly into the brain and form 'blossoms' there. Everything that we want to taste, however, must first be dissolved by the saliva in the mouth; we can taste nothing that hasn't first been transformed into fluid. But what is it that tastes? We would not be able to taste anything if we did not have fluid within us. Our solid human constitution, everything that is solid in the body, does not taste. Our inner fluid mixes with what is dissolved of the food. Thus we can say that our own fluid mixes with the fluid from without. The

solid part of the human organization does not taste anything. Our constitution is 90 per cent water, and here,
around the papillae of the tongue, it is in an especially fluid
state. Just as water shoots out of a geyser, so do we have
such a spurting forth of fluid on the tip of the tongue.

Saliva that has been spit out of the mouth is no longer
part of me, but as long as that fluid is within the little gland
of the tongue, it belongs to me as a human being, just as my
muscles belong to me. I consist not only of solid muscles but
also of water, and it is this fluid that actually does the
tasting because it mixes with what comes as fluid from
without. What does one do when one licks sugar? One
drives saliva from within towards the taste buds. The dissolved sugar penetrates the fluid, and our 'fluid man', as it
were, permeates himself with the sugar. The sugar is
secreted delicately in the taste buds of the tongue and
spreads out in one's own fluidity, giving us a feeling of
well-being.

As human beings we can only taste, but why is this so? If
we had fins and were fishes — which would be an interesting existence — every time we ate, the taste would penetrate
right through our fins. But then we would have to swim in
water, where we would find everything, even the delicate
substances, well dissolved. The fish tastes all the traces of
substances that are in the water and follows the direction of
its taste, which is constantly penetrating into the fins. If
something pleasant flows in its direction, the fish will taste
it, and its fins will immediately move towards it. We human
beings cannot do what the fish can because we have no fins;
in us they are completely lacking. But since we cannot use
the sensation of taste to move around, we intensify it
within. Fishes have a highly developed sense of taste, but
they have no inward sense of it. We human beings have the
taste within, we experience it; fishes exist in the totality of
the water and experience taste together with the

surrounding water. People have wondered why a fish swims far out into the ocean when it wants to lay its eggs. They swim far out, not only into the Atlantic Ocean but also into other parts of the earth's oceans, and then the young slowly return to European waters. Why is this? Well, European fishes that swim around in our rivers are fresh-water fishes, but the eggs cannot mature in fresh water. Fishes sense by taste that a trace of salt flows towards the outlet of a river; they then swim out into the sea. If the sun shines differently on the other side of the earth, they taste that and by this sense swim half-way around the globe. Then the young taste their way back again to where the parent fishes have dwelt. So we see that fishes follow their taste in every way.

It is extremely interesting that the water that flows in the rivers and is contained in the seas is full of taste, and the fact that fishes swim around in them is really due to the water's taste. It is actually the taste of the water that makes them swim around; the taste of the water gives them their directions. Naturally, if the sun shines on a certain portion of water, everything that is in the water at that spot is thoroughly dissolved by the heat of the sun. It is changed into another taste, and that is why you see a lot of fishes swimming around there; it is the taste.

It is really a strange matter, gentlemen, because we would actually be swimming, too, if we went only by our taste. When I taste sugar the fluid man within me wants to swim towards it. The urge to swim is indeed there; we want to swim constantly according to our taste, but the solid body prevents us from doing so. From that element which continually would like to swim but cannot—we really have something like a fish within us that constantly wants to swim but is held back—we retain what our inner soul being experiences through taste. With taste we live completely within the etheric body, but the etheric body is held fast by the water in us, and that water in turn is held by our physical body. It is the most natural thing to say that man has an etheric body that is really not disposed to walking on the earth. It is suited only for swimming; it is in fact fishlike, but because man makes it stand erect it becomes something different. Man has within him this etheric body that is actually only in his fluid organization, and it is indeed so that he would constantly like to swim, swim in the elements of water that are contained even in the air. We would like to be always swimming there, but we transform this urge into the inner experience of taste.

You see, such aspects really lead one to comprehend the human being. You cannot find this in any modern scientific book because people examine not the living human being but only the corpse, which no longer wants to swim. Nor does it participate any longer in life. We participate in life because actually we are the sum of everything existing in the world. We are fishes, and the water vapour that is similar to us is something in which we would like to be constantly swimming about. The fact that we cannot do so results in our pouring it into us and tasting it. The fishes are really cold creatures. They could taste things marvellously well that are dissolved in the water, but they do not do so because they immediately move their fins. If the fins would disappear from the fishes, they would become higher animals and would begin to have sensations of taste.

The nerve bulbs that I told you about last time are differently formed 'onions'. They penetrate into the mucous membrane of the nose, but they do not sit within a groove from which fluid seeps out; they reach all the way to the surface. That is why these nerve bulbs can perceive only what comes close to them. This means that we have to let the fragrance of the rose come up to the nerve bulb of our nose before we can smell it. Thus one part of the human body has the function of fashioning in a special way these nerve bulbs, which are spread out over the whole skin, in order to sense smells permeating the air.

Not only does the outer air waft towards man, but also the breath streams out from within him. The breath constantly passes through the nose, and within this breath lives the air being of man. We are water, and as I told you earlier, we are also air. We do not have the air within us just for the fun of it. Like the water within me, my breath is not solid. Just as when I reach out my hand and feel that I have stretched out something solid, so I stretch what I contain in my air organism into my nose. There I grasp the fragrance of the rose or carnation. Indeed, I am not only a solid being but continually a being of water and air as well. We are the air as long as it is within us and is alive. When we stretch our 'air hands' through the nose and grasp the fragrance of a rose or carnation—bad odours, too, of course—we do not touch it with our hand but rather grasp it with the nerve bulbs, which attract the breath from within so that it can take hold of the fragrance.

This is something that is manifest also in the dog. I have told you that as soon as the nose smells, the tail wags. Just as in fishes the fins start to move about, so, too, in dogs the tail starts to move. But what does this tail that can only wag really want to do? This is most interesting. The tail can only wag, but what does it really want to do? You see, gentlemen, the dog would really like to do something quite different. If it were not a dog but a bird it would fly under the influence of smell. Just as fishes swim, a dog would fly if it were a bird. Well, of course, a dog has no wings, and so he uses the substituted organ and just wags his tail. It isn't enough for flying, but it involves the same expenditure of energy. In human beings it is the same. Because we always have delicate sensations of smell that we do not even notice, we would constantly like to fly.

Think now of the swallows that live here in summer.

What arises as scents from the flowers is pleasing to them, and because it is pleasing to their organ of smell they remain here. But when autumn comes or is just approaching, the swallows, if they could communicate among themselves, would say, 'Oh, it's beginning to smell bad!' The swallow has an extraordinarily delicate sense of smell. You remember that I told you that people of savage tribes could smell someone as far away as Arlesheim. Well, for swallows the odour arising in the south is perceptible when autumn is approaching; it actually spreads out all the way to the north. While in the south it smells good, up north it begins to smell of decay. The swallows are attracted to the good odour and fly south.

Whole libraries have been written about the flight of birds, but the truth is that even during the great migrations in spring and autumn the birds follow the extremely delicate dispersion of odours in the whole atmosphere of the earth. The organ of smell in the swallows guides them to the south and then back again to the north. When spring arrives here in our lands, it starts to smell bad for the swallows down south. When the delicate fragrances of spring flow southwards to them, they fly back north. It is really true that the whole earth is one living being and that the other beings belong to it.

In our body, things are so organized that the blood flows to the head and then away from it. On the earth, things are so arranged that the migratory birds fly to the equator and then back to their point of departure. We, too, are influenced by the air because the air we breathe drives the blood to the head. In so far as we are beings of air, we are completely permeated with smell. For example, a person who walks across a field that has just been fertilized with manure is really going there together with his airy being. The solid man and the fluid man do not notice the manure, but the man of air does, and then there arises in him, understandably enough, the urge to fly away. When the manure's stinking odour rises from the field, he would actually like to fly off into the air. He cannot do so because he lacks the wings and thus reacts inwardly to what he cannot fly away from; it becomes an internal process of the soul. As a result, man inwardly becomes permeated with the manure odour, with the evaporations that have become gaseous and vapour-like. He becomes suffused with the bad odour and says that he loathes it. His loathing is a reaction of the soul.

In the fluid man there exists the more delicate airy form that, in a way, he takes from the fluid organization of himself. It is through this that he can taste. Likewise, something lives in this airy form that we constantly renew in us through inhaling and exhaling. Each moment it is expelled and reborn; it is born 18 times a minute and dies 18 times a minute. It takes years for the solid form to die, but the airy form dies during exhalation 18 times a minute and is born during inhalation. It is a continuous process of dying and being born. What is extracted within is the astral body. As I told you the other day, it is the astral body that reverses the forces of tail-wagging that should really be down below. Because these forces are pushed up and against the sense of smell, we are able to think. The brain grows to meet the nose under the influence of the astral body, and no one can really understand the brain who does not look at the whole matter in the way I have just done. This understanding results from a correct observation of our senses.

On account of our sense of smell we would always like to be flying. The bird can fly but we cannot; at best we have these solid shoulder-blades. Why can the bird fly? Gentlemen, the bird has something peculiar that enables it to fly; it has hollow bones. Air is inside them and the air that the bird absorbs through its organ of smell comes into contact with the air that it has in its bones. Indeed, the bird is primarily a being of air. Its most important aspect consists of air; the rest is merely additional growth. The many feathers a bird may have are actually all dried up. The most significant thing, even in the ostrich, is that a bit of air is still contained in each downy feather and all this air is connected with the air outside. The ostrich walks because it is too heavy to fly but, of course, the other birds do.

We human beings have only our shoulder-blades attached to our back, which are clumsy and solidly shaped. Although we would constantly like to fly with them, we cannot. Instead, we push the whole spinal marrow into the brain and begin to think. Birds do not think. We have only to observe them properly to realize that everything goes into their flight. It looks clever, but it is really the result of what is in the air. Birds do not think, but we do because we cannot fly. Our thoughts are actually the transformed forces of flying. It is interesting that in human beings the sense of taste changes into forces of feeling. When I say, 'I feel well,' I would really like to swim. Since I cannot, this impulse changes into an inner feeling of well-being. When I say, 'The odour of the manure repulses me,' I would really like to fly away. But I cannot, and so I have the thought, 'This is disgusting; this odour is repulsive!' All our thoughts are transformed smells. Man is such an accomplished thinker because he experiences in the brain, with that part I described earlier, everything that the dog experiences in the nose.

As human beings, we owe a lot to our nose. You see, people who have no sense of smell, whose mucous membrane is stunted, also lack a certain sense of creativity. They can think only through what they have inherited from their parents. It is always good that we inherit at least something; otherwise, if all our senses were not rudimentarily developed, we could not live at all. A person born blind also has inherited the interior of what the eye possesses. He has this primarily because he is not only solid but also a person of fluid and air.

We have now seen how strange all this is. We perceive solid substances with our sense of touch through the nerve bulbs that penetrate the skin everywhere; we become aware of watery substances with our sense of taste; what is of air, the vaporous, is recognized by us through the nerve bulbs that penetrate into the mucous membrane of the nose. We also sense something else around us, though in a more general way; that is, heat and cold. So, as human beings we are partly solid, partly water, partly air, and also partly warmth, since we are usually warmer than the surrounding world.

You see, science does not really know that the aspect of tasting concerns the part of us that is water and that the element of smell pertains to the part of us that is air. Because the nerves of taste come into the taste buds, it is the scientific opinion that these nerves actually taste. But this is nonsense. In the mouth, it is the fluid of the watery organization of man that tastes, and in the nose it is the element of air that smells. Furthermore, the part of us that is warmth perceives heat and cold. The internal warmth in us directly perceives the external warmth, and this is the difference between the sense of warmth and all the other senses. Warmth is produced by all the organs, and as human beings we harbour a world of warmth within us. This element of warmth perceives the other world of warmth around us. When we touch something that is hot or cold, we naturally perceive it just on the spot where we have touched it. But when it is cold in winter or hot in summer, we perceive this coldness or heat in our surroundings; we become a complete sense organ.

We can see how science errs in this regard. According to scientific books, the human being is some kind of compactly shaped form. All the bones are drawn on the paper; the muscles and nerves are all there. But this is utter nonsense because it represents no more than one tenth of the human being. The rest is up to 90 per cent water, and then we must account for the air and the warmth within. In fact, three more aspects — of water, air and warmth — should be sketched into the image of the human being drawn up by materialistic science. Man cannot be comprehended in any other way. Only because we are warmer than our surroundings and are also a portion of a world of warmth do we experience ourselves as being independent in the world. If we were as cold as a fish or a turtle, we would have no ego; we could not speak of ourselves as 'I'. We could never think if we had not transformed the sense of smell within us, or, in other words, if we had no astral body. Likewise, we would have no ego if we did not possess a portion of warmth within us.

Now, someone might say that the higher animals have their own body temperature, too. Yes, gentlemen, but they are burdened by their warmth. The higher animals would like to become an I but cannot. Just as we cannot swim or fly, the higher animals would like to become an I but cannot do it. You can discern that in their forms; they would really like to become an I, and because they cannot they assume their various shapes.

So, as human beings we have four parts in us: the solid person, which is the physical, material part; the fluid person, which carries the more delicate body — the life body or etheric body — within itself; the air being, the person of air who constantly dies and is renewed in the physical realm but who contains the astral body, which remains throughout life; and the portion of warmth, the ego being.

The sense of warmth is distributed delicately over the whole human being. Here science does something peculiar. When we examine the human being from a purely materialistic standpoint, we discover these nerve bulbs that I have described to you. Now, people say to themselves, 'If I touch this box, I feel it and its solidness because of the nerve bulbs.

If the box were cold, I would also feel the cold through such a nerve bulb.' They constantly look for these nerve bulbs of warmth and these nerve bulbs of feeling, but they never find them. Someone will examine a piece of skin, and because some of these nerve bulbs for feeling look a little different he thinks that they belong to something else. But it is all nonsense. There are no nerve bulbs sensitive to warmth, because the whole human being is perceptive to warmth. These nerve bulbs are used only for sensing solid, water and vaporous substances. Where the sense of warmth begins, we become no more than a bit of warmth that perceives exterior heat. When we are surrounded by an amount of heat that enables us properly to say 'I' to ourselves, we feel well, but when we are surrounded by freezing cold that takes away from us the amount of warmth that we are, we are in danger of losing our ego. The fear in our ego makes the cold outside perceptible to us. When somebody is freezing he is actually always afraid for his ego, and with good reason, because he pushes the ego out of himself faster than he actually should.

These are the aspects that will gradually lead us from observation of the physical to observation of the non-physical, the non-material. Only in this way can we begin to comprehend man. Having mentioned all this, we shall be able to continue with quite interesting observations next time.

How the soul lives within the breathing process

Gentlemen, I said last time that we have several matters still to discuss. I would like to consider them today. Maybe during the Christmas holidays you could confer among yourselves and decide what should be brought up during the next lecture.

The human being has his senses for perceiving the world. We have examined the eye and the ear, considered the sense of touch, which is spread out over the whole organism, and have discussed the senses of taste and smell. All these senses are significant only for man becoming acquainted with his surroundings and, as I have already explained, for enabling him to shape his body. But man does not live by virtue of the senses; he lives through the process of breathing. If you ask why he is an erect being, why his nose is in the middle of his face, for example, you have to answer that it is because of his senses. But if you look for the reason why he is alive, you have to consider his breathing, because the breath is related to all aspects of life. In one respect, human beings breathe just as the higher animals do, although many animals do breathe differently. A fish, for instance, breathes while swimming and living under water.

If we now look at human breathing we first need to consider the process of inhalation. The breathing process is initially one of inhalation. From the air around us we inhale the oxygen that is required for our existence. This then permeates our whole body, in which carbon in minute particles is deposited; or rather, in which it swims or floats. The carbon that we contain in our bodies is also found elsewhere in nature. As a matter of fact, carbon exists in a great many forms. For instance, carbon is found in coal and in every plant, which consists of carbon, mixed with water and so on, but carbon is the main component of the plant. The graphite in a pencil contains carbon, and the diamond, which is a valuable gem, is also carbon. The diamond is transparent carbon; hard coal is opaque carbon. It is rather interesting that something like coal exists in nature. It is certainly not elegant or attractive, yet is of the same substance as a valuable gem, which, depending on its size, for example, is fit for a crown. Coal and diamonds contain the same substance in different forms. We, too, have in ourselves carbon of various forms.

When we breathe in oxygen it spreads out everywhere in our body and combines with the carbon. When oxygen combines with solid coal, a new gas, carbon dioxide, arises. This is a combination of oxygen and carbon, and it is this gas that we then exhale. Our life involves integrating our body into the rest of the world by inhaling oxygen and exhaling carbon dioxide.

If we inhaled only pure oxygen, however, and never exhaled, we would have to contain an immense amount of carbon, and the carbon dioxide would have to remain in us. Yes, we would be forever expanding, finally becoming gigantic, as big as the earth itself. Then we could always be inhaling. But we do not possess that much carbon; it must be constantly renewed. We could not survive if we only inhaled. We have to exhale to acquire carbon anew, and the carbon dioxide we produce is lethal. Indeed, if oxygen is life for us, carbon dioxide is death. If this room were now filled with carbon dioxide, we would all perish. Our life alternates between the life-giving air of inhalation and the deadly air of exhalation. Life and death are constantly within us, and it is interesting to see how they initially enter into the human being.

To comprehend this you must realize that bacteria and bacilli—microscopically small living beings—exist everywhere in nature. Whenever we move, multitudes of these little bacteria fly about us in the air. Countless tiny living beings exist within the muscles of animals. As I have already mentioned, they can rapidly increase in numbers. No sooner does one appear—particularly one of the smallest kind—then the next moment there are millions. The infectious diseases are based on their capacity for tremendous multiplication. These minute beings do not actually cause the illness, but a feeling of well-being is engendered in them when something is ailing in us. Like the plant in manure, these little beings feel well in the stricken organs of our body and like to remain there. Anyone who claims that they themselves cause disease is just as clever as one who states that rain comes from croaking frogs. Frogs croak when a rain shower comes because they feel it and stay in water that is stimulated by what is active in the rain, but they certainly do not cause the rain. Likewise, bacilli do not bring about a disease like flu; they only appear whenever the flu appears, just as frogs mysteriously emerge whenever it rains.

One must not say, however, that research with bacilli has no use. It is useful to know that man is exposed to a certain illness, just as one knows that frogs croak when it rains. One cannot pour the baby out with the bathwater and say that it is unnecessary to examine the bacilli, yet one must realize that they do not cause the illness. One never gives a proper explanation by merely stating that for cholera there are these bacilli, for flu there exist these other bacilli, and so on. That is only a lazy way out for people who do not want to examine the actual causes of illnesses.

Now, if you take these infinitesimally small living creatures away from their habitat, they cannot continue to live. For example, cholera bacilli taken out of the human intestines die. This bacillus can survive only in the intestines of men or of animals like rats. All these microscopic creatures can live only in specific environments. Why? That these tiny beings need a specific environment is an important factor. You see, if you consider the cholera bacillus at the moment when it is within the human intestines, the force of gravity does not have as strong an effect on it as when it is outside. The force of gravity immediately ruins it when it is out of its element. Man, too, was initially a tiny living being just like these countless little creatures. As an egg, an ovum, the human being also was such a microscopic living being, such a miniature living creature. With this, gentlemen, we come to an important chapter.

Compare a cholera bacillus, which can exist only in the human intestines, with the human being. All these bacilli need to live in a place where they are protected from the earth. What does this imply? It means that an effect other than that of the earth influences them. The moonlight that shines sometimes in one way, sometimes in another has its effects on the earth, and it is indeed so that the moon influences all these living creatures. It can be seen that these creatures must be protected from the earth so that they can surrender themselves to the cosmos, especially to the influence of the moon. Now, in its earliest stage the human egg also surrenders to the moon's influence. It gives itself up to the moon just before fertilization. Just as the cholera bacillus exists in the intestines, so this tiny human egg exists in the female and is initially protected there. The female organism is so constituted, however, that the human egg is protected only in the beginning. The moment it passes too far out of the body it becomes vulnerable; then the earth begins to affect it.

Women discharge such human eggs every four weeks. At first they are given up to the moon's influence for a short time and are protected. But when the female organism dispatches the human egg during the course of the monthly period, it comes under the influence of the earth and is destroyed.

The human organization is so marvellously arranged that it represents an opposite to the bacilli. Cholera bacilli, for example, remain in the intestines and are careful not to venture too far out. Left to their own devices, they remain where they can be protected from the earth's influence. The human egg also is initially protected from the earth's influence in the mother's body, but then it moves outwards because of the blood circulation of the mother, and comes under the influence of the earth's gravity. With the occurrence of the monthly period, which is connected with the moon's course and influence, an ovum is destroyed; the human ovum is really destroyed. It is not an actual human egg yet, however, for it has not been protected from destruction through fertilization.

What really happens through fertilization? If left only to the earth's influence, this human egg would perish. Through fertilization it is enfolded in a delicate, etheric substance and is protected from the earth. It is thus able to mature in the mother's body. Fertilization signifies the protection of the human egg from destruction by the earth's forces. What is destroyed in the infertile egg passes over into the environment; it does not just disappear. It dissolves in the totality of the earth's environment. Eggs that cannot be utilized for the earth continually spread abroad through its whole environment. This is a continual process.

We can now look at something that people rarely consider. Let us draw our attention to the herring in the ocean. They lay millions upon millions of eggs, but only a few are ever fertilized. Those that are fertilized become protected from the influence of the earth. It is a little different in man's case, because he isn't a herring — at least not always* — but

---

*Play on words. In German, 'Hering' is a very skinny person.

all these herring eggs that are not fertilized and are cast off in the ocean extricate themselves from the earth's influence by a kind of evaporation. If you consider the herring and all the other fishes, all the other animals and also human beings, you can say to yourselves, 'My attention is directed to something that continually arises from the earth into cosmic space.' Gentlemen, not only does water evaporate, but infertile eggs are also always evaporating upwards from the earth. Much more happens in cosmic space than materialistic science assumes.

If someone were sitting up there on Venus, for example, the vapours that arise and condense again as rain would hold little interest for him, but what I have just described to you, rising constantly into cosmic space, would be perceived up there as a greenish-yellow light. From this we may conclude that light emerges from the life of any given cosmic body. We will also be led to the realization that the sun, too, is not the physical body materialistic science pictures it to be but is rather the bearer of even greater, mightier life. It is as I have explained earlier; something that radiates light must be fertilized, just as the sun must be fertilized in order to radiate light through life. So then we have this difference: when a human egg is not fertilized it spreads out, it evaporates into cosmic space; when it is fertilized it remains for a while on the earth.

What happens is like inhalation and exhalation. If I only exhaled, I would give my being up to cosmic space as does the infertile human egg. Consider how interesting it is that you exhale, and the air that you have exhaled contains your own carbon. It is a delicate process. Just imagine that today you have a tiny bit of carbon in your big toe. You inhale, and oxygen spreads out. The small amount of carbon that today is in your big toe combines with the oxygen, and tomorrow this little particle of carbon is somewhere out there in the atmosphere as carbon dioxide. That is really what happens.

During his lifetime man constantly has in himself the same substance that the human egg contains when it is fertilized. If we only exhaled and never inhaled we would always be dying; we would continually be dissolving into the atmosphere. By inhaling we guard ourselves against death. Every time we inhale we protect ourselves from death.

The child that is still maturing in the mother's womb has come into being from the fertilized human egg and is protected from disintegration. The child takes its first breath only at the moment of birth when it comes into the world. Before that it must be supplied with oxygen from the mother's body. But now with birth something quite significant happens. At birth man for the first time receives from the outer world the capacity to live. After all, man cannot live without oxygen. Although in the mother's womb he exists without oxygen from the outer air, he does get it from the body of the mother.

Thus one can say that when man emerges from his mother's body and comes into the world, he actually changes his whole life process. Something radically different happens to it. He now receives oxygen from outside, whereas before he was able to assimilate it in the body of his mother. Just ask yourselves if there is a machine anywhere in the world that can supply itself with heat first in one way and then in another? For nine or ten months man lives in the body of his mother before he appears in the external world. In the womb he is supplied with what life gives him in a completely different manner from the way he does after he has taken his first breath.

Let us examine something else connected with this. Imagine that your sleep has been somewhat disturbed. You are awakened from a fitful sleep by a quite frightening dream in which you perhaps experience that you come home to a locked house and cannot get in. Someone in the house is expecting you so you struggle to unlock the door.

You may have experienced something like this. In dreams we do indeed experience such conditions of anxiety.

Now, if you examine what actually happens when the human being has such nightmares, you always discover that something is amiss with the breathing. You can even experimentally produce such nightmares. If you take a handkerchief and plug up your mouth or cover your nose, you will dream the nicest nightmares as nightmares go because you cannot inhale properly.

It is rather strange that our having such conditions of anxiety depends simply on inhalation and exhalation, in other words, on oxygen and carbon. We can deduce from this that we live in the air with our soul element. We do not live in our muscles or in our bones with our soul element but rather in the air. It is really the case that our soul moves along with the air during inhalation and exhalation. Thus we can say that the soul element seeks out the air in which it floats after the child has taken its first breath. Before that it absorbs oxygen in a completely different way.

Where does the human being get oxygen prior to birth? In the prenatal state an actual breathing process does not yet exist. There is no breathing while the human being is in the mother's womb; everything takes place through the circulation. Various vessels that are torn away at birth pass into the embryo from the mother's body, and with the blood and fluids oxygen also passes into the embryo. With birth man carries his basic life principle out of the watery element into the air. When he is born he transposes the life principle from the fluid element in which it existed before birth out into the air.

From this you can conclude that before conception the human being is first an entity that, like the bacilli, is not fit for the earth at all. Initially he is a being alien to the earth. Later on, he is shielded from the earth's forces and can develop in the mother's body, but when he is actually born and emerges from the surroundings of the maternal womb, he is exposed to the forces of the earth. Then he becomes capable of life only by becoming accustomed to an activity that enables him to live in the air. Throughout his earthly life man protects himself against the forces of the earth by living not with the earth at all but by living with the air.

Just imagine how hard it would be if you had to live with the earth alone! A man who steps on the scales finds that he weighs a certain amount — a thin one less, a fat one more. Now imagine that you had to grab yourself by the hair and carry your whole body all the time, constantly carry your own weight. Wouldn't that be an exhausting chore! Yet, although you do indeed carry it around with you, you do not feel this weight at all, nor are you aware of it. Why? Your breathing protects you from the heaviness of the earth. In fact, with your soul you do not live in the body at all but rather in the breathing process.

You can now easily comprehend why materialistic science does not find the soul. Materialistic science looks for the soul in the body, which is heavy. In its research it dissects a dead body that no longer breathes. Well, science cannot discover the soul there, because the soul is not to be found in such a body. Materialistic science could find the soul only if our constitution were such that in walking around everywhere we would have to carry our own bodies, sweating profusely from the effort. Then it would make sense to seek for the soul with materialistic means. But the way things really stand, it makes no sense at all. We sweat for other reasons. When we emerge from the maternal womb, we do not live within our solid substances. As it is, we are only 10 per cent solid substance. Nor do we live in our fluid element, to which we bestow life. With our soul we actually live in our breathing.

Gentlemen, please follow me now in a train of thought that belongs to the most significant matters of the present

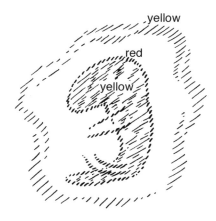

yellow

red

yellow

Fig. 12

time. Let us picture to ourselves a human foetus [Fig. 12]. Through birth it emerges into the outside world and becomes a fully-fledged human being who now inhales air with his lungs and exhales again through his nose. It should be quite self-evident to you that when a person is born, he actually lives with his soul in the breathing process. As long as he exists in the mother's womb, he lives in a watery element. In a sense, he emerges from the water into the air when he is born. As earthly man you can live only in the air, not in water. But before birth you lived in water, and up until the third week you were even shaped like a little fish to enable you to live there. You lived in water up to the time of birth, but the earth does not allow you to live in that element. What does it signify that before birth you lived in water? It means that your life cannot derive from the earth at all, that it must originate from beyond the earth because the earth does not permit you to live. We must lift ourselves up from the earth into the air to live.

Because we have lived in water up to the moment of birth, we may conclude that our life is not bestowed by the earth. Our life of soul is not given us by the earth. It is impossible for the earth to bestow this life of the soul on you. Hence we may understand that it comes from beyond the earth. When we comprehend how life is actually contained in the breathing process, and how life already exists in the embryo but in a fluid element, we immediately realize that this life has descended from a spiritual world into the mother's ovum.

People will frequently call such statements unscientific. Nevertheless, we can study a lot of science and reach the conclusion that what the illustrious scientists do in their science is much less logical than what I have just told you. What I have now told you is absolutely logical. Unfortunately, things are such in our age that children are already drilled in school to turn a deaf ear to something like this; or if they happen to hear it, they will say at most, 'He's crazy. We've learned that everything grows out of the human egg.' Well, that is just as ridiculous as learning that the human head grows from a head of cabbage. A human head can grow from a cabbage no more than the human element, the whole human activity during life, can be derived from the human egg. But children are already taught these completely nonsensical things in school.

I have already given you an example of this. Even the smallest children are told that once the earth, along with the whole planetary system, was one huge primeval fog [Fig. 13]. Of course, the fog does nothing when it is still, and so it is made to rotate. It starts to revolve quickly, and as it turns it becomes thinner and thinner. Eventually individual bodies split off, and a round one remains in the middle. The children are shown with a demonstration how this can be imitated. The teacher takes a piece of cardboard, sticks a needle through it, and puts a small drop of oil into a glass of water. He now turns the piece of cardboard and the oil drop, which floats on top of the water, begins to move. It

Fig. 13

starts to rotate, and tiny oil drops split off. A large drop of oil remains in the middle. This is a little planetary system with its sun. You see, children — so he says — we can do it on a small scale. So it is quite plausible that there once existed a nebula that revolved, and from this nebula celestial bodies gradually split off, leaving the large star remaining in the middle. [Fig. 14]

Fig. 14

But now, gentlemen, what is the most important factor in this experiment? Why does the drop of oil rotate in the glass of water? Because the teacher turns the piece of cardboard. Likewise, a great cosmic teacher had to sit somewhere out there in the universe to turn things around, spinning off celestial bodies! Gentlemen, when from the beginning someone teaches children such things, they become 'clever' as adults. When a person tries to be logical and expresses doubt, they call him a dreamer because *they* know how the world began!

You see, such thoughts contain absolutely no reality. This rotating, primeval nebula thought up by Kant and Laplace has no reality at all; it is really quite foolish. To postulate such rotating nebulas is really rather stupid. The only grounds for it are the supposedly spiral nebulas observed through telescopes. Out in the wide cosmic spaces there are indeed such spiral nebulas; that is correct. But if by looking out there with a telescope and seeing these spiral nebulas a man should say, 'Well, yes, our whole solar system was once such a nebula too' then he is about as clever as one who takes a swarm of insects in the distance for a dust cloud. This can happen, but the swarm of gnats is alive while the dust cloud is lifeless. The spiral nebula out in space is alive; it has life within it. Likewise, the whole solar system had its own life and spirituality in earlier times, and this spirituality continues to work today.

When the human egg is shielded in the body of the mother by fertilization, it can unite with the human spirit. When we gradually grow old, the heaviness slowly makes itself felt by the fact that our substances are seized by the earth's gravity. Suppose a person's digestion is amiss and, as a result, the life forces do not properly pass through it. Then all kinds of tiny solid particles form in the muscles. They become filled up with these small solid bodies, which are minute uric acid stones, and then we have gout. We begin to be conscious of heaviness, of gravity.

When we are healthy and oxygen invigorates us through our breathing, such uric acid deposits are not formed, and we do not become afflicted with gout. Gout occurs only if

oxygen does not pass through our body in a truly invigor-
ating manner and does not assimilate carbon correctly. If
oxygen does not pass through our organism in the right
way, carbon will cause all kinds of problems; then there will
be present everywhere such minute particles in our blood
vessels. We feel that as an effect of the earth in moving
around. In fact, we have to be shielded from the earth. We
remain alive only because we are constantly protected from
the earth and its influences by the breathing process. The
only reason the earth does not damage us is that we are
constantly being shielded from it. We would always be sick
if we were always exposed to the earth.

You see, in the middle of the nineteenth century, when
natural science had its greatest materialistic successes,
people were completely stunned by its accomplishments
and scientists wanted to explain everything by way of what
happens on the earth. These scientists were extremely
clever, and they liberated man from much that had
encumbered him. Nothing is to be said against them; they
can even be praised. Yet they were so completely stupified
by scientific progress that they tried to explain the whole
human being as if only the earth had an influence on him.
They did not realize that when the earth's influences begin
to take effect on man he first becomes nervous and then
becomes ill in some way. He is well only by virtue of being
constantly shielded from earthly influences.

Eventually, however, man is overcome by these earthly
influences. How do they make themselves felt? The earthly
influences assert themselves because man gradually loses
the art of breathing. He gradually forgets how to breathe
properly. When he cannot breathe properly any more, he
returns to his condition before conception. He dissolves into
the cosmic ether and returns to the world from which he
came. With his last breath, man sinks back into the world
from which he emerged. When we correctly understand

breathing, we also comprehend birth and death. But nowhere in modern science do we find the right understanding of breathing.

To sum up, man first learns to live with the world through the female ovum, then learns to exist independently on the earth for a certain length of time by virtue of fertilization through the male, and finally returns to the condition where he again can live on his own outside the earth. Gradually one learns to comprehend birth and death, and only then can one begin to have the right concept of man's soul, of what is not born and does not die but comes from without, unites itself with the ovum in the mother, and eventually returns to the spiritual world.

The situation today is such that we must comprehend the immortal soul element, which is not subject to birth and death. This applies especially to those who are active in science. This, indeed, is necessary for mankind today. For hundreds and thousands of years, men have had a faith in immortality that they cannot possibly retain today because they are told all kinds of things that actually are nothing and fall apart in the face of science. Everything that a man is asked to believe today must also be a matter of knowledge. We must learn to comprehend the spiritual out of science itself, the way we have done here in these lectures. That is the task of the Goetheanum and of anthroposophy in general: to correctly understand the spiritual through natural science.

You see, it is difficult to get people somehow to comprehend something new. It is Christmas time now, and people could say to themselves, 'Well, we must find a new way to understand how the spirit lives in the human race.' If people would stop to think how the spirit lives in mankind, and if they would try to arrive at this understanding through real knowledge, we would find everything renewed. We could even celebrate Christmas anew, because we would observe this holiday in a manner appropriate for the modern age. Instead, on the one hand, people continue to observe only what is dead in science and, on the other, they perpetuate the old traditions to which they can no longer attach any meaning. I would like to know what meaning those people who exchange gifts can still see in Christmas. None at all! They do it merely from habit, as an old custom. Side by side with this, a science is taught that is full of contradictions. No one wishes to consider the fact that science presents something that can lead to the realization of the spiritual.

Today, one can say that if Christianity is to have any meaning at all, one must once again embark on attaining a real knowledge of the spirit. This is the only thing possible; it is not enough just to perpetuate the old. For what does it imply to read the Bible to people on festive occasions, or even to children in school, if along with this one tells the child that there was once a primeval nebula that simply rotated? The head and the heart end up completely opposing one another. Then man forgets how to be a human being on the earth because he no longer even knows himself.

Anyone is a fool who thinks that as human beings on the earth we consist only of what is heavy, of the body that is put on the scales and weighed. This part we do not need at all. It is nonsense to think that we consist of these material substances that can be weighed. In reality, we do not become aware of the body at all, because we shield ourselves from it in order to stay well. The curing of illness consists in expelling the earthly influences that are affecting the sick person. All healing is actually based on removing the human being from the earth's influence. If we cannot remove man from the earth and its influences, we cannot cure him. He then lies down in bed, allows himself to be supported by the bed and gives himself up to weight. When one lies down one does not carry one's own self.

So we have the old customs on the one hand and, on the other, a science that does not enlighten man as to what he really is as a human being. Nothing positive can come from all this. It is true that the World War, with all the consequences that still afflict us today, would not have occurred if human beings had been aware of their own humanity in some degree beforehand. Even now, they do not want to know. Even now, they still want to get together at congresses without any new thoughts and just repeat the same old things. Nowhere are they able to conceive new thoughts. What at first existed in mankind as confused ideas became a habit and then became our social order today. We are not going to get anywhere in the world again until from within we really feel the true nature of the human being.

This is really what those who understand the aims of anthroposophy conceive of as Christmas. Christmas should remind us that once again a science of the spirit must be born. The science of the spirit is the best spiritual being that can be born. Mankind is much in need of a Christmas festival. Otherwise, it does away with the living Christ and retains only the cross of Christ. Ordinary science is only the cross, but we must arrive at what is living once more. We must strive for that.

Well, gentlemen, that is what I wanted to mention on this particular day in addition to the other things. With this, I wish you all pleasant holidays!

Why do we become sick? Influenza, hay fever, mental illness

Question: For many years I have suffered from hay fever. Now I have heard that it must be treated early in the year. If injections are administered as early as January or February before a person begins to suffer, they are supposed to be more effective. Should I go along with this remedy?

Dr Steiner: What you have said is correct, but there is one small catch. You see, the remedy that is in use here is meant to be applied prophylactically; that is, it is meant to work ahead of time. In fact, it should be used weeks before the symptoms of hay fever arise. The problem, however, is that patients come in only when they are already afflicted with the malady. Just today we received an interesting letter about another hay fever remedy. The inventor of this other remedy writes that his medication brings only a little relief to individual hay fever attacks. He believes that our remedy can permanently cure hay fever, especially if it is taken twice at wide intervals. Naturally, we would much prefer patients to be treated in January or February rather than in May or June. Understandably, however, people generally see a doctor only after an illness has been contracted.

Yet, our hay fever remedy works in such a way that if given to the patient even during the external appearance of the illness, which is only the final result of an inner affliction, it protects him from a renewed attack. It is particularly effective if applied again a year later. After that, the application need not always be repeated. Even though the illness affects only one organ, this remedy treats its basis in the whole bodily organization. To explain this, I would like to go into more detail concerning the causes of internal illnesses and how they arise in the first place.

Of course, it is quite simple to comprehend why one becomes indisposed if one breaks a leg or sustains a concussion due to a fall. In these cases the injury is external and the cause easily understood; the cause is externally visible. In the case of internal illnesses, however, one usually does not really consider where they come from and how they suddenly assert themselves. This pertains to another question raised earlier of why one may become infected when in contact with certain people. An external cause also seems to be present here.

Ordinary science offers a simple explanation for this. Bacilli are transmitted from an ill person who has influenza, for example, and then these are inhaled and bring about the disease in another. It is like someone injuring a man by hitting him with a mattock. In this case the injury is caused by a patient bombarding another person with a multitude of bacilli. Matters are not at all that simple, however; they are much more complicated. You will understand this when you realize that in everyday life a person constantly becomes a bit indisposed and then must cure himself. The point is that all of us are really a bit sick when thirsty or hungry, and we cure ourselves by drinking and eating. Hunger is the beginning of an illness, and if it is allowed to continue we can die from it. After all, we can die of starvation and even sooner of thirst. So you see that even in our everyday lives we bear something like the beginning of a disease. Every act of drinking or eating is in truth an act of healing.

We must make clear to ourselves now what in fact happens when we become hungry or thirsty. You see, our body is inwardly always active. Through the intake of food, the body receives nutrients. External substances are absorbed through the mouth and the intestinal passages into some part of the body. Now, you must understand that the human organization immediately rebels against these nutritional substances; it does not tolerate them in their original forms and destroys them. Food substances must actually be disintegrated. In fact, they are annihilated, and this begins in the mouth. The reason for this is that there is continuous, never-ceasing activity in our body. This activity must be observed in the same way as fingers or hands are. Ordinary science simply records how a piece of bread is eaten, dissolved in the mouth, and then distributed in the body, but we must also take into consideration that the human body is continually active. Even if nothing is put into it, if nothing goes into the body for five hours, say, still its activity does not cease. You may even be like an empty sack, but things have not quieted within. You remain in constant inward activity, and things are still bustling around. Only when this internal activity can become occupied with something is it content. That is especially the case after a meal when it can dissolve and disintegrate the food substances; then it is content.

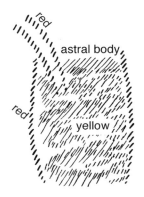

Fig. 15

This internal activity that we possess is quite different from man in general, for the human being can become lazy. The internal activity is never lazy, it never ceases. If I don't eat anything, it is as if I had an empty flour sack in which there is activity even if I avoid all tangible substance. This activity — for reasons that I shall tell you later on — is identified in spiritual science as the astral body. It is never lazy, and if it can stay active destroying and dissolving the food substances, it is filled with inward comfort; it then has a feeling of inner well-being. But if I take in no food substances, then the astral body is not satisfied, and this dissatisfaction is expressed as hunger. Hunger is not something at rest within us; it is an activity, a soul-spiritual activity that cannot be stilled. We can truly say that this inner activity is in love with the food substances, and if it does not receive them it is just as dissatisfied as any jilted lover. This dissatisfaction is the hunger, and it is by all means something spiritual.

So the activity that is executed internally consists of disintegrating food substances. What is useful is transmitted into the blood vessels, and the rest is eliminated through urine or faeces. This is the healthy, normal and regular activity of the human being in which the astral body works properly to dissolve the food substances. It absorbs into the body what is useful and discharges what is not.

We must assume, gentlemen, that this activity of man is no ordinary activity; rather, it contains something immensely wise. Now dissolved and transformed food substances are constantly being transmitted through blood vessels to the inner organs, and the nourishment that goes into the lungs is completely different from what goes to the spleen. The astral body is much smarter than the human being. Man can only stuff the provisions into his mouth, but the astral body can distinguish them. It is like sorting two substances, throwing one in one direction to be used there and the other in another direction. This is what the astral body accomplishes. It selects certain substances to dispatch to the lungs, spleen, larynx and other organs. A wise distribution is at work within. The astral body is immensely wise, much wiser than we are. The most educated person today would not know how to send the proper substances into the lungs, larynx or spleen; he would not even know what to say about it. But internally man can do this through his astral body.

The astral body, however, can become stupid — not as stupid as the human being can become, but stupid in comparison to its own cleverness. Let us assume that it thus becomes stupid. Man is born with a certain predisposition and is inwardly endowed with certain forces. The activity that the astral body develops for food substances occurs even if somebody sits down all day, immobile like an oriental idol. His astral body still remains active, but that is not enough. We must also do something externally, and if we have no work to do we must go for a stroll; the astral body demands that we at least walk around. This differs with each individual. One person needs more physical activity, another less.

Let us suppose now that someone has certain predispositions from birth that make him into a sedentary person. It pleases his stupid head — or we could say his stupid ego — to sit around a lot. Now, if he is predisposed to sit around, but the astral body is predisposed to move, then his astral body will become stupid. This will also happen if somebody overexerts himself walking. In both cases the astral body will become stupid and will no longer accomplish things correctly. It will no longer properly sort out the food substances and transmit them to the appropriate organs; it will do all this clumsily instead. The astral body becomes too disorganized to send the right substances to the heart or larynx. Substances improperly transmitted to the heart, for example, will remain somewhere else in the body. They are not put in the organ where they belong but, since they are basically useful, neither are they eliminated with the faeces. Instead, they are deposited somewhere else in the body. But a man cannot tolerate having something deposited in his body that is not part of its proper activity; he cannot stand that.

So what happens with these improper deposits due to the malfunctioning astral body? What happens to us on account of that? Well, suppose we have in our body certain deposits that should have been directed to the larynx. Because someone's astral body does not function properly, 'larynx refuse' is secreted everywhere in his body. The first thing that happens is that his larynx becomes weak. The organ does not receive sufficient sustenance, and thus the person suffers from a weakened larynx. But apart from that, his body contains larynx refuse, which is dispersed every-where. As I have already told you, the human body is 90 per cent water, and the refuse dissolves in this whole fluid organization. The pure, animated fluid that a person requires within him is now polluted. This is what happens so often within ourselves. Deposits meant for certain parts of the body dissolve in our fluid organization, con-taminating it.

Say that the refuse of the larynx is dissolved in us and comes into contact with the stomach. It cannot cause damage there, because the stomach has what it needs and was not deprived of anything. But the bodily fluids flow everywhere in the human organism and penetrate into the area of the larynx, which is already weakened. It receives this polluted fluid, this water in which the larynx refuse is dissolved, and specifically from this the organ becomes diseased. The larynx refuse does not affect the other organs, but it does cause the larynx to become afflicted.

Let us now consider a simple phenomenon. A sensitive

person finds it pleasant to listen to another person speak beautifully. But if someone crows like a rooster or grunts like a pig, he will not find this so pleasant to hear, even if he understands what is being said. It is not at all pleasant to listen to a person crowing or grunting. Listening to someone who is hoarse is a particularly uncomfortable and constricting experience. Why do we experience such sensations while listening to another? It is based on the fact that in reality we always inaudibly repeat whatever the other is saying. Listening consists not only in hearing but also in speaking faintly. We not only hear what another says but also imitate it with our speech organs. We always imitate everything that someone else does.

Now imagine that you are near a person who is sick with flu, and though you may not be listening to him and inwardly imitating his speech, you feel sorry for him. This makes you quite susceptible and sensitive to him. The flu patient's fluid organization contains many dissolved substances, which contaminate the pure, living fluid I told you about and make it instead unhealthy for him. I can even describe to you the nature of the fluid such a person has within himself.

Imagine that you have a piece of ground where you plant various things. Not everything thrives in every kind of earth, but suppose you want to plant onions and garlic in this particular spot. Should the earth be unsuitable, the onions would be small and the garlic buds still smaller, so you should also add to this soil something that contains sulphur and phosphorus. Then you would have the healthiest onions and garlic buds, and they would smell strong, too!

Now, when a man has influenza refuse within his body, the same substances are dissolved in his fluid organization that had to be added to the ground in order to produce the finest onion and garlic plants, and before long the sick person begins to smell like these plants. Now, I take part in this, though I may not even be aware that I am sitting in this odour of onion or garlic, because it need not be strong. The odour exuded by a person who is sick with the flu causes the patient's head to feel dull, because a certain organ in the head, the 'sensorium', is not properly supplied with the substance it needs. As a result of having 'flu refuse' within us, an organ in the mid-section of the head is not properly supplied. This odour is always like that of onions or garlic and can be detected by someone with a sensitive nose. Just as we tune in on and imitate a shrill and rasping voice, so do we join in with what an ill person evaporates. As a consequence, our own astral body, our own activity, becomes disorganized. This disorder causes a chemical basis that in turn makes us contract the flu. It is like making soil suitable for onions and garlic. At first, then, the illness has nothing to do with bacteria but simply with the relation of one person to another.

If you want to plant predominantly onions and garlic in a garden, and you add to the earth substances containing phosphorus and sulphur, you can now sit back and say, 'Well, I've done my duty. I want to harvest onions and garlic, and so with some kind of organic fertilizer I have added sulphur and phosphorus to the garden.' But it would be foolish to think that this is all it would take to grow the onions. You would first have to plant the bulbs! Likewise, it would be foolish to maintain that in man's interior, bacteria are already growing in the environment that is being prepared. They first have to be introduced into it. Just as the onion bulb thrives in soil rich in phosphorus and sulphur, so do the bacilli thrive within a sulphuric environment in the body. Bacilli are not even necessary for one person to catch the flu from another. Instead, by imitating with my fluid organization what is happening in the patient's fluid organism, I myself produce a favourable environment for the bacilli; I myself acquire them. The sick person need not bombard me with them at all.

When we look at the whole matter, we must reply in quite a specific way to the question of what causes us to be stricken with a certain disease. We become sick when something injures us, and even in the case of internal illnesses something is actually injuring us. The impure fluid, in which substances are dissolved that should have been digested, injures us; it injures us internally.

Now we can turn our attention to illnesses like hay fever. The incidence of hay fever depends much more on the time of year than on the pollen in the air. More than anything else, what makes a man susceptible to catching hay fever is the fact that his astral body is not properly excreting; it is not properly executing the part of its activity that is directed more to the external surface. As a result, when spring approaches and everything begins to thrive in water, a person makes his whole fluid organization more sensitive and thus susceptible to this illness by dissolving certain substances in it. By dissolving various substances in this fluid organization, the fluids in a person's body always become a little diluted. The fluid organization in a man who has a tendency toward hay fever is always somewhat too large. The fluids are being pushed aside in all directions by what is dissolved in them. That is how a person becomes sensitive to everything that makes its appearance in spring, especially to pollen, those particles from plants that are now particularly irritating.

If the nose were not enclosed, hay fever could be induced by many other irritants. Pollen does enter the nose, however, and it cannot be well tolerated if one already has hay fever. Pollen does not cause hay fever but it aggravates it.

Our hay fever remedy is based on drawing together again the extended fluid organization in the body so that it becomes a bit cloudy and once again secretes what it had

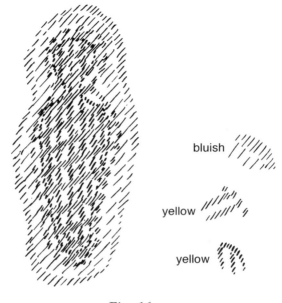

Fig. 16

initially dissolved. It is really quite simple and based on nothing more than contracting the fluid organism to its normal size. It first becomes a little cloudy, and you have to watch that what is secreted from the fluidity is not later retained in the body. That is why it is beneficial for a person to perspire somewhat after having been inoculated with the remedy; it is good if he can move about and do something that induces perspiration right after the inoculation. The inoculation is always somewhat problematic when given to a person who is suffering from constipation, and the patient should first be asked if he is constipated. Otherwise, if the fluid organization is contracted, things accumulate too much and are not eliminated right away. This, of course, is not good. A person who is constipated should be given a laxative along with the inoculation.

Healing entails not only applying a medication but also adjusting life accordingly, so that the human body reacts in an appropriate manner to what has been given it. This naturally is of tremendous significance; otherwise, the person can be made even sicker. If you inoculate somebody with a remedy that is quite effective, even exceptionally good, but you do not see to it that the patient's digestion functions properly and that everything the remedy brings about is eliminated, you naturally drive him further into the illness.

With truly effective remedies it is important that the doctor should know not only which medicine cures which disease but also what questions to ask the patient. The greatest medical art lies in asking the right questions and in knowing the patient well. This is extremely important. Yet it is strange, for example, that we meet doctors who frequently have not even asked the patient his age, though this is significant. While he may use the same remedies, a doctor can treat a 50-year old in a manner completely different from the way he treats one who is 40, for example. Doctors should not be so schematic as to say, 'This medication is right for this illness.' For instance, it makes a great difference if you want to cure someone who is also constantly afflicted with diarrhoea or someone who has chronic constipation. Such remedies could be tested, and here experiments with animals would be much less objectionable than they are in other areas. Regarding constipation or diarrhoea, you can easily learn how some remedy reacts in the general physical organism that human beings have in common with the animals by giving the same medicine to both a dog and a cat. The dog regularly suffers from constipation, and the cat from diarrhoea. You can acquire a wonderful knowledge by observing the degree of difference in the medication's effect in the dog or the cat. Scientific knowledge really is not attained by university training in how to do this or that with certain instruments. True science results, rather, when common sense is exercised a little; then people know what kinds of experiments to conduct.

In sum, it is of prime importance to realize that an illness has its basis in the whole human organization. The individual organ becomes afflicted because the activity of the astral body directs substances to it that have been precipitated from within. The development of certain inner diseases like influenza, hay fever and even typhoid fever becomes comprehensible when we understand how substances improperly deposited in our bodies are dispersed in our fluid organism.

We are not only a 'material being' but also a 'water being', and, as I have already explained to you, an 'air being' too, whose form changes every moment. One moment the air is outside, and the next it is within.

Just as the solid substances that we contain within our bodies as refuse dissolve in the water, so does that water itself constantly evaporate within us. Within the muscles of your little finger, for example, are minute evaporations of water. Water constantly evaporates throughout your whole body. Furthermore, what is evaporating in the fluid organism penetrates into what you inhale as oxygen, which is also a vapour or gas. When water on the ground evaporates, it rises up into the atmosphere, and when water constantly evaporates in delicate processes within our fluid being, it penetrates into the air that we inhale. We cannot tolerate solid substances being dispersed in the fluids, and neither can we tolerate fluids evaporating into the air organism.

Take the case of a person whose lungs have become afflicted because something has occurred like the process that I have just described. This person can become afflicted with a lung disease, which can be cured if it arose from the wrong substances being deposited in the water organization. But let us assume that the lung's affliction is not pronounced enough to become apparent. After all, the human organs are sensitive. The condition does not reach the point where the lungs become so strongly afflicted that they are inflamed, but they do become a little indisposed. The person can tolerate this slight indisposition, but substances now enter into his fluid organism that really should penetrate the lungs. In this case, the fluids within the lungs have the wrong kinds of substances dissolved in them; and these substances evaporate, especially if the lungs are not completely well.

Thus, in the case of quite obvious internal diseases, the water organization receives something inappropriate from the solid substances, and in this case something inappropriate reaches the point of evaporation and mingles with the oxygen that is inhaled. It is a fact that water evaporating inappropriately and uniting with oxygen damages the nervous system in particular, because the nerves require healthy oxygen, not oxygen that has evaporations in it from the contaminated fluid of our water organization. Contaminated fluid evaporates into the lungs, and this fluid may be responsible for their slight indisposition. Something that should not evaporate does, and this is damaging to the nervous system. The person does not become ill in an obvious, external way, but he does become insane.

It can be said that internal physical illnesses are based on something in man that causes improper substances to be dispersed in his fluid organism. But so-called mental illnesses are in reality not mental at all, because the mind or spirit does not become ill. Mental illnesses are based on body fluids evaporating improperly into oxygen and thereby disturbing the nervous system. This can happen when some organ is so slightly impaired or indisposed that it cannot be detected externally. You see, then, that man must continually process substances correctly so that nothing inappropriate disperses in his fluids and that his fluids in turn do not improperly evaporate. But even in everyday life there is a process that causes improper evaporation of water, and this becomes noticeable when we are thirsty. We cure the thirst by drinking; we free our water, so to speak, from what is inappropriately evaporating within it and wash away what is incorrect.

So we can say that in hunger there is actually the tendency to physical illness, and in thirst there is the predisposition to mental illness. If a man does not properly nourish himself, he forms the basis for organic diseases, and if he does not quench his thirst rightly, he may bring about some form of mental illness. In some circumstances, the improper quenching of thirst is difficult to detect, especially if it occurs in infancy. At this stage one cannot clearly distinguish between assuaging thirst and hunger since both are satisfied by milk. Therefore, if through the mother's milk or that of a wet nurse something harmful comes into the organism, this can much later cause the fluid organism to evaporate incorrectly and thus lead to some mental disorder. Or let us say a person is wrongly inoculated. An ill-chosen inoculation with one or another cow lymph or diseased human lymph can afflict the organs that work upon the water, even though the water itself does not become directly diseased. As a result of an inappropriate inoculation, a person's evaporation processes may not function correctly, and later he may be disposed to some kind of mental illness.

You will have noticed, gentlemen, that nowadays a great many people become afflicted with dementia praecox, so-called 'youthful insanity', which extends, however, quite far beyond the years of youth. This illness, in which people begin mentally to deteriorate in their youth, originates in great part from the wrong kind of feeding during the earliest years of childhood. It is not enough merely to examine chemically the baby's milk; one must look into completely different aspects. Because people have ceased to pay attention to feeding in our age, this illness arises with such vehemence.

You will have realized from all this that it does not suffice simply to train doctors to know that a certain remedy is good for a certain illness. One must rather seek to make the totality of life healthier, and for that one must first discover all that is related to a healthy life. Anthroposophy can provide this understanding. It aims at being effective in the field of healing and seeks to understand questions of health correctly.

Fever versus shock. Pregnancy

Questions are raised concerning pregnancy and the possible effects of outer events during pregnancy.

Dr Steiner: Gentlemen, these are extremely important aspects of life. Generally, no significant influence can be exerted on the child during pregnancy except indirectly by way of the mother, since the child is connected with the mother, as I have said here already, by numerous delicate blood vessels. The unborn child receives everything it requires, including its nourishment, from its mother. Later, it acquires a completely different breathing process.

We can best consider the matters that you have brought up if we deal further with the general basis of human states of illness and health. In pregnancy, it is even more difficult than in the case of common hunger and thirst to say where the tendency towards illness begins and where it ends. Other things also enter into pregnancy that prove beyond doubt that the mother's condition of soul has an extraordinary influence on the developing child. You only have to observe what happens, for example, if the mother, especially in the early months of pregnancy, is badly frightened. As a rule, the child will be affected for its whole life. Naturally, you cannot say that a physical change occurs in the child but only that the mother suffers a fright. How can a mother's fright affect the child?

Modern science basically gives the most inadequate answers here, because it really knows nothing, or claims to know nothing, of what influences the human soul and spirit. We can best approach these difficult questions — and they are indeed complicated — if we focus on two phenomena of life that man experiences primarily in illness, that is, fever and shock. These are two opposite conditions that man undergoes, fever and shock.

What is fever? You know that our normal body temperature is 98.6°. If it rises any higher, we say that we have a fever. The fever is visible outwardly through a person becoming hotter. What is shock? Shock is actually the opposite condition. Shock occurs when a person is incapable of developing sufficient warmth within. If you take an overdose of a poison such as henbane (*Hyoscyamus niger*), for example, which is also used as a remedy, you risk going into shock. Through such shock, all the membranes in the abdomen of the mother, where the child is developing—the membranes of the intestines but also those of the organ in which the child rests during pregnancy, the so-called uterus, the womb, in other words all the membranes of the abdomen—become slack. It is as if a sack were stretched too far, becoming worn out and unable to hold anything any longer. With the introduction of henbane, undigested food backs up, and the proper functioning of the abdomen, which I described recently, is disrupted. A large amount of food then accumulates in a man's abdomen that he cannot assimilate.

In order to understand what is at work here, we must take a closer look at the human organism. What actually happens when the abdomen does not work properly? Although it is the abdomen that isn't working properly, you will find that something is actually wrong with the front portion of the brain. A very interesting relationship!

Consider the human being—the abdomen, the chest, the diaphragm, which is about here [*Rudolf Steiner sketches on the blackboard*, Fig. 17]. There we have abdomen, chest and head. If something is out of order in the abdomen, then something is also not functioning properly in the front part of the brain. The two therefore belong together. In the

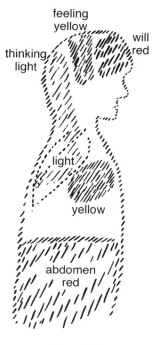

Fig. 17

human being they belong inwardly together, the forebrain and abdomen. We can also say that the heart with its arteries, as I have described them to you, is connected with the midbrain. Finally, the chest with the lungs and the breathing process is related to the back portion of the brain.

Every time something is amiss with the breathing, something is also wrong in the back part of the brain. Whenever a person has difficulty breathing and doesn't receive enough oxygen, one can observe that something is wrong with the back of the brain. When a person suffers from disorders of the heart, especially if the rhythm of the heart's activity is disrupted so that the pulse is irregular, then something is wrong in the midbrain. In a disorder of the abdomen, one always finds some irregularity in the forebrain. Everything is remarkably interrelated in the human being.

You see, people often don't want to believe these things, because in the formation of the forehead they see the noblest aspect of the human being and the less noble in the abdomen. And if one speaks the truth about these things, such people find this 'lower region' unworthy of man. You will have realized from my lectures, however, that the digestive system is in turn related to the limb system in such a way that it represents a most significant aspect of the human being.

Once I knew a man who had quite an unusual forehead. A Greek forehead is different [*sketching*, Fig. 18]. In Greek statues we find foreheads that slope backwards. This man actually had a pronounced bulge, and his forebrain was actually pushed out. I am convinced that this man, whose brain was pushed forward so much, possessed a particu-

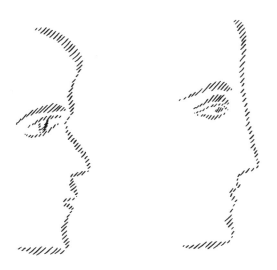

Fig. 18

larly well-formed abdomen and never suffered from diarrhoea or constipation, for example; he never suffered from stomach-aches and the like. The man in question was, in fact, a person of unusual sensitivity, but this sensitivity depended on his always feeling inwardly comfortable. This indicates that his powerful, protruding forehead never permitted disorders of the abdomen. You can see from this that a man's forehead is related in a remarkable way to his abdomen.

If I give someone too large a dose of henbane, he goes into shock. What causes this shock? Something goes wrong with the forebrain, because everything possible collects in his abdomen. Oddly, however, when a person complains of a stomach-ache, caused perhaps by mild constipation, I can give him henbane in highly diluted form, and he will become healthy. He gets a slight fever and becomes well.

Here you see a strange fact. If I give too much henbane to a perfectly healthy person, he goes into shock. He will suffer severe abdominal distress, his head will feel cold, his abdomen will swell, the intestines will slacken, and the abdominal functions will cease. What do you see from this? You see that I have introduced too much henbane into the stomach. The stomach should react with vastly increased digestive activity, because henbane is extremely difficult to digest. Being poisonous simply means that a substance is difficult to digest. The stomach therefore must become furiously active. The brain is not strong enough, the front part of the brain. These things are thus related in the human body. The brain is not strong enough to stimulate the stomach sufficiently; the brain becomes cold and the person goes into shock.

What happens now if I give a person a minute, diluted dose of henbane? In this case, the stomach has less to do, and the brain is strong enough to regulate this minor task. Through introducing a minute amount of henbane, which the brain can manage, I have stimulated the brain into working harder than before. If the brain can overcome it, it is like asking a person to do a job that he can manage; then, he does it well. If I ask him to do a job in one day that actually requires ten, he would simply give up. This is the case with the brain. It contains, as it were, the workman in charge of the abdomen. If I ask too little of the brain, the workman remains lazy. If he is stimulated through his activity, he does well. If I ask too much of the abdomen, however, he refuses to participate and the person goes into shock.

What is the cause of fever? Fever is actually the result of an overactivity of the brain, which penetrates the entire human being. Assume that a person suffers from a disorder in some organ, say the liver or the kidneys, or especially the lungs, in the way I discussed with you recently. The brain begins to rebel against it. If the lungs no longer function correctly, the back portion of the brain rebels and stimulates the front part into rebelling against this lung disease, and hence fever occurs.

This shows that man becomes warmer from his head downwards and colder from below upwards. This is very interesting. The human being actually is warmed downwards from above. With fever we are concerned with our head. If there is an inflammation in the big toe, we produce the ensuing fever with the head. It is interesting that what lies farthest down is regulated by the foremost parts of the brain. Just as in the case of the dog, whose tail is regulated by his nose, so it is with the human being. If he struggles with a fever in his big toe, the activity that begets this fever lies entirely in the front of his brain. It is no slight to his dignity that, if man has an infection in his big toe, the fever originates entirely from the front, from a point above his nose. The human being thus always becomes warmer from above and colder from below.

This is related to why shock can be induced if excessively large doses of certain substances are administered to the human being but why a healing rise in temperature can be produced if we do not overtax the brain but stimulate its activity only with small doses. The activity of the brain, however, is stimulated all day not only by substances that we introduce into the brain; what we see and hear also stimulate it constantly. Also when you eat, you not only fill your stomachs, but you taste your food as well. Taste is stimulated, as is the sense of smell, all of which stimulates the brain.

Consider a woman who is pregnant. The child is in the first period of the pregnancy, which entails a tremendous increase in the mother's abdominal activity. Except during pregnancy, such activity in the abdomen is never necessary; in men, it doesn't occur at all. The abdominal activity is thus increased in an unprecedented way. When abdominal activity is increased, the sensory nerves above all are stimulated, because the abdomen and the forebrain belong together.

What does it mean when a person is hungry? I have explained to you that here a certain activity that really should be continuous cannot be performed. When hungry, a person craves food, which means that at the same time he longs for the stimulation of his taste buds. He can alleviate this by eating.

When a woman is pregnant, however, and must provide in her abdomen something for the growing child, much is stimulated also in the brain, particularly in the sensory nerves, the nerves of taste and smell. Eating does not satisfy these nerves of taste and smell, because the food doesn't go directly to the child but to the stomach. An excess of activity is required. The abdomen must work overtime in a certain way, and so the need arises in the head for smells and tastes which go beyond the normal.

The best care for the unborn child naturally requires an understanding of these matters.

Pregnant women are thus often not at all satisfied when they obtain what they momentarily crave; as soon as they have it, they crave another taste. Being also extremely moody, their taste is subject to abrupt change. One can appease them, however, by being kind to them and paying heed to what, in one's own opinion, is only a figment of their imagination. In the early months of pregnancy, women live in fantasies of tastes and smells. If you tell a pregnant woman that it is just her imagination, this is a real emotional slap to her. What is developing in her quite naturally due to the connection between the brain or head and the abdomen is repulsed. But if one cheers her up by being attentive, neither denying her wishes nor taking them literally, it is much easier to satisfy her. If, for example, one buys her something with vanilla flavour the second she craves it, by the time it is brought to her it may no longer be the right thing; she might say, 'Yes, but now I want sauerkraut!' It is well that it should be so! You must realize that if something so extraordinary is to take place in her abdomen it is because the child's development must demand it, and the pregnant woman must therefore receive special consideration.

Indeed, this shows us a lot more. It shows us that a powerful influence is exerted on the child by the environment of soul and spirit in which the mother lives. With some insight, the following can be understood. There are children who are born with 'water on the brain', that is, with hydrocephalus. In most cases this can be traced back to the fact that the mother, who perhaps rightly sought stimulation in life, was bored stiff during the first months of pregnancy, particularly the first few weeks. Perhaps her husband frequently went out alone to the local pub and she, being left at home, was extremely bored. The result was that she lacked the energy required to influence the brain cells. Boredom makes her head empty; the empty head, in turn, imparts emptiness to the abdomen. It does not develop sufficient strength to hold the forces of the child's head together properly. The head swells up, becoming hydrocephalous. Other children are born with abnormally small heads, particularly the upper portion of the head, that is, with acrocephalus. Most of these cases are connected with the fact that during the first weeks of pregnancy the mother engaged in too much diversion and amused herself excessively. If such matters are observed properly, a relationship can always be noted between the child's development and the mother's mood of soul during the early weeks of pregnancy.

Naturally, much is accomplished with medicine, but regarding these questions we have as yet no real medicine today but only a kind of quackery, because all the interrelationships are not correctly discerned by a merely materialistic science. These relationships require individual observation in most instances, and during the embryonic life of the human being, and therefore during pregnancy, they can be observed particularly well. Consider the significantly increased abdominal activity during pregnancy; the abdomen must be terribly active. This, in turn, calls for the strongest possible activity of the forebrain. It is not surprising, therefore, that some mothers actually become a little crazy during the first stage of pregnancy. They become a little crazy, because the abdomen and the forebrain, which actually thinks, are closely related. One arrives at very remarkable and interesting results if one looks for the relationships between the abdomen and what humanity accomplishes spiritually. It is curious and strange that spiritual science must call attention to these matters, whereas materialistic science completely fails in this area.

It would be extraordinarily interesting, for example, to

consider the following. You see, there were a great many philosophers in England—Hobbes, Bacon, Locke, Hume. These philosophers, even including John Stuart Mill, led essentially to the great rise of materialism. These philosophers all had such heavy thoughts that they could not penetrate the spiritual with their thoughts. They clung to matter with their thoughts. It would be extraordinarily interesting to examine the digestions of all these philosophers, these many philosophers. I am convinced they all suffered from constipation! Starting with Hobbes in the seventeenth century, and proceeding all the way into the nineteenth, this whole philosophy that brought us materialism was actually caused by the constipation of individual philosophers! This materialism could have been prevented—what I say now is not in earnest, I'm only joking!—if one had given Hobbes, Bacon, Locke, and the others regular laxatives in their youth. Then all this materialism most likely would not have arisen.

It is indeed odd, you see, that something that people frequently call materialistic must be pointed out by spiritual science. But the reason for this is that when the human being is really observed, the spirit is revealed where others see only matter. Anthroposophy does not assume that the abdomen is only a chemical factory. I once told you that the liver is a wondrous organ, that the kidney with its functions is also a marvellous organ. Only by comprehending these organs will one find the spirit everywhere. If you stop finding the spirit in some area, if you think that digestion is a process that is too materialistic to be studied in a spiritual way, you then become a materialist. Indeed, materialism came into being through spiritual arrogance. I have told you this before, though it sounds remarkable: when the ancient Jews of the Old Testament had bad thoughts during the night, they did not blame these bad, unhealthy thoughts on their heads but on their kidneys. When they said, 'This night God has affected my kidneys,' they were more correct than today's medicine. The ancient Jews also said that God reveals himself to man not through man's head but directly through the activity of his kidneys and generally through his abdominal activity.

Considering this viewpoint, it is most interesting, though I don't know if you gentlemen have seen it, to watch an Orthodox Jew pray. When a devout Orthodox Jew prays, he does not take his phylactery out of a pocket that he wears over his heart or that hangs over his head. He wears his phylactery over his abdomen and prays with it in this position. People today naturally no longer know what the relationship is here, but those who long ago gave the ancient Jews such commandments were aware of the relationship. In western regions of Europe, people don't have much opportunity any more to see this, but in eastern European regions it makes quite a special impression to observe how the old Jews pray. When they prepare for prayer, they take the phylactery out of their trouser pocket; it then hangs around them and they pray.

This knowledge that humanity once possessed by means of various dreamlike, ancient clairvoyant forces has been lost, and humanity today is not advanced enough to rediscover the spirit in all matter. You can comprehend nothing if you simply take your ordinary thoughts into a laboratory and mechanically execute experiments, and so on. You are not thinking at all while doing this. You must experiment in such a way that something of the spirit emerges everywhere; for that to happen, your experiments must be arranged accordingly. And so one can say that it is peculiar that anthroposophy, the science of the spirit, has to point out how the human brain, the so-called noblest part, is connected with the lower abdomen, but it is simply so. Only a true science leads to these facts. Similarly, any number of things can cause a disorder of the heart, for example. It can come through an internal irregularity, but in most cases an irregular activity of the heart can be traced to some disorder in the midbrain, where the feelings are particularly based [see Fig. 17 on p. 149]. It is interesting to discover that just as the abdomen is related to the forebrain, so this forebrain is related, from the viewpoint of the soul, to the will, and the midbrain is related to feeling. Actually, only the back part of the brain is related to thinking. If we look into the brain, we see that the hindbrain is related to breathing and to thinking. Breathing has, in fact, a pronounced relationship to thinking.

Picture the following case. A person lacking the benefits of Waldorf education, in which these things are frequently discussed, develops in his youth in such a way that he turns out to be a scoundrel. His feelings are confused, causing him to be malicious. What does this mean? It means that the soul does not work correctly in the midbrain. If the soul is not properly nourished, the heart's rhythm becomes irregular. You can cause an irregular rhythm of the heart and all sorts of diseases of the heart by developing into an ill-tempered person.

Naturally, if a woman in early pregnancy goes into a forest, let us say, and has the misfortune of discovering a person who has hanged himself from a tree and is already dead — if he is still twitching, it's even worse — she sustains a terrible shock. It becomes an image in her, and probably, unless other measures can be taken — usually by life itself, not by artificially induced means — she will give birth to a child who is pale, with a pointed chin and skinny limbs, and who is unable to move around properly. With a pregnant woman, a single such frightening sight suffices to affect the unborn child. In later life, when one is 18, 19, or 20 years old, to be a scoundrel only once won't hurt; one must become a habitual scoundrel, and that takes longer. With a pregnant woman, however, a single incident is enough to have a dire effect.

The results of such experiments can reach much further. Imagine a young mother-to-be who is busy with her work. She hasn't been told that army manoeuvres are being held nearby. Cannons begin to thunder, and her ears are given a frightful shock. Since hearing is strongly connected with the hindbrain as well as with the breathing, such a fright can cause a disorder of the breathing system of her developing child.

You might ask, 'What is he saying? Why, he wants us to pay attention to every little detail in life!' Yes, gentlemen, if a healthy educational system and healthy social conditions existed, you wouldn't have to think at all about many of these things, since they would develop by force of habit like other routine matters. I don't believe that there are many men who, when they habitually beat their wives in the middle of every month, give it too much thought. They do it out of habit. There are such husbands. Why do they beat their wives? Because they have run out of money, they cannot go down to the local pub, so they amuse themselves at home by abusing their wives. These are habits that people form. Well, gentlemen, if we had a sound educational system for everybody, we would acquire different habits. Were it known, for example, that army manoeuvres would be held one morning and that there would be explosions, it should as a matter of course be called to the attention of any pregnant woman in the area. Something like this can become a habit. Sound education and socially acceptable conditions can give rise to a number of habits that need not be thought about any longer but simply carried out. This is something towards which we must work. Essentially, however, this can be accomplished only through proper education.

This is why the science of the spirit in particular will be in a position to explain the material world correctly. Materialism only looks at the material realm but is ignorant of all that lives in the material. It observes fever but does not know that fever is called forth by tremendously expanded brain activity. Materialism is always greatly astonished by shock but does not rightly recognize that shock comes from a drop of body temperature, because the proper 'internal combustion' can no longer continue. Thus we can say that the way the head of a pregnant woman is stimulated is strongly connected with her child's development.

People pay no heed to what is contained in spiritual culture. A sound education will also gradually permeate everything we read and are told. Some day, for example, when people pay attention to what anthroposophy says, novels will perhaps be published for pregnant women. When pregnant women read them, they will receive impressions of ideal human beings. As a result, beautiful babies will be born who will grow to be strong, fine-looking human beings. What a woman does with her head during pregnancy becomes the source of the activity taking place in her abdomen. She shapes and forms the child with what she imagines, feels and wills.

Here, spiritual science becomes tangible to the point where one can no longer say that the spirit has no influence on the human being. For the rest of his life, unless education sets it right later on, a person is under the influence of what his mother did during the first months of pregnancy. The later months are not as important, because the human being has already been shaped, and definite forms have become fixed, but the first months are of particular importance and are full of significance. When one sees the physical origin of the human being in the womb, something reveals itself that in every respect points to spiritual science.

If one thinks reasonably, one can say to oneself that the warmth streaming down from above and the cold streaming up from below must always meet in the right way in the abdomen. One must care for the abdomen in the right way.

This is something that must be seen, so that what comes from above can meet what comes from below in the right way. When we are clear that a person is so strongly influenced by his mother's experiences of soul and spirit that he can end up with a large or a small head, a ruined heart or breathing system, then we see that a person is, in fact, completely influenced by soul-spiritual considerations.

It can also happen that a mother-to-be, in the first or second months of pregnancy, could run into somebody with an unusually crooked nose, the likes of which she has never seen before. Unless some corrective measure is taken, in most cases the child will also grow a crooked nose. You will even be able to see that in most cases if the woman was startled by the sight of a person whose nose was twisted to the right, the child will be born with a nose twisted to the left. Just as a man's right hand is connected with the left speech centre in the brain, just as everything is reversed in the human being, so the twist of the nose is also reversed. We can conclude that if someone has a crooked nose, he most likely has it because his mother was frightened by someone with a crooked nose. A person has many other features. Materialistic science, when it doesn't know the origin of something, always talks of heredity. If one has a crooked nose — well, that's inherited; the red skin tone of another — that's inherited, too. Things are not like this, however. They arise from causes such as I have related. The concept of heredity is one of the most ambiguous held by modern science. If you look at a person and see a twisted nose or a birthmark, this does not necessarily indicate that the mother saw the same birthmark. She might have seen something else that caused the child's blood to flow in the wrong direction. These are all deviations from the normal human form, but there is indeed a normal human form.

One cannot simply say that deviations from the normal human form do not come from bodily but from spiritual experiences while still maintaining that the entire human being comes merely from the belly of the mother, from that which is within the material realm! If one wishes to explain abnormalities spiritually, one must certainly also explain the entire human being spiritually. Naturally, the mother no more than the father can produce a human being spiritually. To do so would require all the creativity which makes up the human being, which is infinite. We are led to understand, therefore, that man already exists prior to birth as a spiritual being, and as soul he is united with what is made available to him corporeally. Only regarding abnormal features can the embryo be influenced spiritually. It is much more remarkable, however, that I have a nose in the middle of my face or that I have two eyes! If I am born with a crooked nose, that is an abnormal feature, but recall the nose in the middle of the face with its marvellous normal form, which I recently explained to you, and the eye — what a wondrous thing! All this does not grow out of the mother's womb; it is something that already exists in the soul realm before the human being arises in the womb.

Here, correctly understood, natural science points to what human life is like in the spiritual world before conception. Today's materialists will naturally say that this is fantasy. Why do they say this? All the ancient people who, in primordial human times, still possessed certain dream-like perceptions, which we no longer have, knew that man exists before he appears on earth. Throughout the Middle Ages, however, it was forbidden by decree of the Church to think of so-called pre-existence, which means pre-earthly existence; the Church forbade it. When a materialist holds forth from his pulpit today, this is only the continuation of the medieval pulpit, and though he no longer speaks the language of those preachers, using instead his own brand of propaganda, he only says what medieval sermons stated long ago. Materialism has simply taken over the medieval preachings, and, though they are not aware of it, today's materialists basically elaborate on what the Church taught. Materialism stems basically from the Church of the Middle Ages. Then, no soul was permitted to have existed before its earthly life. The intention was to teach people that God creates the soul when conception takes place. If a couple were in the mood to let conception occur — we know that in many instances this can be a mood of the moment — the Good Lord had to move quickly and create a soul for them! This is what the Church edict really implied and what one was supposed to believe.

It is not a sensible viewpoint, however, to make God the servant of the moods of human beings, so that he must hurriedly produce a soul when they happen to be in a mood to let conception take place. If you give this some thought, you discover what is actually contained in the materialistic viewpoint, which undermines human dignity. A real and true knowledge of the human being leads us instead to the realization that the soul is already there, has always lived. It descends to what is offered it through the human seed and its fertilization.

Anthroposophy has not, therefore, arrived back at the spirit because of some arbitrary fantasy but simply because it must, because it takes scientific knowledge seriously, which others do not. People study natural science, which would lead to the spirit, but they are too lazy to come through natural science to the spirit on their own. That would require a little effort on the part of their heads. Instead, they allow some old teachers to deprive them of the spirit, and yet they still manage to be religious! Then they are dishonest, however; it is like keeping two different sets of accounts. A person who is consistent in his reckoning must ascend from nature to spirit, and matters such as those we have discussed today, for example, will lead us there.

The brain and thinking

This was the first lecture given to the workmen after the burning of the Goetheanum. As a demonstration of their sympathy, all present stood when Rudolf Steiner entered.

Dr Steiner: It is difficult to put into words the sorrow I feel. I know of your deep sympathy, so let me be brief. May I take this opportunity to call attention to the fact that as early as 23 January 1921, here in this hall, I read from a brochure a statement made by an opponent, indeed, one can already say an enemy, that went like this:

> There are plenty of spiritual sparks of fire that strike like lightning against the wooden mousetrap. It will require quite a bit of cleverness on Steiner's part to work in a conciliatory manner so as to prevent a real spark of fire from bringing the Dornach grandeur to an inglorious end some day.

You see, with such inflammatory talk it is not surprising when something like the fire occurs, and in view of such vehement hostility it was something that could easily be feared. You can understand why it was easy to fear. It is true, however, that even now one can see what certain groups think about the matter. We need only consider the antagonism contained in the poor taste of newspapers, which now, after the Goetheanum has been destroyed, ask, 'Didn't that "clairvoyant" Steiner foresee this fire?' That such attitudes are also evidence of a great stupidity is something I don't wish to talk about now. It points to a malicious degree of hostility, however, that some people find it at all necessary to publish such statements! One learns from this what people think and how crude things are today. It is indeed crude!

You can be sure, however, that I will never let anything divert me from my path, come what may. As long as I live, I shall represent my cause and will continue in the same way as I have done up to now. Also, I naturally hope that there will be no interruption to any of our work, so that in the future we can work together here in the same way as we have before; at least, that is my intention. Come what may, my thought is that the building will have to be reconstructed in some form; to be sure, no effort will be spared towards that end. We must therefore go on in the same way as before; this is simply an inner commitment.

Today, I wish to make use of our time by saying a few things to you that relate to the subject we discussed a little before this sad event. I tried to show you that a true science must work towards once more recognizing the soul-spiritual aspects of the human being. I don't believe you have any idea how emotionally charged the reaction is that this matter calls forth today within scientific circles. These scientific circles, as they call themselves today, which are taken to be something special by the layman, are the very ones that stand ready to make common cause with all existing hostile forces when it is a matter of proceeding against the anthroposophical movement. You must see that the hatred against the anthroposophical movement is by no means a slight matter. During the days when the tragedy took place, a report reached me, for example, of the formation of an association that calls itself 'The Association of Non-Anthroposophical Experts on Anthroposophy'. They are people who naturally have nothing to do with the accident here but who are part of the whole opposition. The report concludes with the words, 'This calls for a life-or-death struggle. The side that has the Holy Spirit will gain victory.'

It is obvious from the idiotic things said by these people, who want a life-or-death struggle, that the spirit — leaving the Holy Spirit completely aside — is not with these people. That is evident at once from the minutes of their meeting. Nevertheless, the spirit of hatred that exists is expressed in the sentence, 'This calls for a life-or-death struggle.' People do wage this struggle, and the number of opponents is indeed not small. So-called scientific groups participate in these affairs today and in a most intensive way.

You see, I must continue to stress this, because the authority of science is so strong today. In order to know something, one turns to a so-called scientific expert, because this is the way things are arranged. Laymen don't know the means by which such persons become 'experts' and that one can be the greatest idiot and yet be an 'expert' with certificates and so on. These matters must be fully understood, and it is therefore important to get to the bottom of things and understand what really lies at their foundation. The very first sentences taught little children in school today — not directly, but indirectly — are mostly rubbish! Things that are considered self-evident today are in fact rubbish.

One is attacked from all sides today for saying that it is nonsense that the brain thinks; for it is agreed everywhere that the brain thinks and that where there is no brain, there can be no thinking, that there are no thoughts where no brain exists. Well, from my lectures you will have seen that the brain naturally plays its part in, and has a significance for, thinking. But if those people, who in fact make little use of their brains, claim that the brain is a sort of machine with which one thinks, then this is mere thoughtlessness. It is not surprising when a simple, uneducated person believes this, because he is not in possession of all the facts and so he believes in the voice of authority. No logic and real thinking, however, are contained in the statement that the brain thinks, and today I shall give you a number of examples to prove it.

If you look at a small beetle, you can easily see that it has a small head. If you dissect the head of such a beetle — the burying-beetle, for instance — you discover nothing like a brain, which is supposed to be the thinking apparatus. Naturally, the tiny beetle has no brain in this sense but only a little lump, a lump of nerves, you could say. It does not have even the beginnings of a complete brain.

Now, I will relate a scene to you as an example, but before I give you this example I must tell you that these burying-beetles always follow the lifelong habit of laying their eggs, and maggots hatch from them that only later change into beetles. As soon as they have emerged from the eggs, these tiny maggots require meat for their nourishment. They could not live without it. So, what does the burying-beetle do? It searches in the field for a dead mouse or a dead bird or a mole, and having discovered one — a dead mouse, for example — it runs home again, only to return not alone but with a number of other beetles. These beetles that it has returned with run all around the mouse. Picture the mouse here [*sketching*]; the beetle has discovered it; it runs off and then returns with a number of other burying-beetles. You see them run all around it. Occasionally, you notice that they all run away. At other times, you will see the beetles arrive, run around the dead mouse, and then start digging. First they dig the ground under the mouse and then all around it. The mouse gradually sinks deeper and deeper into the earth as they continue digging. They dig until the mouse finally falls into the ground. They then fetch the females, who lay their eggs in it. Finally, they cover the hole completely so that passers-by won't notice it. I mentioned earlier that sometimes you can observe the beetles leave without returning. When you look into this, you find that the ground is too hard to dig. The beetles seem to have realized that here they could do nothing. Whenever they stay and begin digging, the ground is soft.

It is unbelievably strange but true that only 10 or 12 beetles return with the one that makes the discovery, never 40 or 50. Only as many beetles return as are required to do the work. The first beetle doesn't bring more helpers than it needs, nor does it bring fewer. It arrives with just the right number to do the job. This sounds unbelievable, but what I am telling you is not a fairy-tale. People have been able to demonstrate this phenomenon with all kinds of experiments. It's absolutely true.

The person who first described the activity of these beetles wasn't a superstitious person but one who had sound judgement. He was a friend of the botanist Gleditsch, and was a scientist in the first half of the nineteenth century, an age when science was still on a sounder footing. He was involved in experimental work and once used toads in his experiments. These tests were intended for something completely different — you know that electricity was first discovered through work on a frog's thigh — and he needed to dry a dead toad. What did this natural scientist do? He took it outside and pinned the dead toad to a small piece of wood to let the sun dry it quickly. After a while he returned to check it and found a number of beetles around it hard at work. He decided to leave the dead toad alone and watch what these fellows, the beetles, were up to. What did they do? They continued digging until the wood fell and the toad had a place in the ground, in the hole; then the females came to lay their eggs in it. That done, the beetles covered the toad and the wood it was pinned to with earth. Now, if a human being were to do that, one would think he also buried the stick in order to hide every trace. So you see, the burying beetles do exactly what a clever human being would do; indeed, I am convinced that a number of stupid people wouldn't do anywhere near as well. You see, therefore, that what is called cleverness, intelligence, is present without the beetles possessing it.

One might call this nonsense and say that it need not be looked upon as intelligence, that it is stupid to say it is intelligence since it is simply instinct. Of course, I consider it stupid for a person to use the word 'instinct' in this case, thus getting on the wrong track. One needs a word, however, and 'instinct' is used for everything, so that one need not think at all. One must learn to know the facts themselves — it is all the same what one calls them — one must learn to know the facts. Still, one might object by saying, 'All right, but what he has told us is still nonsense. The beetles are born with this ability; they pass it on genetically. One need not think of intelligence here. It is inherent in their physical nature, and there is no need to think that these beetles possess intelligence.

Now I shall tell you another story that was told by a person of incontestable authority, a story that has also been reported by others but above all by Darwin, an incontestable source; after all, people swear by Darwin, don't they? He observed this activity in wasps, not beetles. Wasps have brains that are no larger than those of beetles. Their larvae also require meat as soon as they hatch. Now, these wasps are weaker than beetles, even when they band together, so they cannot handle moles or dead toads but prefer smaller creatures that they can handle without help. This is why wasps gather little animals like flies and such for their young.

Darwin, who is considered to be the greatest natural scientist of the nineteenth century, observed a wasp who needed such an insect, a female wasp, heavy with eggs, looking for an insect into which to lay them. Finding a fly, a dead fly, on the ground, she tried to fly away with it, but it was too difficult for her. What did the wasp do? It bit off the fly's head and hindquarters and flew off with the breast and wings, which it could manage. Without the head and hindquarters of the fly, the wasp could now fly. Now — as I said, Darwin watched all this — a strong breeze was blowing and the wasp could not fly forwards because the fly's wings caught the wind. The two wings caught the wind, and it could not fly forwards. Again, what did the wasp do, laden with the fly? It landed on the ground, bit off the two wings, and flew away with the fly's breast without the wings.

In this case it is impossible to say that this is anything else but deliberate, since the wasp, after all, accommodated itself to the wind. This cannot be inherent in the wasp, to bite off the wings. It must be what is called intelligence that motivates the insect. The wasp tells itself that if the wings are discarded, the wind won't catch in them. It is impossible for this to be inherited; what exists there is what one calls deliberation; consequently, one must admit that intelligence is really at work here. Here intelligence is at work.

Now you can see how scientists proceeded in the nineteenth century. I purposely mentioned to you Darwin, who observed this. What was his conclusion, however? Darwin said that everything that confronts us in animals is produced only through heredity and through natural selection, and so forth.

In order to set up theories, people simply suppress what they themselves know. This is the essential point, that people suppress what they know to set up convenient theories. Such theories are by no means scientific and only throw sand in the eyes of the public. Darwin was certainly a great man, and nobody has acknowledged his positive accomplishments in a more kindly way than I. I have written everything possible in Darwin's favour, but, oddly enough, we must realize that even those who have made significant contributions have suffered from the malady of having no eyes for facts. In spite of the great scientific triumphs made in the external world, it is characteristic of scientists of the nineteenth century that people completely lost their sense for facts, and the facts were simply suppressed.

Now, let's go further. Let's consider other insects. In these matters one must study insects, because they can illuminate our subject particularly well; we can be quite sure that in their case they do not owe their intelligence to having a large brain, because this they certainly don't have. Therefore one must study insects in this matter. Indeed, not only are they able to illuminate the things I have just described but many others as well. Insects lay their eggs, and a mature insect never emerges from them but only little worms. With butterflies, which are insects, it is even more complicated. First, a little worm appears, a caterpillar; it pupates, and finally from the chrysalis emerges the butterfly. This is certainly quite a transformation, but this transformation actually occurs with all insects. You see, there are some insects that, when they are fully mature, feed only on plants. I am not agitating for vegetarianism, as you know, gentlemen, but these insects are vegetarians. They eat only plants. The strange thing is that their larvae, the maggots, require meat when they hatch. These insects therefore have a great peculiarity, that they are born with a completely different food preference from that which they later acquire. They convert to plant food only when they are fully developed insects. When they are still little children and look completely different — like maggots or worms — they feed on meat.

What do these mature insects do? They seek out other insects, mostly caterpillars, and lay their eggs on their backs. They themselves no longer have an appetite for meat, but they know that maggots requiring meat will hatch from their eggs. Therefore they lay their eggs in the body of such a caterpillar or some such animal. Though one can marvel at this cleverness, there is much more. One can even say that these newly hatched maggots are already clever. Consider that some maggot species depend on *living* flesh for food. When it is time to lay the eggs, this insect, which has a stinger, punctures another living insect that is larger, and lays many eggs within it. Sometimes numerous eggs are deposited, filling the caterpillar's body, and from these the maggots hatch. The maggots are then within the body of this other insect. These eggs are only deposited in live insects, because if the animal in which the eggs are laid were to die, the eggs would be lost, since the maggots can only survive on living flesh. Consider, therefore, that if a maggot were to destroy a vital organ in the host insect, thus causing its death, all the other maggots hatching from the eggs would perish. These little creatures are so clever, however, that nothing is ever eaten in the living caterpillar except those parts not needed for its survival. All vital organs are spared, and the caterpillar stays alive. Regardless of how many eggs are deposited, only so much is consumed as to ensure the host insect's life.

You see, these things are known but are simply suppressed. People know it but suppress it, and it isn't well received, naturally, when one points them out, because this not only shows up the incapability but the downright dishonesty of official science.

In the case of animals and insects you can see that it is possible to say that they certainly do not possess intelligence, because they have no apparatus for intelligence, that is, brains. Nevertheless, intelligence is working in what they do, and it must be admitted that intelligence is there. The animals do not deliberate; deliberation would require a brain. Animals don't deliberate, but what takes place in their activities is intelligent. Indeed, it happens that animals even have something similar to memory. They have no recollection but something akin to it. You can observe this, for instance, if you are a beekeeper. Here stands a beehive.

The bees hatch. For the sake of an experiment, you move the hive to a nearby spot. The bees return to the first location. Naturally, this is 'instinct', and there is no need to be surprised about it; they fly in the direction from which they flew away. Now, however, they begin to look everywhere for the hive and fly around seeking it. They arrive at the new location but do not enter the hive immediately. Instead, they swarm around it for a long time, and one can definitely conclude that they are examining it to see if it is their own! The burying-beetle does the same when it examines the ground to see if it is hard or soft. While bees have no recollection, the above incident shows that they nevertheless possess something similar to memory, namely, they must determine whether it is the same beehive. We do this with our memory; bees do it with something similar.

You see, what works as intelligence through the human head is at work everywhere. Intelligence is at work everywhere; even in insects there is marvellous intelligence. Picture the wonderful intelligence at work when the larvae that hatch inside the caterpillar's body do not feed immediately on its stomach. If they did, all the maggots would perish. Compared with the tactics employed by humans during war, the intelligence ruling the insect arouses respect and exposes the foolishness of human beings. In this regard, human beings have no reason to claim sole possession of intelligence.

I'll tell you something else now. You are all familiar with paper. You all know that the paper we have today was invented no earlier than four or five hundred years ago. Before this, parchment and all sorts of materials were used for writing. Civilized man discovered so-called rag paper just four or five centuries ago. Before this, man wrote on leather and so on. How was paper discovered? One had to discover how to mix together certain substances in a specific way. Perhaps one of you has been in a paper factory. At first the paper is in a liquid form, and it is then solidified. It is produced in a purely artificial way through various chemical and mechanical means. Perhaps you've not only seen paper but also now and then a wasps' nest. A wasps' nest is built like this [*sketching*]. It is attached to something and formed so the wasps can fly into it. It is grey, not white — but paper can be grey, too — and this wasps' nest is real paper. If one asks what a wasps' nest is made of chemically, one finds that it is identical with paper. It is real paper.

Wasps, however, have been building their nests for thousands and thousands of years, not just four or five hundred. You can see, therefore, that wasps manufactured paper much earlier than humans. That's simply a fact: the wasps' nest is made of paper. If, thousands of years ago, people had been clever enough to examine the substance of a wasps' nest, they would have discovered paper then. Chemistry was not that advanced, however; neither was writing, through which some things have also come about that do not exactly serve man. In any case, the wasp has made paper for an immeasurably longer time than the human being has.

Naturally, I could go on, not for hours but for days, to speak of how intelligence pervades everything and is found everywhere. Man simply gathers this intelligence that is spread out in the world and puts it to use. Owing to his well-developed brain, he can put to his own use what permeates the world. Thanks to his brain, he can utilize for his own benefit the intelligence contained in all things.

Our brain is not given us for the purpose of producing intelligence. It is sheer nonsense to believe that we produce intelligence. It is as stupid as saying, 'I went to the pond with a water pitcher to fetch water. Look, it contains water now. A minute ago there was none; the water, therefore, materialized from the walls of the pitcher!' Everybody will say that is nonsense. The water came from the pond; it was not produced by the pitcher. The experts, however, point to the brain, which simply collects intelligence because it is present in everything, like the water, and claim that intelligence emerges from within it. It is as foolish as saying that water is produced by the pitcher. After all, intelligence is even present where there is no brain, just as the pond does not depend on the water pitcher. Intelligence exists everywhere, and man can take hold of it. Just as the water from the pitcher can be put to use, so man can make use of his brain when he gathers the intelligence that is present everywhere in the world. To this day, however, he is not making use of it in a particularly outstanding manner.

You can see that it is a matter of correct thinking. But those who never think correctly — for they show that they cannot think correctly — claim that intelligence is produced by the brain. This is as foolish as claiming that water from a pond is produced by its container. Such foolishness, however, is science today. Actually, these matters should be obvious; one should simply realize that intelligence is something that must be collected and gathered together.

Now, you can take your brain and resolve to gather intelligence somewhere. It doesn't collect intelligence by itself any more than the empty water pitcher, which, when you put it away, remains empty. By itself the water pitcher cannot fetch water, nor does the brain collect intelligence by itself. You cannot leave the brain to its own devices and expect it to function any more than the water pitcher. What must be present so that the brain can gather intelligence? The empty water pitcher alone can be compared to the belief that man consists only of blood, nerves and brain. Something else must be present that does the collecting and that gathers intelligence by means of the brain. It is the soul-spiritual element of man that does the collecting. It enters man as I described recently in the lecture on embryonic development. It has previously existed in the soul-spiritual world and only makes use of the physical. If the facts are not suppressed, if one sees that intelligence, like water, pervades everything and, like water in a pitcher, must be gathered together, then — if one is a serious scientist and not a charlatan — one must search for the gatherer. This is simply what follows from the use of clear reason. It is not true that anthroposophical science of the spirit is less scientific than ordinary science; it is much more scientific, much more scientific.

The day before yesterday, there was an example of the kind of logic people employ. As you know, a natural scientific course was recently held here. I have already told you of experiments conducted in Stuttgart concerning the task of the spleen. We confirmed that the spleen has the task of serving as a sort of regulator of the digestive rhythm. The blood circulation has a definite rhythm, as found in the pulse with its 72 beats per minute. These are related to the intake of food. People also pay a little heed to the rhythmic intake of food; they are not too good at it, however, and frequently have no set mealtime. Worse still, people indiscriminately partake of foods that are beneficial to them and those that are not. There is no regularity here as there is in the blood. If, for example, I eat at one o'clock instead of two o'clock, this is an irregularity. The blood circulation, after all, doesn't work that way and doesn't produce a different pulse when it requires nourishment. This is where the spleen takes over. We have tried to demonstrate this with experiments and have been successful to a degree. More experiments are needed and must be done soon, but we have been able to show to some extent that the spleen is a regulator. Though we might have irregular eating habits, the spleen keeps food in the intestines as long as the blood needs it. If we don't starve ourselves too much — if we starve ourselves too much even the spleen would be unable to function properly — the spleen supplies the blood with fat taken from our own body.

You see, because we were completely honest, Dr Kolisko quite honestly stated in her book that in my medical course I indicated that the spleen has this task, and she then proceeded with experiments to confirm this. Then a professor in Munich said that was too easy, because Dr Kolisko had already received the suggestions from anthroposophy and so had them up her sleeve. It is not supposed to be hypothetical-deductive science if one starts with indications or suggestions and then conducts experiments to prove them. He therefore said that this isn't hypothetical-deductive science.

Why does the professor say that? Because people do not wish to work with a thought as their guideline. Instead, they want a lot of material delivered to their laboratories, and they blindly begin to experiment until they happen on some result. They call this hypothetical-deductive science, but there is no hypothesis in it at all. Occasionally, the most significant discoveries are made by chance. Then, well — even a blind dog sometimes finds a morsel! How could we progress, however, if in our laboratories our work did not follow and test our ideas?

The professor in Munich says that it is not hypothetical-deductive science for one to work with indications. Now, imagine that somewhere experiments had been conducted that proved the spleen's function but that a fire had destroyed the reports of the work. Only the final result would be known. Couldn't somebody come along and say that he would repeat these experiments? It would not be any different from our starting out with these indications. The same professor would also have to object to that as being unscientific. Now, wouldn't that be absurd? The only difference here is that I have made my indications by tracing the spiritual course of the matter, but I have done it in such a way that it can readily be followed according to anatomical science. Then, through experiments, another person seeks affirmation of what has been precisely indicated. Our task here was simply to show correct physical proof for what I had said. There is no logical difference between my knowledge acquired by spiritual-scientific means and what another person has already found earlier by means of experiments.

What does it tell us when someone considers it correct, hypothetical-deductive science that something has been discovered by physical means, though the descriptions of the tests may have been burned, while anything done by anthroposophy is not considered hypothetical-deductive science? This is dishonest and shows that people immediately denounce anything coming from anthroposophy. People aren't really concerned about hypothetical-deductive science; they are so foolish that they don't notice that this is logical nonsense. They say that ours is not hypothetical-deductive science, not because it would be logical to say so, but only because it derives from anthroposophy. People are too foolish to comprehend what comes from anthroposophy. Naturally, their lack of comprehension makes them angry, and therefore they denounce it. The real reason anthroposophy is considered heresy is that those who are engaged in so-called science do not think and cannot understand anthroposophy. This is an aspect of our entire civilization. It is possible today to be a great scientist or scholar without really being able to think. In the future, one must truly cultivate honesty, an honesty that takes into account all the facts, not only those that conveniently fit one's pet theory, thus throwing sand in the eyes of the public.

The hatred of anthroposophy is based in large part on anthroposophy's honesty, something people don't want to grant it. If people had a keener sense for truth, they would often stop writing after the first sentence. Since all their arguments against anthroposophy would collapse, however, if anthroposophy were properly studied, they invent all kinds of fabrications concerning it. People inventing fabrications about anthroposophy don't care about truth, and once they start telling lies, they go further. The serious defamations of anthroposophy thus arise. What is the result? A person who cannot see through all this believes that anthroposophists engage in devilry. Such a person cannot see through this, because he naturally believes those in 'authority', who do not speak the truth. Anthroposophy suffers most of all from these lies that are circulated about it, whereas its one aim is to focus on the facts and be a real science.

In view of the painful tragedy that has struck here, we must at least look into the real state of affairs and realize how anthroposophy is being slandered out of a spirit of pure falsehood.

I myself am absolutely opposed to any agitation coming from our side. Naturally, I cannot stop everything, but when I speak to you, I am strictly pointing out facts. This is all I have done today, and from these facts I have drawn a general characterization of scientific life. You must admit to yourselves that where such facts are ignored there is no desire to create real science but only a desire to throw sand in the eyes of the public, even if in a quite unconscious way. People would have to be much more clever to see through this.

We shall continue on Monday. If you have something to ask, I would like you to speak entirely from your hearts. I, for one, don't wish to be deterred by the great tragedy that has struck here. This is why I didn't want to waste my time lamenting but wanted to tell you something useful.

The effects of alcohol

Dr Steiner: Does anyone have a question on his mind?

A question is asked concerning alcohol, its negative effects, etc.

Do you mean the extent to which alcohol generally is detrimental to health? Well, alcohol's initial effect is quite obvious, because it influences what we have been describing in man all along, that is, the entire constitution of the soul. In the first place, through alcohol, a person suffers a form of spiritual confusion so strong that he becomes subject to passions that otherwise are weak in him and can easily be suppressed by his reason. A person thus appears more sensible if he has had no alcohol than if he drinks. To begin with, alcohol has a stimulating influence on the blood, causing increased blood circulation. This, in turn, arouses a person's passions; for example, he may more readily become furious, whereas otherwise he can control his anger more easily. So you can see that the first effect of alcohol is exercised on man's reason — indeed, on his whole life of soul.

After alcohol has remained for a certain length of time in the organism, it causes another symptom that you know well, called a hangover; the appearance of a hangover shows you that the entire organism objects to the initial effect of alcohol. What does it mean for a person to have a hangover? As a rule, it appears in the morning after an evening of too much drinking. Due to the drinking the night before, the circulation of a person's blood is strongly agitated. The increased movement that otherwise would have taken its course at a much slower pace uses up a lot of energy.

Pay close attention to this! Let us assume that the body accomplishes a certain activity within 24 hours. When somebody consumes a goodly amount of alcohol, the same activity is completed in perhaps twelve or even six hours. The body thus deprives itself of inner activity. People who are in the habit of drinking every once in a while, therefore, instinctively do something before the hangover appears: they eat heartily. Why do they do this? They eat heartily either to avoid a hangover altogether or so that its effects the next day are at least milder, so that they can work.

What happens if a person has drunk himself into a visible state of intoxication and then consumes, let us say, a large hot dog? He stimulates again what has been used up by the previous excessive activity. But if, because he is not a habitual drinker, he doesn't do this — habitual drinkers remember to eat — and he forgets to eat that hot dog, he then will suffer the hangover, basically because his body is no longer able to engage in increased inner activity. When the body does not function correctly, however, waste products, in particular uric acid, are deposited everywhere. Since the head is the most difficult to supply, the waste products are deposited there. If a person has, through alcohol consumption, depleted the inner activity of the body during the night, he walks around the next morning with his head in the condition that is normal for his intestines, that is, filled with refuse. An immediate revolt by the body is brought about when, through the intake of alcohol, too much activity is demanded of it.

As I have mentioned to you before in these lectures, man has a much higher tolerance — I don't mean only regarding alcohol but generally — and can take much more abuse than is normally assumed. He is capable of readjustment for a long time. Some people even make use of a most deceptive, most questionable antidote against a hangover. When they come home or get up the next morning with a powerful hangover, what do they do? Surely you have seen this; they continue drinking, making the morning pint into a special cure.

What does this continued drinking signify? During the night, through the agitation of the blood, the body has been deprived of functioning activity. This activity is now missing in the morning. Through renewed drinking, the body is stimulated once again, so that the last remnants of activity are also consumed. Since, with these last remnants, the major part of the refuse is also disposed of, the hangover disappears to a degree from the head but remains that much more in the rest of the body. People are, however, less aware of that. Additional drinking in the morning thus unconsciously transfers the hangover to the rest of the organism. Only now, when this occurs, does the real misery for the body begin. Those alcoholics who drive away a hangover with more drinking are in the worst shape, because gradually, as this is repeated, the entire body is ruined.

Still, however, because man can endure a good deal, it is almost impossible to ruin the body that quickly. Therefore the first thing that happens to a real alcoholic is that he suffers from a form of delirium. This does not as yet indicate total ruin. When delirium tremens, as it is called in medicine, sets in, people see certain kinds of animals, mice and the like, running all over the place. They suffer a form of persecution complex. Delirium tremens is connected with the phenomenon of people seeing themselves surrounded and attacked from all sides by small animals, especially mice. This is something that even has a historical background. There are structures called 'mice towers' [Mäusetürme] which have usually come by their name through somebody in some earlier time having been incarcerated in them who suffered from delirium tremens; and, though some real mice might well have been there too, this person was plagued by thousands upon thousands of mice that he merely imagined all around himself.

You can see, therefore, that the effects of alcohol can only very slowly ruin the body; the body resists these alcohol-induced effects for a long time.

What happens when people who have been drinking heavily for some time are suddenly bothered by their con-science and, having some energy left, stop drinking? It is an interesting fact that if they had not suffered from delirium tremens before, now, after abstaining from alcohol, they sometimes get it. Here we find something of interest, when people's consciences suddenly stir. They have been drink-ing for a while, let us say, drinking since early in the morning, and then suddenly their conscience stirs and they stop drinking. What happens then? If they had not had delirium tremens earlier, they struggle with it now. This is the interesting fact, that sometimes those who have been drinking for a long time begin suffering from delirium tremens when they *stop* drinking.

This is one of the most important signs that man must be viewed in such a way that the head is seen to work differ-ently from the rest of the body. In the last lectures I men-tioned many aspects of this to you. As long as a person suffers only in his head from the side-effects of drinking, his overall condition is still tolerable; the effects have not yet permeated the entire body. When they have penetrated, however, and the person gives up alcohol, the rest of the body really revolts by way of the brain and he suffers from delirium tremens just because he discontinued drinking.

One thus can say that it is the blood which bears the bodily counterpart for the most important functions of the soul. You probably know that some people suffer from persecution complexes, seeing all sorts of figures that are not there. Particularly in earlier times, such persons were bled — not a bad remedy, really. You must not believe that all people in the past were as superstitious as is generally assumed today. Bloodletting was not something derived from superstition. People were bled primarily by applying leeches somewhere on the body that drew off blood. The blood thus became less active. Not necessarily in the case of alcoholics, but for other attacks of insanity the blood thus became less active, and the person fared better.

As I have mentioned, the nervous system is very closely related to the foundations of our properties of soul, but it is much less important for the human will. The nervous system is important for reason, but for the human will it has much less significance than the blood.

Now, when you see that alcohol pre-eminently attacks the blood, it is clear from the body's strong reaction to alcohol's effects that the blood is well protected against alcohol. The blood is extraordinarily well protected against the assault of alcohol on human beings. By what means is the blood so strongly protected against this assault? We must ask further, then. Where do the most important ingredients of the blood actually originate?

Remember that I told you that blood consists of red corpuscles containing iron, which swim around in the so-called blood serum, and it also consists of white corpuscles. I told you that the most significant components of blood are the red and white corpuscles. We shall now disregard the corpuscles connected with the spleen's activity, which, in our tests in Stuttgart, we termed the 'regulators'. There are many components in the blood, but we want now to focus only on the red and white corpuscles, asking where in the body these corpuscles originate. These corpuscles originate in a most special place. If you examine the thigh bone from the hip to the knee, if you think of the bone in the arm, or any long bone, you will find in these bones the so-called bone marrow. The marrow is in there, the bone marrow. And you see, gentlemen, the red and white corpuscles originate in this bone marrow and migrate from it first into the arteries. The human body is arranged in such a way that the blood, at least the most important part of it, is produced in the inner hollows of the bones.

If this is the case, you can say to yourself: in so far as its production is concerned, the blood is indeed well protected from harm. In fact, alcohol must be consumed for a long time and in large quantities to damage the bone to the point of penetrating it to the innermost part, to the bone marrow, and destroying the bone marrow so that no more red and white corpuscles are produced. Only then, after the effects of drinking alcohol have reached the bone marrow, does the really ruinous process begin for the human being.

Now it is true that regarding their intellects and soul qualities human beings are in many ways alike; regarding the blood, however, there is a marked difference between man and woman. It is a difference that one is not always aware of but that is nevertheless clearly evident. This is that the influence on human beings of the red and white corpuscles that are produced within the hollows of the bone is such that the red corpuscles are more important for the woman and the white are more important for the man. This is very important: the red corpuscles are more important with the woman and the white with the man.

This is because the woman, as you know, has her menstrual period every four weeks, which is actually an activity that the human body undertakes to eliminate something that must be eliminated, red corpuscles. A man, however, does not have menstrual periods, and you can easily tell that his semen is not derived directly from red blood. It has its origin in white corpuscles. Although considerably transformed, in the end they turn into the main ingredient of semen. Thus, regarding what affects human reproduction, we must go to the protected bone marrow to investigate the means by which the human reproductive capacity can be influenced physically. Indeed, the human reproductive capacity can be physically affected precisely through the bone marrow within the bone.

After having been produced in the bone marrow, the red and white corpuscles naturally enter the bloodstream. When a woman now drinks alcohol, it is the red corpuscles that are particularly affected. The red corpuscles contain iron, are somewhat heavy, and possess something of the earth's heaviness. When a woman drinks, it affects her in such a way that there is too much heaviness in her. When a pregnant woman drinks, therefore, her developing child becomes too heavy and cannot inwardly form its organs properly. It does not develop properly inwardly, and its inner organs are not in order. In this round-about-way, gentlemen, the harmful influence of alcohol is expressed in the woman.

In men, alcohol primarily affects the white corpuscles. If conception takes place when a man is under the influence of alcohol, or when his system is generally contaminated by the effects of alcoholism, a man's semen is ruined in a way, becoming too restless. When conception takes place, the tiny egg is released from the mother's organism. This can only be seen with a microscope. From the male, a great number of microscopic sperm are released, each one of which has something resembling a tail attached to it. The seminal fluid contains countless numbers of such sperm. This tail, which is like a fine hair, gives the sperm great restlessness. They make the most complicated movements, and naturally one sperm must reach the egg first. The one that reaches the egg first penetrates it. The sperm is much smaller than the egg. Although the egg can be perceived only with a microscope, the sperm is still smaller. As soon as the egg has received it, a membrane forms around the egg, thereby preventing penetration by the rest of the sperm cells. Generally only one sperm can enter the egg. As soon as one has penetrated, a membrane is formed around the egg, and the others must retreat.

You see, therefore, it is most ingeniously arranged. Now, the sperm's restlessness is greatly increased through alcohol, so that conception occurs under the influence of semen that is extraordinarily lively. If the father is a heavy drinker when conception occurs, the child's nerve-sense system will be affected. The woman's drinking harms the child's inner organs because of the heaviness that ensues. The man's drinking harms the child's nervous system. All the activities are damaged that should be present in the right way as the child grows up.

We can therefore say that if a woman drinks, the earthly element in the human being is ruined; if a man drinks, the element of movement, the airy element that fills the earth's surroundings and that man carries within himself, is ruined. When both parents drink, therefore, the embryo is harmed from two different sides. Naturally conception is still possible, but proper growth of the embryo is not. On the one hand, the egg's tendency towards heaviness tries to prevail; on the other, everything in it is in restless motion, and one tendency contradicts the other. If both parents are alcoholics and conception occurs, the masculine element contradicts the feminine. To those who understand the entire relationship, it becomes quite clear that in the case of habitual drinkers exceedingly harmful elements actually arise in their offspring. People do not wish to believe this, because the effects of heavy drinking in men and women are not so obvious, relatively speaking. This is only because the blood is so well protected, however, being produced, after all, in the bone marrow, and because people must do a lot if they are to affect their offspring strongly. Weak effects are simply not admitted by people today.

As a rule, if a child is born with water on the brain, one

does not investigate whether or not, on the night conception occurred, the mother was at a dinner party where she drank red wine. If that were done, it would often be found to be the case, because wine causes an inclination towards heaviness, so that the child can be born with hydrocephalus. If, however, the baby has a congenital twitch in a facial muscle, one normally does not check to find out if the father had perhaps been drinking too much the evening conception occurred. Seemingly insignificant matters are not investigated; people therefore assume that they have no effect. Actually, alcohol always has an effect. The really disastrous effects, however, occur with habitual drinkers. Here, too, a striking, a very remarkable thing can be noted.

You see, the children of a father who drinks can develop a weakness somewhere in their nervous systems and thus have a tendency towards tuberculosis, for example. What is inherited by the children need not be connected with the effects *felt* by the alcoholic father. The children need not have a tendency towards mental confusion, for example, but instead, towards tuberculosis, stomach ailments, and the like. This is what is so insidious about the effects of alcohol, that they are passed on to totally different organs in human beings of the next generation.

In these matters, the great effect on human development of minute amounts of substances must always be taken into consideration. Not only that, but in each instance one must consider how these substances are introduced into the human being. Consider the following example. Our bones contain a certain amount of calcium phosphate. Our brain also contains some phosphorus, and you will recall from earlier lectures that phosphorus is most useful since without phosphorus the brain actually could not be used for thinking. We therefore have phosphorus in us. I have already told you that phosphorus has a beneficial effect when the proper amount is consumed in food so that it is digested at a normal rate. If too large an amount of phosphorus is introduced too quickly into the human stomach, it is not useful but instead harmful.

Something else must also be considered, however. You know that in earlier days matches were made with heads of phosphorus, but they are rarely seen any more. When I was 13, 14 and 15 years old, I had an hour's walk from our home to school every day. There was a match factory about halfway where phosphorus matches were manufactured by workmen. At any time, one could see that a number of these workmen had corroded jaws — this was in the 1870s — and, starting from the jaw, their bodies were gradually destroyed. Beginning with the upper and lower jaws — especially the upper — the bones were eaten away.

Knowing the harmful effect that phosphorus can have on people, one realizes that such a match factory is actually about the most murderous place there is. In matters connected with the progress of human civilization, it is always necessary to look at the numerous harmful effects that man can suffer in this way. I always saw a number of these workmen going into this match factory with bandaged jaws. That is where it started, and then it spread. Of course, phosphorus was obviously already contained in the upper jawbone, but what kind of phosphorus was it?

You see, the phosphorus that first enters the stomach along with food and then travels internally through the body into the jaws is not harmful, provided the amount is not too large. Matches, however, are manufactured first by cutting long wooden strips into tiny sticks; these are then fitted into frames so that one end sticks out. They are dipped first into a sulphur solution and then into a phosphorus solution. The workman who dipped the matches simply held the frame in his hand and always got splattered. Just think how often in a day a person who cannot wash his splattered hands might touch his face during working hours. Though the amounts of phosphorus with which the person comes in contact in this way are minute, they nevertheless penetrate his skin. This is a mystery of human nature: a substance that is often extraordinarily useful when taken internally and assimilated first through the body can have the most poisonous effect when it comes in contact with the body from outside. The human organism is so wisely arranged inwardly that an overdose of phosphorus is eliminated in the urine or faeces; only the small amount required is allowed to penetrate the bones, the rest is eliminated.

There are, however, no provisions for the elimination of externally absorbed influences. This problem could, of course, have been alleviated. Remember that in the last century little thought was given to humanitarian considerations. It would have helped if bathing facilities had been made available so that every workman could have had a hot bath before leaving work. A great deal could naturally have been accomplished by such an arrangement, but it simply was not done.

I only mention this to you to illustrate how the human body works. Minute, detrimental influences from outside, even substances that the body otherwise needs to sustain itself, can undermine human health, indeed, can generally undermine the entire organization of the human being.

Man can withstand a good deal, but beyond a certain point the organism fails. In the case of drinking alcohol, the organism fails at the point at which alcohol prevents the correct functioning of life-sustaining activities, the invisible life-sustaining activities.

When a person is exposed to phosphorus poisoning, the inner activity that otherwise would assimilate phosphorus is undermined. It is undermined from outside. It is actually quite similar in the case of alcohol. When a person drinks too much alcohol, drinking always more and more, so that imbibing alcohol is no longer merely acute but has become chronic, the alcohol works directly as alcohol in the human being. What is the direct effect of alcohol? Remember that I once told you that man himself produced the amount of alcohol he requires. I told you that in the substances contained in the intestines a certain amount of alcohol is constantly produced by ordinary food, simply because man needs this small amount of alcohol. What do we need it for? Remember that in an anatomy lab specimens are preserved in alcohol, because otherwise they would decompose. The alcohol prevents what was a living body from decaying. The alcohol produced in the human being works in the same way in the human organism; that is, it prevents decay of certain substances needed by man. Man's inner organization really prescribes how much alcohol he should have, because he has certain substances that would otherwise decay and must be conserved.

Take now the case of a person who drinks too much alcohol. Substances that should be eliminated are retained in the body; too much is preserved. If a person repeatedly exposes blood that circulates in the body to alcohol, he conserves this blood in his body. What is the consequence? This blood, having a counteracting influence, blocks the canals in the bones; it is not eliminated quickly enough through the pores and so forth. It remains too long in the body. The marrow in the hollows of the bone is consequently stimulated too little to make new blood, and it becomes weak. It so happens that, in the so-called chronic alcoholic, the bone marrow in time becomes weakened and no longer produces either the proper red corpuscles in the woman nor the proper white corpuscles in the man.

Now, at a point such as this, I always have to make the following observation. Certainly, it is very nice when people come up with social reforms such as the prohibition of alcohol and so forth. It certainly sounds fine. But even such a learned man as Professor Benedict — I told you about his collection of criminals' skulls and how Hungarian convicts objected to having their skulls sent to Vienna because they would be missing from the rest of their bones on Judgment Day — even Professor Benedict said, and rightly so, 'Here people speak against alcohol, but many more have perished from water than from alcohol.' Generally, that is quite correct, because water, if it is contaminated, can be present in much larger quantities. Considered simply from a statistical point of view one can naturally say that many more people have died from water than from alcohol.

Something else must be taken into consideration, however. I would like to put it like this. The situation with alcohol is like the story contained in Heinrich Seidel's *Leberecht Hühnchen*. I don't know whether you are familiar with it, but it is the tale of a poor wretch, a poor devil who only has enough money to buy one egg. He also has a great imagination, however, and so he thinks, 'If this egg had not been sold in the store but instead had been allowed to hatch, a hen would have developed from it. Now, when I eat this egg, I am actually eating a whole hen.' And so he imagines, 'Why, I, who have a whole hen to eat, am really a rich fellow!' But his imagination is not satisfied there, so he continues, 'Yes, but the hen I am now eating could have laid any number of eggs from which hens again would hatch, and I am eating all these hens.' Finally, he calculates how many millions and millions of hens that would amount to, and he asks himself, 'Shouldn't that be called gorging myself with food?'

You see, this is the case with alcohol, not in a funny sense as in this story but in all seriousness. Certainly, if you take the time from 1870 to 1880, and you investigate how many people died throughout the world from water and from alcohol, statistics would show that more people died from impure water. In those days, people died more frequently from typhoid fever and related illnesses than today, and typhoid can, in many instances, be traced to contamination of the water. So, in this way, gentlemen, it is easy to conclude that more people die from drinking water.

One must think differently, however. One must know that alcohol gradually penetrates the bone marrow and ruins the blood. By harming the offspring, all the descendants are thus harmed. If an alcoholic has three children, for example, these three are harmed only a little; their descendants, however, are significantly hurt. Alcohol has a long-term negative effect that manifests in many generations. Much of the weakness that exists in humanity today is simply due to ancestors who drank too much. One must indeed picture it like this: here is a man and a woman, the man drinks too much, and the bodies of their descendants are weakened. Now think for a moment what this implies in a hundred, and worse, in several hundred years! It serves no purpose to examine only a decade, say from 1870 to 1880, and to conclude that more people died from water than from alcohol. Much longer periods of time must be considered. This is something that people don't like to do nowadays, except in jest as did the author of *Leberecht Hühnchen*, who naturally was looking over a long span of time when picturing how to wallow in so much food.

If this matter is examined from the social viewpoint, consideration must go beyond what is nearest at hand. Now the use of alcohol can be prohibited, but when it is, strange phenomena appear. You know, for example, that in many parts of the world the sale of alcohol has been restricted or even completely prohibited. But I call your attention to another evil that has recently made its appearance in Europe, that is, the use of cocaine by people who wish to intoxicate themselves. In comparison to what the use of cocaine will do, particularly in damage to the human reproductive forces, alcohol is benign! Those individuals who take cocaine do not hold cocaine responsible for the damage it does, but you can see from the external symptoms that its use is much worse than that of alcohol. When a person suffers from delirium tremens, it becomes manifest in a form of persecution complex. He sees mice everywhere that pursue him. A cocaine user, however, imagines snakes emerging everywhere from his body [Fig. 19]. First, such a person seeks an escape through cocaine, and for a while he feels good inside, because it brings about a feeling of sensual pleasure. When he has not had any cocaine for some time, however, and he looks at himself, he sees snakes emerging everywhere from his body. Then he runs to have another dose of cocaine so that the snakes will leave him alone for a while. The fear he has of these snakes is much

Fig. 19

greater than the fear of mice that is experienced by an alcoholic suffering from delirium tremens.

Certainly, one can prohibit this or that, but people then hit on something else, which, as a rule, is not better but much worse. I therefore believe that enlightening explanations, like the one we presented today regarding the effects of alcohol, for example, can be much more effective and will gradually bring human beings to refrain from alcohol on their own. This does not infringe on human freedom, but understanding causes a person to say to himself, 'Why, this is shocking! I am harmed right into my bones!' This becomes effective as feeling, whereas laws work only on the intellect. The real truths, the real insights, are those that work all the way into feeling. It is therefore my conviction that we can arrive at an effective social reform—and in other spheres it is much the same—only if true enlightenment in the widest circles of people is made our concern.

This enlightenment, however, can come about only when there is something with which one can enlighten people. When a lecture is given nowadays on the detrimental effects of alcohol, these things are not presented as I have done today—though that should not be so difficult, because people know the facts. But they do not know how to think correctly about these facts that are familiar to them. The listeners come away from a lecture given by some dime-a-dozen professor, and they do not know quite what to make of it. If they are particularly good-natured, they might say, 'Well, we don't have the background to comprehend everything he said. The educated gentleman knows it all. A simple person can't understand everything!' The fact is that the lecturer himself doesn't fully comprehend what he is talking about. If one has a science that really goes to the root of things and considers their underlying foundations, however, it is possible to make it comprehensible even to simple people.

If science is so unreal today, it is because true humanness was excluded from it when it originated. Teachers at the universities can rise from lecturer to assistant professor, in Germany from 'extraordinary professor' to full professor. The students are in the habit of saying, 'The full professor knows nothing extraordinary, and the assistant professor knows nothing fully.' The students sense this in their feelings, gentlemen; the sorry state of affairs thus continues. Regarding social reforms, science essentially accomplishes nothing, whereas it could be effective in the most active way. A person who is sincerely concerned about social life therefore must emphasize again and again that dry laws on paper are much less important—though naturally they too are needed—but they are much less important than thorough enlightenment. The public needs this enlightenment; then we would have real progress.

Particularly facts like those that can be studied in the case of alcohol can be made comprehensible everywhere. One then arrives at what I always tell people. People come and ask, 'Is it better not to drink alcohol, or is it better to drink it? Is it better to be a vegetarian or to eat meat?' I never tell anyone whether or not he should abstain from alcohol, or whether he should eat vegetables or meat. Instead, I explain how alcohol works. I simply describe how it works; then the person may decide to drink or not as he pleases. I do the same regarding vegetarian or meat diets. I simply say, this is how meat works and this is how plants work. The result is that a person can then decide for himself.

Above all else, science must have respect for human freedom, so that a person never has the feeling of being given orders or forbidden to do something. He is only told the facts. Once he knows how alcohol works, he will discover on his own what is right. This way we shall accomplish the most. We will come to the point where free human beings can choose their own directions. We must strive for this. Only then will we have real social reforms.

If I am here on Wednesday, we will be able to have the next lecture.

The power of intelligence as the effect of the sun. Beaver lodges and wasps' nests

Dr Steiner: Much knowledge is required to really answer a question like the one posed last time, and we have already considered it from a number of different angles. Because anything relating to reproduction of living beings must be thoroughly understood, I wish to make use of the time today to speak a bit more about this question from a completely different perspective.

There's something peculiar about a remark recently made by an American who came to the conclusion, based on statistics — a favourite innovation of our time that is increasingly pursued in America — that the people who acquire the greatest intelligence are always born in the winter months. Naturally, these statistics should not be taken to mean that a person born in the summer months would have to be stupid. The statistics refer only to the majority. In any case, this American made the statement that, according to statistics, those born between December and the middle of March grow up to be the smartest people.

Something is indicated here that is difficult to study in humans, because with human beings everything possible can interfere. It does indicate, however, that living beings in general — and man is first of all a living being — depend in a certain respect on the course of the year and its influence on them.

Statements like the one made by this American surprise people today only because they know far too little about the real processes of nature. Perhaps this American will meet the same fate as that of a certain professor who once measured human brains; he drew up statistics and found in every instance that women's brains are smaller than those of men. Since, in his opinion, a smaller brain indicates less intelligence, he concluded that all women have less intelligence than men — and became famous! He became famous for finding that the brains of women are smaller than those of men. Now, sometimes autopsies are performed on famous people after death, just because they are famous, and this happened to the professor. His brain was removed, and it turned out that the brain of this man was much smaller than all the women's brains he had examined!

Similarly, if he were not embarrassed to make it known, it might turn out that this American was himself born in the summer. If he were born in the summer, one would have to say that according to his own theory he could not be too clever, and therefore his theory could not be particularly valuable. But you see, there is something behind all these matters after all, and this something can lead to the most significant issues when studied in the right way.

I wish to tell you something today that definitely pertains to the question posed by Mr R. You see, the conditions relating to reproduction can actually be studied only in animals and plants, because in humans they depend on so many other factors that they cannot be studied properly. If you take what I told you the day before yesterday, that is, that humans, women as well as men, influence the egg cell or semen through drinking, you will see that this alone makes it impossible to accurately study their reproduction. Now animals are rarely in the habit of getting drunk. In them conditions thus remain much more pure, and one can study the matter more purely. The most important aspects of the problem make dissection of animals for the purpose of such study quite unnecessary. Through dissection one really discovers the least of all. To begin with I shall tell you

Fig. 20

something that is not based on dissection but on positive results that were obtained by people who did not work according to theories but with practical experience. What I will relate to you has to do especially with the beavers in Canada.

These beavers can be encountered around here only in zoos or, stuffed, in laboratories, and they actually appear to be rather clumsy. Such a beaver has a rather clumsy head and body, the front legs are quite thick, and the hind feet are webbed so he can swim. Its strangest feature is its tail, which looks almost like an instrument; it is quite flat and is, in fact, the beaver's most ingenious aspect. What he has behind him is his most ingenious tool. People who have observed beavers do not know at first what they use these tails for, and they have thought up all sorts of incorrect ways of explaining them.

The beaver is a most unusual animal. When one becomes acquainted with a beaver in its own habitat, it is found to be an extremely phlegmatic animal, something that is also evident in those in our zoos. It is so phlegmatic that one cannot really do anything with it. You can attack a beaver, grab for it, but it will not defend itself. The beaver itself will never attack no matter how much it is provoked. It is a completely phlegmatic creature.

These beavers live mainly in such areas as large swamps or small rivers, and they live in a most remarkable way. When spring arrives, a beaver looks for a spot near a lake or river, digs a burrow in the mud, and spends the entire summer living like a true recluse alone in this burrow. This beaver sits the whole summer in this reclusive summer dwelling like a phlegmatic monk passing the time in his summer house! It is only a hole that he digs in the earth, but he does it in total isolation.

When winter approaches—already when late autumn comes—the beavers emerge from their burrows and congregate in groups of two to three hundred. They come in all their 'phlegma' and form communities. Naturally, those that had mated earlier are among them. A female beaver had prepared her isolated home so that it was suitable for children; the male lived nearby in his own burrow. Now, all these families gather together.

In their slow, phlegmatic way, the beavers proceed to look for a suitable locality. Though it is sometimes difficult to observe because of their phlegmatic temperament, one group will prefer a lake, another a river, which they follow downstream to a point that appears particularly suited to their purposes. After they have investigated the area, the whole group gathers together again. Near the lake or river, there are usually trees. It is really remarkable how these clumsy beavers now suddenly become extraordinarily skilful. They make use of their front feet—not their hind feet, which are webbed so they can swim—more cleverly than a man handles his tools. Using their front paws and sharp teeth, they gnaw branches off trees and even cut through tree trunks. Then, when a group of them has enough branches and felled trees, they drag them either into the lake they have chosen or into the river.

These animals then push the branches and trees in the lake to the selected spot. Those who have dragged their trees into the river know full well that the river itself will carry them. They only steer the branches so that they won't drift to the side. In this way, all the branches and trees are transported to the spot they have chosen either on the lake's shore or alongside the stream.

Having arrived there, those who have chosen a lake — having transported the trees to the shore — immediately begin constructing so-called lodges. The others, who have picked a river, do not begin with the building of lodges; they first proceed to construct a network of branches. These are interlaced with each other [*sketching*, Fig. 21] until they form a proper network. When the beavers have built up such a wall, they add a second by fetching more branches, all of the same length; in this way, they make a wall two metres or more thick. Thus, you see, the animals dam up the river; the water must flow over it, and underneath it they have free space. Only now, having finished their dam, this wall, do they build their lodge into the wall so that the river flows over it.

When the beavers have accumulated enough branches, and their wall appears thick enough to them, they haul in other material such as ordinary chunks of earth. They

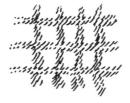

Fig. 21

fashion a kind of loam from it and putty up the dam on all sides. The beavers first erect a wall, just like real architects. Those who select the lake site, however, don't need a dam and therefore don't try to build one.

After this wall is built—in the case of those who choose the lake, it begins immediately—the beavers begin constructing little lodges from the same material. They look like clay barrels [*sketching*, Fig. 22], but they are real little houses, constructed like braided mats. They are puttied up so well that the small amount of water that seeps into the space can do the beavers no harm. Such a beaver lodge is never constructed in a part of the stream where the water freezes. Imagine how ingenious this is! As you know, water only freezes on its surface; if one dives deep enough, one comes to still or flowing water, neither of which freezes at that depth. Precisely at the level where the water never freezes, these beavers build their dwellings.

Each of these lodges has two floors. There is a floor built in here [*sketching*], and below it is the entrance. The beavers

Fig. 22

can run up and down in the lodge; they live upstairs and keep their winter supplies downstairs. They haul in the food they need for the winter, and when it is all stored, the beaver family moves into this lodge, always remaining near the other families.

There the beaver families live until spring, when they once again move to their solitary dwellings. During the winter, the food supplies are brought up from the lower floor, and in this way the beavers sustain themselves. As I said, when summer comes, they seek out their solitary burrows, but during the winter they are together. They lead their social life in beaver villages on the bottom of lakes or in streams by the side of the dam they have so skilfully constructed.

From all that has been observed, even beavers in zoos work solely with their teeth and front paws, never with their tails. Although it is formed most ingeniously, the tail is never used for work. There are many descriptions that claim that beavers employ their tails in working on their constructions, but that is an illusion; it is simply not true. Beavers do possess especially well-developed front legs and teeth, and they use them more cleverly than a man uses his tools.

You know that natural history classifies the various animal species, and among the mammals are the beasts of prey, bats, the ruminants, and so forth. Among the mammals are also the so-called rodents. Our rats, for example, are rodents. The way the beaver is formed actually puts it in the rodent family.

In any book on natural history, you will find that the rodents are described as the most stupid of mammals, hence the beaver is reckoned among the least intelligent of mammals. One can say that the beaver, when studied as a single animal, appears above all as a terribly phlegmatic little rascal. Its phlegmatic temperament is so great that it can appear about as clever as phlegmatic humans appear: they show no interest in anything. The beaver is therefore awfully stupid, but it also accomplishes all these extraordinarily clever feats! One can therefore say that Rosegger's saying about man does not apply to beavers: 'One's human, two are a crowd, and three a bunch of animals.' Rosegger said this not about beavers but about human beings. He means that when many people meet together, they become stupid. There is something true in this. In a crowd, people become confused and can do stupid things, though there certainly are intelligent people among them!

We can say that the opposite is the case with beavers. One is stupid, but several are a bit brighter! When two or three hundred gather together in the autumn, they become most clever, they become real architects. Though we humans do not tend to be particularly sensitive to the special beauty of the constructions of beavers, this is due to our human taste, but the beaver lodge is really as trim as the beaver is clumsy.

Now, much research can be done on why the beavers are so clever when they congregate. An important indication lies in the fact that the beavers begin their activity in the autumn; by day, however, one sees little of this activity. The construction of such a dam and beaver village—it is really an entire village that they lay out—takes place very quickly and is often finished in a matter of days. They are seen doing little during the day, extraordinarily little, but they work feverishly at night. Thus, the beaver's cleverness is brought about first by winter and second by night. Here lie the real clues for the study of this whole matter.

When people study, however, the first principle should be to avoid too much speculative thinking. This might sound strange, but you will understand what I mean. Man does not become especially intelligent through speculation. As a rule, if he ponders over something that he has observed, nothing particularly clever will result. If one wishes to understand the phenomena of the world, therefore, one should not rely too much on speculation; one's speculation is not at all the important thing. Should the facts call for it, one should think, but one's main attention should not be directed towards brooding over something one has observed as a means of figuring it out. Instead, other facts should be looked at, compared with the problem at hand, and a connection sought between them. The more one connects various facts, the more one learns to understand nature. People who have only brooded over nature have really not discovered anything more weighty than what they knew in the first place.

When a person becomes a materialist, he speaks materialistically about nature, because that is where he is coming from. He does not discover anything new. When a man speaks idealistically about nature, he does so because he is already an idealist. In almost all instances, it can be proven that through speculation people discover only what is made evident to them through what they already are. Correct thinking only results when one simply allows the facts to guide one.

Now I will add another group of facts to those concerning the beaver, facts that will lead you to the correct clues, not through speculation but simply through a comparison of the facts. I have already referred to the wasps and told you of an observation about wasps made by Darwin. Today, I would like to point this out again.

The wasps make ingenious nests for themselves. Though faintly resembling honeycombs, the walls of these wasps' nests do not consist of wax but of actual paper. Secondly, the whole process differs from that of the bees. There are wasps' nests, for example, that are built first by digging up the ground; then something resembling a pouch is made. It is constructed somewhat like a beaver lodge, but it is put together with tiny twigs or whatever wood the wasps can find, which they work and shape in the right way so that they end up with a covering, a pouchlike covering that is somewhat thick. It is in this that they build their little nest. There they build their different floors. The cells are hexagonal, just like the bee's honeycomb, and are enveloped by a paper covering. They are like the floors in a building, and there are sometimes many of them, one above the other.

Everything inside the nest is fashioned of paper. The pouchlike outer covering, however, is not made of paper but of other materials, that is, of tiny twigs or bits of wood that are first split before being used. All this is woven into a network and then puttied up. That is what the outer covering consists of, and it is either built in a hole in the ground or fastened with a natural putty to something up in the air. Within the pouch are the individual cells, into each of which an egg will be laid.

This is the story, then, with wasps. You can imagine that wasps are extraordinarily susceptible to the weather. Only some of one year's wasps survive until the following spring, but it doesn't matter if the others don't survive as long as one or two females from a nest remain. In winter the females seek out a sheltered little nook where they can just about get by, and they hibernate there. In spring, these females emerge from their hiding places and are ready to lay their eggs. Interestingly enough, a special variety of wasp hatches from all these eggs in spring. These wasps that are hatched in spring, growing very quickly and not yet having cells, immediately begin to construct such cells. Flying around in whole swarms, they look everywhere for materials with which to build a nest properly. This work continues all summer long. These wasps construct cells.

The wasps that hatch from eggs laid in spring have a specific characteristic; that is, they are all sterile and cannot reproduce. With these wasps there is no reproduction.

Their reproductive organs are so stunted that reproduction is out of the question. So the first thing the wasp does in spring is to produce an army of workers for itself that are sexless and terrible drudges; they toil throughout the summer.

I have known natural scientists who considered it a goal worth striving for to manipulate humans so as to produce sexless individuals. They would not have families and would only toil, leaving reproduction to a select few, as with the wasps.

Well, the fact is that the sexless wasps toil away all summer. When summer is over, the female begins to lay eggs that produce males and females. As a rule, it is the same female that laid the sexless eggs earlier. Now she lays eggs from which, in autumn, males and females emerge.

The males develop into rather puny creatures. By comparison, the sexless wasps are quite robust workers. The males turn out to be stunted and cannot do much of anything. They have just enough time to feed for a while, mate, and then die. Truly, these male wasps play a rather sorry role. They are hastily hatched in autumn, they must feed a little, and then they impregnate the females; after that, having accomplished their goal, they die. That is all they do.

Among some types of wasps the males are a bit hardier. Here things are really curious. Though it is only an exception, it resembles the behaviour of certain spiders. With certain spiders, something remarkable is the case. You see, the female spiders consider the males good for nothing but fertilizing them. The males are permitted to approach the females only when they are ready for fertilization, never before. Before, the females generally don't permit the males to come near them; first they must be mature enough for the fertilization. Now, as I said, the following also occurs occasionally, as an exception, among wasps. Among spiders, which are, after all, lower creatures, when a female notices a greedy little male approaching, she places herself in a spot that is not easily accessible to him and even more difficult for him to leave. There the female waits for him, lets fertilization occur, and then lets him try to leave. When he comes up against an obstacle, the female quickly pursues him and bites him until he's dead. Here, the female spider herself sees to it that the male dies. Such is the case with some spiders. Just imagine, when the male has carried out his function, he must be killed, because he no longer serves a purpose.

Among wasps, however, the males die as a rule by themselves, because they have expended so much energy during their mating activity that they have no strength left and so perish. The sexless wasps die at the same time. After toiling all summer, they all die in the autumn. The sexless and the male wasps die, and only the females remain. Of these, many also succumb to the cold of winter. Only those few survive that have found a secure shelter. They make it through to spring, lay eggs, and the whole cycle starts anew. So, in spring and summer only sexless wasps are born. Not until late autumn, approaching winter, can the sexually active wasps be born.

These are the facts, you see, that must be observed. It is very important to connect these with other facts, since this shows us how much the sex life of animals is connected with the seasons of the year. The sex life of animals is very strongly connected with the course of the year.

Let us assume that it is summer. The earth is extraordinarily exposed to the sun's effects. The sun sends down light and warmth to the earth. Direct exposure to sunlight causes one to sweat; one notices the sun's effects by one's own condition. Neither the beaver nor the female wasp expose themselves directly to sunlight; they are always in some cavelike dwelling. In their holes they benefit from the sun's light and heat only indirectly through the earth. Thereby, as winter approaches they receive quite definite qualities. Just think, towards winter the wasps receive a quality that makes them capable of producing sexually active offspring.

What does this signify? The female wasp is exposed throughout the summer to the sun's heat and light and produces sexless wasps. You can therefore say that the effects of the sun are such that they actually destroy the sexuality of the wasps. It is quite obvious from this fact that the sun with its light and heat, which are reflected by the earth, has the effect of destroying the reproductive tendencies. This is why, when spring comes and warmth and sunlight prevail, the wasps produce sexless offspring. Only when winter approaches, when therefore the sun's heat and light no longer have the same intensity, do the wasps gain the strength to produce offspring with reproductive organs. This clearly demonstrates that the seasons of the year have a definite influence.

Now, if we turn from the wasps to the beavers, we must say that the beaver is an extremely stupid, phlegmatic animal! It is stupid and phlegmatic to the highest degree. Fine. But where does it spend the summer? It stays in the ground in its solitary burrow, allowing heat and light that comes into the burrow to penetrate its body, so that it actually absorbs all the summer sunlight and warmth. When this absorption is completed in the autumn, the beaver begins to look for other beavers, and together they become clever. It employs a cleverness that it does not possess as a single animal. Now, suddenly, as they gather together, the beavers become clever. Naturally, as single animals they could never construct all those beaver villages. The first step of choosing a suitable site is clever in itself.

This clearly illustrates what I pointed out last time: the cleverness that is in a creature must first be gathered, just as water is collected in pitchers. What does the beaver do while as a single animal it lives like a hermit in its summer house? The beaver gathers sunlight and the sun's warmth for itself—or so we say, because all we can perceive is the sun's light and warmth. In truth, the beaver gathers its intelligence. Along with sunlight and warmth, intelligence streams from the cosmos down upon the earth, and the beaver gathers it for itself; now the beaver has it, and it builds. With the beaver you can see in reality what I recently presented to you as a picture.

Something else now becomes comprehensible: the beaver's tail. Compare it with what I said about the dog's tail, the dog's tail being its organ of pleasure and therefore the soul organ of the dog. The dog wags its tail when it is happy. In the beaver's case it is so that within its tail, which the animal does not use as a tool but which is formed most ingeniously, the beaver has its accumulated intelligence. The animal directs itself by means of this. This means that the beaver is really directed by the sun's warmth and light. These are contained in the tail and have become intelligence. This is really the communal brain of the beaver colony.

These tails are the means by which the sunlight and warmth produce cleverness. The beaver does not employ its tail as a physical instrument; it uses its front paws and teeth as physical instruments. The tail, however, is something that has an effect; it has an effect just as when a group is being driven forward by somebody from behind. In that case, it is somebody driving them. Here it is the sun, which, through the beavers' tails, still has an after-effect in winter and constructs the beaver village. It is this intelligence, which comes down from the sun to the earth with light and warmth, that does the building.

Naturally, what descends as soul and spirit from the universe affects all the other creatures, including the wasps.

How does it affect the wasps? When the female is exposed to the sun—meaning the sun's earthly effect, which it enjoys in its earthen hole—the force in the wasp's offspring that can bring forth more offspring is destroyed. The wasp can produce only sexless insects under the sun's influence. Only when the wasp is not so strongly exposed to the sun's heat, in autumn, and is still full of vitality—not subdued as in winter—does the force develop in it to bring forth sexually active wasps. This once again demonstrates plainly that what comes from the earth produces the sexual forces, whereas that which comes from the universe produces intelligence and kills sexual forces. In this way a balance is brought about. When the wasp is more exposed to the earth, it develops sexual forces; when the wasp is exposed more to heaven—if I may use this word here—it does not develop sexual forces but produces sexless wasps instead. These sexless insects have in themselves the cleverness to construct a whole wasps' nest. Who, in fact, builds this nest? The sun builds it through the sexless wasps!

This is a most important point, gentlemen. In truth, the wasps' nests, as well as all the beavers' constructions, are built by the cleverness that flows to earth from the sun. This is plain to see when all the facts are brought together. That is why I said to you that all speculation indulged in after something has been observed doesn't do a bit of good. Only when facts are compared and related to each other is a sound opinion gained.

People simply look at the isolated facts, and this is why there is so much that is not to the point. They think to themselves, 'Now, when one observes beavers, one observes beavers, and afterwards one speculates about beavers. When one observes beavers, what does one care about wasps?' But one discovers nothing if one fails to observe something that is seemingly so far removed from the beaver as the wasp. If one were to look at the wasp, one would see that wasps' nests are also constructed through the cleverness that comes to us from the sun.

The sun's effects can still be observed in a tame beaver in a cage, although the animal need not be tamed, because it is so phlegmatic, but needs only to be in captivity. When the sun's effects cease to be so strong and instead the earth influences it, even the caged beaver begins its winter activities. It tries to bite through the wires of its cage. This is said to be the beaver's instinct. Anybody can say 'instinct'; that is just a word. Such words are like empty containers into which everything is poured that one knows nothing about. If one wishes to explain something like instinct, however, one reaches the point where one must say: it is indeed the sun! Gentlemen, it really is so. In this manner, through the pure facts themselves, one comes to recognize how the cosmic surroundings of the earth affect living beings.

Now it is no longer so surprising that some American chap comes along and says that those humans born in the months from December to March most readily acquire intelligence. In the case of human beings, matters have become quite complicated. Everything in man tends towards his becoming independent from all that animals are still dependent upon. You must therefore consider the following. Persons born between December and March were conceived between March and May. Their births date back to conceptions that took place in the spring nine months earlier, between March and May, and hence to a time approaching summer. According to everything I have explained today, the sun's effects are always stronger then. So, what does the sun do? It subdues human sexual forces just a little — not completely, because man is more independent than the animals — and these subdued sexual forces become forces of intelligence. That is why such a person has an easier time of it, while those born in summer must work somewhat more at acquiring their cleverness. That can happen, but it is true that humans have different predispositions. Those conceived in spring and born the following winter tend to acquire forces of intelligence more easily than those born at other times.

All this must be known so that these differences can be compensated for through education. In man, this can be done. Wasps, however, cannot be educated to produce sexless offspring that build nests in winter, nor can beavers be educated to overcome nature, as we say, to a certain degree. You can see from this that man differs from animals in this respect. In the animals, the soul-spiritual element depends completely on cosmic development. It simply depends on the sun for wasps' nests and beaver lodges to be built.

Something else can be seen in the beaver. In the autumn, these beaver hermits that have spent the entire summer in seclusion come together in groups of two and three hundred, and only then, as groups, can they employ the intelligence bestowed by the sun. They can use it as groups, not individuals. Individually, they could never accomplish this; it must be the work of the group.

With human beings much can be accomplished by the individual that animals can only accomplish in groups. This is why in anthroposophy we say that the soul life of animals exists only in groups — hence, group souls. Man, however, has his individual soul.

Now, this is most interesting. I once told you what the human thigh bone looks like, for example. In the beaver, it really is not the same, but a human thigh bone looks like an extraordinarily delicate, beautiful work of art. In it there are beams, quite ingeniously constructed. A human being is actually built up in such a way that, when observing him correctly, one can say: he builds up everything in himself that the beaver builds outwardly. By nature he builds

Fig. 23

everything in himself that the beaver builds outwardly. The question then arises: where does all that is so wisely and ingeniously constructed within a human being originate? If the beaver construction originates from the sun and its surroundings, the human organization also originates from the sun. We are, indeed, not earthly beings but sun beings and have only been placed on the earth. What for? You can see when you consider the following.

From the earth the wasps have the power to produce sexual offspring. Man must be on the earth in order to have his reproductive force. By comparison, he has another force that is more rational, which he gets from cosmic surroundings. We can see quite clearly that man gets his intelligence from cosmic surroundings, and the reproductive force he gets from the earth. One could go further and show how the moon is related to the earth, but there is no more time today. We can go into that another time. You can see, however, that if facts are viewed correctly they lead you to realize that the world is really a unity and that we are dependent also upon the earth's surroundings, which consist not merely of a shining, warming sun but also of a clever sun, an intelligent sun. This is extremely important, because the individual questions that you pose can be answered better in this way. You see that the reproductive force, which I described to you last time, is affected by drinking. Why are they related in such a way that a little drinking does not make such a difference but heavy drinking does? You can figure this out from the following.

What is alcohol? Wine demonstrates what alcohol actually is, because wine, which only wealthy people can afford to drink, has the most harmful effect. Beer is less harmful for the reproductive organs than wine. Beer affects other organs more—the heart, kidneys, and so forth—but the alcohol in wine and, of course, especially the alcohol in hard liquor, affects the reproductive organs.

Where does the substance contained in wine and hard liquor originate? It originates through the influence of the sun's forces! This substance needs the whole summer to mature. Now you can see why it becomes harmful to the reproductive organs. When one drinks, the reproductive organs are subjected to what has been internally absorbed in the way food is, to what should be absorbed solely by way of the sun itself, the sun's shining. This takes its toll. Man drinks something that the sun produces outside of him. It becomes a poison through this. When the warmth of the sun is taken into the system in the right way, however, the organism itself produces the small quantity of alcohol it needs, as I have explained. In drinking alcohol, man really admits an enemy into his system, because what is introduced externally in the right way turns into a poison when it is internally consumed, and vice versa. I have demonstrated this to you in the case of phosphorus. So, what works in alcohol is what the sun has produced in it, because the sun has matured it. When the sun shines on us, it is the other way around; then we must absorb warmth and light from outside. When we consume alcohol, however, we warm ourselves inwardly. The same force that is our friend when we make use of it outwardly becomes our enemy when we use it internally.

The same is also true in nature. There are forces in nature that work beneficially from one direction, but when they work from the opposite direction they work as poisons. We can gain understanding only when we examine this in the right way.

I wanted to add this so that you could understand better everything that relates to Mr E's question. Now think all this over. Should you wish to ask further questions, I hope to be here next Saturday.

The effect of nicotine. Vegetarian and meat diets. On taking absinthe. Twin births

A question is raised concerning the effects of vegetarian and meat diets, and of nicotine.

Concerning conception, how is it possible that women bear sons if none of the ancestors had sons? How can the birth of two sets of twins be explained?

What influence does absinthe have on semen?

What is the difference between the ages of wasps and bees?

Dr Steiner: The matters I have discussed regarding bees naturally refer only to bees and not to wasps. Bees differ from wasps, so my statements refer to bees, not wasps.

Now we shall try to go into these questions. The first asked about the influence of nicotine and therefore of the poison that is introduced into the human body through smoking and through tobacco in general. First, we must be clear how the effect of nicotine shows itself. The effect of nicotine shows itself above all in the activity of the heart. Through nicotine, an increased, stronger activity of the heart is called forth. The heart is not a pump, however, but only reflects what goes on in the body: the heart beats faster when the blood circulates faster. Nicotine therefore actually affects the blood circulation, animating it. One must therefore be clear that through the introduction of nicotine into the human body the blood circulation is stimulated. This, in turn, calls forth a stronger activity of the heart.

Now, this whole process in the human organism must be traced. You must be clear that everything occurring in the human organism is actually carefully regulated. One of the most important points regarding the human organism, for example, is the fact that the pulse rate of the adult is 72 beats a minute, and this holds true even into old age.

By comparison, as I have mentioned to you before, man takes about 18 breaths a minute. When you multiply 18 by 4, you get 72. This means that on average the blood substance pulses four times as quickly through the body as does the breath. Of course, these are average figures; they differ slightly in each human being. The fact that this ratio varies in people accounts for the differences between them, but on average it is 1:4; that is, the blood circulation is four times more intense than that of the breathing rhythm.

If I now introduce nicotine into the human organism, I can do it for two reasons—first, because of a strong liking for tobacco, and second, as a remedy. Every substance that is poisonous is also a remedy. Everything, one can say, is both poisonous and healing. If, for example, you drink several buckets of water, they naturally have a poisonous effect, whereas the proper amount is a means of sustenance, and when it is introduced in unusually small amounts, it can even be a remedy. As a matter of fact, water is generally a potent remedy when certain methods are employed. It can therefore be said that even the most commonplace substances can be poisons as well as remedies. This is why the effect that a given substance has on the human organism must be known.

If I introduce tobacco into the human organism, it first stimulates the blood circulation. The blood becomes more active, circulating more vigorously. Breathing, however, is not stimulated to the same degree by tobacco; the breathing rhythm remains the same. The blood circulation is therefore no longer synchronized with the breathing. When people introduce nicotine into their bodies, they really need a blood circulation different from the one they normally have.

Let us, for example, imagine someone whose system was

adjusted to the exact average of 18 breaths and 72 pulse beats (there aren't any such people, but let's assume it). Now, nicotine causes his pulse rate to increase to, let us say, 76 beats. The correct ratio between pulse and respiration is thus altered. The result is that the blood doesn't receive enough oxygen, since a certain amount is supposed to be absorbed into the blood with each pulse beat. The consequence of nicotine poisoning, therefore, is that the blood demands too much oxygen. The breathing process does not supply enough oxygen, and a slight shortness of breath occurs. This shortness of breath is, of course, so negligible that it escapes notice; after all, as I have told you, the human body can take a lot of abuse. Nevertheless, the use of nicotine always calls forth a definite, very slight shortness of breath. This slight shortness of breath causes with each breath a feeling of anxiety. Every shortness of breath causes a feeling of anxiety. It is easier to control a normal sensation of anxiety than this terribly slight anxiety, of which one is completely unconscious. When something like anxiety, fear, or shock remains unnoticed, it is a direct source of illness.

Such a source of illness is constantly present in a person who is a heavy smoker because, without realizing it, he is always filled with a certain anxiety. Now, you know that if you suffer from anxiety, your heart pumps more quickly. This leads you to realize that the heart of a person who constantly poisons himself with nicotine continuously beats somewhat too fast. When it beats too quickly, however, the heart thickens, just as the muscle of the upper arm, the biceps, grows thicker when it is constantly strained. Under some circumstances, this is not so bad, as long as the inner tissue doesn't tear. If the heart muscle — it is also a muscle — becomes too thick from overexertion, however, it exerts pressure on all the other organs with the result, as a rule, that beginning from the heart the blood circulation becomes disturbed. The circulation of the blood cannot be initiated by the heart, but it can be disturbed when the heart is thickened.

The next consequence of a thickened heart is that the kidneys become ill, since it is due to the harmonious activities of heart and kidneys that the entire human bodily organization is kept functioning properly. The heart and kidneys must always work in harmony. Naturally, everything in the human being must harmonize, but the heart and kidneys are directly connected. It quickly becomes apparent that when something is amiss in the heart, the kidneys no longer function properly. Urinary elimination no longer works in the right way with the result that man develops a much too rapid tempo of life and comes to wear himself out too quickly. A person who takes into his body too much nicotine in relation to his bodily proportions therefore will slowly but surely deteriorate. Actually, he gradually perishes from a variety of inner conditions of anxiety that influence the heart.

The effects of states of anxiety on the activities of the soul can easily be determined. In people who have introduced too much nicotine into their bodies, it becomes noticeable that gradually their power of thought is also impaired. The power of thought is impaired, because man can no longer think properly when he lives in anxiety. Nicotine poisoning, therefore, can be recognized by the fact that such people's thoughts are no longer quite in order. They usually jump to conclusions much too quickly. They sometimes intensify this overly rapid judgement to paranoid thoughts. We can therefore say that the use of nicotine for pleasure actually undermines human health.

In all such matters, however, you must consider the other side. Smoking is something that has only come about in humanity's recent evolution. Originally, human beings did not smoke, and it is only recently that the use of tobacco has become fashionable. Now let us look at the other side of the coin.

Let us assume that a person's pulse beats only 68 instead of 72 times per minute. Such a person, whose blood circulation is not animated enough, now begins to smoke. You see, then his blood circulation is stimulated in the right direction, from 68 to 72, so that his blood circulation and breathing harmonize. If, therefore, a doctor notices that an illness is caused by weak blood circulation, he may even advise his patient to smoke.

As was said before, when the blood circulation is too rapid relative to breathing, one is dealing with terrible conditions of anxiety, which, however, do not become conscious. If for some reason a person's blood circulation is too weak, however, this makes itself felt by the fact that he goes around wanting to do something but not knowing what. This is also a characteristic phenomenon of illness; there are people who go around wanting something, but they do not know what it is that they want. Just think how many people go around without knowing what they want! One commonly says that they are dissatisfied with life. They are the people, who, for example, somehow drift into some profession, which then does not suit them, and so forth. This is really due to a blood circulation that is too weak. With such a person one can actually say that it is beneficial to administer nicotine to cure him. If smoking is agreeable to him, one need not prescribe nicotine in medicinal form, but one can advise him to smoke, if previously he wasn't a smoker.

It is actually true that in recent times people who really do not know what they want have become more and more numerous. It is indeed easy in our modern age for people not to know what they want because, for the last three or four centuries, the majority of them have become unaccustomed to occupying themselves with anything spiritual. They go to their offices and busy themselves with something they actually dislike but that brings in money. They sit through their office hours, are even quite industrious, but they have no real interests except going to the theatre or reading newspapers. Gradually, things have been reduced to this. Even reading books, for example, has become a rarity today.

That this has all come about is due to the fact that people don't know at all what they want. They must be told what they want. Reading newspapers or going to the theatre stimulates the senses and the intellect but not the blood. When one must sit down and read some difficult book, the blood is stimulated. As soon as an effort has to be made to understand something, the blood is stimulated, but people do not want that any more. They quite dislike having to exert themselves to understand something. That is something quite repugnant to people. They do not want to understand anything! This unwillingness to understand causes their blood to thicken. Such thick blood circulates more slowly. As a result, a remedy is constantly required to bring this increasingly thick blood into motion. It is brought into motion when they stick a cigarette into the mouth. The blood doesn't become thinner, but the blood circulation becomes ever more difficult. This can cause people to become afflicted with various signs of old age at a time in life when this needn't yet occur.

This shows how extraordinarily delicate the human body's activity is. Diagnostic results are obtained not only when the blood is examined but also when the manner in which a person behaves — whether he thinks slowly or quickly — is studied. You therefore can see, gentlemen, that if you wish to know something about the effect of nicotine, you must be thoroughly familiar with the entire circulatory and breathing processes.

Now, remember what I recently told you about how the

blood is produced in the bone marrow. Essentially it comes from there. If the blood is produced in the bone marrow and the blood is made to circulate too quickly, then the bone marrow must also work faster than it should. As a result, the bones cannot keep up with their work, and then those creatures develop within the bones, those little creatures that devour us. Doctors such as Metchnikoff believed that these osteoclasts, as such little fellows are called, are the cause of human death. Metchnikoff said that if there were no osteoclasts, we would live forever. He held that they literally devour us. The fact is that the older we get, the more osteoclasts are present. It is true that our bones are gradually eaten by the osteoclasts, but seen from the opposite angle it is like fertilizing a field well — more will grow on it than if it were badly fertilized. For man, the introduction of nicotine into the body has a detrimental effect on the bones, but for these cannibalistic bone-devourers, the osteoclasts, it creates the best environment possible.

This is how it is in the world. A lazy thinker assumes that the world is fashioned by the Good Lord and so all must be well. Then one can ask why God allowed the osteoclasts to grow alongside the bones? If he had not allowed the osteoclasts to grow, we would not be slowly devoured throughout life. Instead, we could abuse our bones so terribly that something else would finally make them deteriorate. In any case, they could last for centuries if these little beasts were not contained within them.

It serves no purpose, however, to think lazily this way. The only useful thing is to examine the facts truly, to know that the delicate forces instrumental in building up the bones have their adversaries. These osteoclasts, too, are part of creation, and we have them within us by the millions. The older you get, the more of these osteoclasts you have. You have cannibals, though they are minute, always within you. Actual cannibals are not the most clever; the cleverest are those that we carry around within us in this way, and they find fertile ground when nicotine is introduced into the body.

You can recognize the extraordinary importance of thoroughly understanding the entire human being in order to determine how a given substance works in the human body.

Now, man constantly eats. He eats animal substances and he eats those of plants. I have told you before that I have no intention of promoting one or another form of diet. I only point out the effects. Vegetarians have frequently come to me saying they are prone to slight fainting spells, and so on. I have told them that it is because they don't eat meat. These matters must be viewed quite objectively; one must not desire to force something. What is the 'objective view', however, regarding eating plants and eating meat? Consider the plant. A plant manages to develop the seed that is planted in the earth all the way to green leaves and colourful flower petals. Now, you either receive your nourishment directly from grains, or you pluck a cabbage and make soup or something. Compare what you get from the plant with what is present in meat, usually an animal's muscle. Meat is a completely different substance from the plant. What is the relationship between these two substances?

You know that there are some animals that are simply gentle vegetarian beings. There are animals that do not eat meat. Cows, for example, eat no meat. Neither are horses keen on meat; they also eat only plants. Now, you must be clear that an animal not only absorbs food but is also constantly shedding what is inside its body. Among birds you know that there is something called moulting. The birds lose their feathers and must replace them with new ones. You know that deer drop their antlers. You cut your nails, and they grow back. What appears outwardly so visible here is part of a continuous process. We constantly shed our skins. I have explained this to you once before. During a period of approximately seven to eight years, our entire bodies are shed and replaced with new ones. This is also the case with animals.

Consider a cow or an ox. After some years the flesh within it has been entirely replaced. With oxen the exchange takes place even faster than with human beings. A new flesh is therefore made. From what did this flesh originate, however? You must ask yourselves this. The ox itself has produced the flesh in its body from plant substances. This is the most important point to consider. This animal's body is therefore capable of producing meat from plants. Now, you can cook cabbage as long as you like, but you won't turn it into meat! You do not produce meat in your frying pan or your stew pot, and nobody has ever baked a cake that became meat. This cannot be done with outer skills, but the animal's body can accomplish inwardly what one can't do outwardly. Flesh is produced in the animal's body, and forces to do this must first be present in the body. With all our technological forces, we have none by which we can simply produce meat from plants. We don't have that, but in our bodies and in animal bodies there are forces that can make meat substance from plant substance.

Now, this is a plant [*sketching*, Fig. 24] that is still in a meadow or field. The forces that have been active up to this point have brought forth green leaves, berries, and so forth. Imagine a cow devours this plant. When the cow devours this plant, it becomes flesh in her. This means that the cow possesses the forces that can make this plant into meat.

Now imagine that an ox suddenly decided that it was too tiresome to graze and nibble plants, that it would let another animal eat them and do the work for it, and then it would eat the animal. In other words, the ox would begin to

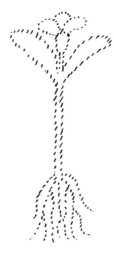

Fig. 24

eat meat, though it could produce the meat by itself. It has the inner forces to do so. What would happen if the ox were to eat meat directly instead of plants? It would leave all the forces unused that can produce the flesh in him. Think of the tremendous amount of energy that is lost when the machines in a factory in which something or other is manufactured are all turned on without producing anything. There is a tremendous loss of energy. But the unused energy in the ox's body cannot simply be lost, so the ox is finally filled with it, and this pent-up force does something in him other than produce flesh from plant substances. It does something else in him. After all, the energy remains; it is present in the animal, and so it produces waste products. Instead of flesh, harmful substances are produced. Therefore, if an ox were suddenly to turn into a meat eater, it would fill itself with all kinds of harmful substances such as uric acid and urates.

Now urates have their specific effects. The specific effects of urates are expressed in a particular affinity for the nervous system and the brain. The result is that if an ox were to consume meat directly, large amounts of urates would be secreted; they would enter the brain, and the ox would go crazy. If an experiment could be made in which a herd of oxen were suddenly fed with pigeons, it would produce a completely mad herd of oxen. That is what would happen. In spite of the gentleness of the pigeons, the oxen would go mad.

You see, such a matter naturally testifies against materialism, because if oxen only ate pigeons and if only the material element were effective, they would have to become as gentle as the pigeons. That would not be the case at all, however. Instead, the oxen would turn into terribly wild, furious creatures. This is proved by the fact that horses become extremely violent when fed a little meat. They begin to grow wild, because they are not accustomed to eating it.

This, of course, applies also to human beings. It is very interesting that historically a part of Asia's peoples is strictly vegetarian. These are gentle people who rarely wage war. In the Near East, people began to eat meat and thus brought about the madness of war. The peoples of the Asian nations transform plants into flesh by making use of the forces that otherwise are left unused, unconscious. Consequently, these people remain gentle whereas the meat eaters of other nations do not remain so gentle.

We must be clear that people have only gradually become mature enough for such deliberations as we are presenting here. When people began to eat meat, it could not be considered in the way we have just done; it all arose from feeling and instinct.

You see, the lion continually devours meat; he is no plant eater. The lion also has very short intestines, unlike the plant-eating animals whose intestines are very long. This is also the case in humans. If a person is born into a certain race or people whose ancestors ate meat, then his intestines will already be shorter. They will be too short for pure vegetarianism. If, in spite of that, he eats only plants, he will have to practice all sorts of measures to remain healthy.

It is certainly possible to be a vegetarian today, and it has many points in its favour. One of the main advantages of eating only vegetables is that one does not tire as quickly. Since no uric acid and urates are secreted, one does not tire as quickly but will retain a clearer head and think more easily—if one is in the habit of thinking! A person who cannot think does not gain anything by freeing his brain from urates, because it is necessary for the whole human organization to harmonize. In any case, through self-control, a person can become a vegetarian today. Then he uses those forces that, in people who eat meat, are simply left unused.

Now, I wish to call your attention to a strange phenomenon. If you look around in the world, you will find that there is an illness that quickly undermines human health. It is so-called diabetes, the sugar sickness. First, sugar is discovered in the urine, and man soon succumbs to the body's deterioration, which is caused by an over-abundance of sugar. It is a truly fatal illness. Sugar is also what keeps the human being inwardly strong, when taken in the right way.

This can even be verified by statistics. Much less sugar is consumed in Russia than in England. This really accounts for the entire difference between the Russian people and the English. The English are self-aware and egotistical; the Russians are unselfish and physically not as vigorous. This is related to the lower sugar consumption in Russia than in England, where a large amount of sugar is eaten in the food. The human body, however, requires the assimilation of an amount of sugar. Just as the bones support a human being, so the amounts of sugar circulating in his body sustain him. If, then, too much sugar is eliminated in the urine, too little is taken up by the body and the health is undermined. This is diabetes.

Diabetes is today more prevalent among Jews. Certainly others also have diabetes, but it occurs with particular frequency today among Jews. These people have a tendency to diabetes. The Jew has more difficulty absorbing sugar, yet on the other hand he requires it. The Jewish diet should therefore actually tend to make it as easy as possible for the human body to make use of sugar and not to eliminate it.

If you read the Old Testament, you will find a variety of dietary rules that to this day are observed in restaurants that serve kosher food. Kosher cooking follows the ancient Mosaic dietary laws. If you study these, you will find the essence lies in the fact that Jews should eat food that allows the greatest assimilation of sugar, since this people has difficulty absorbing it. Pork makes the assimilation of sugar extremely difficult — pork aggravates diabetes unusually in the human being — so the prohibition of pork was calculated particularly to prevent diabetes. You see, you must read the Old Testament even from a medical standpoint; then it becomes terribly interesting. It is fascinating to trace what the various prohibitions and kosher preparations of foods are intended to accomplish. Even the so-called *Schaechten*, the special way of butchering and killing poultry, for example, is intended to retain just the right amount of blood in the meat a Jew consumes so he can assimilate from it the right amount of sugar.

In recent times, Jews have gradually neglected their dietary laws, although they still remain within their racial relationships. Since the dietary rules are really rules for a specific racial group, to abandon them is detrimental, and they therefore succumb more readily to diabetes than other people. That is how it is.

We can therefore say that a meat diet produces unused

forces in the human being that work in the human body improperly to produce waste. Naturally, this waste can then be eliminated again, but it is often a quite complicated task. One can say that when some matters are rightly expressed, they look quite peculiar. Some people work in their own particular way all winter long and eat in their own way too. They consume with pleasure just enough food to give them a slight stomach upset every day, which they keep under control by drinking the necessary amount of alcohol. Come April or May they are ready for Karlsbad or some other health spa, since by that time they have accumulated a goodly amount of waste in their organisms, in their bodies. What they really need now is a thorough cleansing. The system must be cleaned out. They go to Karlsbad. You know that the waters of Karlsbad cause vigorous diarrhoea, which purges the system. This done, they can return home and begin all over again. As a rule, no more is necessary than to go to Karlsbad every year, but if they are kept from going once, they suffer from diabetes or some related problem.

From the standpoint of an affluent society, it does not sound too bad to say that so-and-so is going to Karlsbad. In reality, it means using manure buckets to put one's body back in order; this is what drinking the waters and taking the baths at Karlsbad accomplishes. The system is thoroughly purged and is then all right again for a while.

Naturally, this is no way to raise the level of national health. Ultimately, the quality of all foods processed and sold on the market is geared to the eating habits of a person who can afford to go to Karlsbad or a similar spa. One who cannot afford to go to Karlsbad also has to eat, but he can't be purged without the money. No other foods are available to him. Therefore we must start with medicine in order to set social life on the right course.

Naturally, one could expound on this subject much

longer. If I have forgotten something today, however, I shall try to tell you about it in the course of time.

Concerning absinthe, I only wish to add that it actually works quite similarly to the alcohol in wine. The difference is that while wine directly ruins our physical substance — though sleep evens matters out somewhat — absinthe also ruins our sleep. With absinthe, a person gets a hangover during sleep, and he is therefore prevented from sleeping well. One must sleep, however, if one drinks alcohol. Ordinarily, too much drink must be slept off — this is testified to by the expression, 'to sleep it off'. Sleep has a beneficial effect on alcohol intake and evens matters out. For this reason, absinthe is more damaging than ordinary alcohol, because sleep itself is ruined.

Now you need to consider how our hair, for example, grows more rapidly during sleep. A person who shaves knows that when he sleeps particularly late on a given day, he is more in need of a shave when he wakes. Have you noticed this? [*Answer: 'Oh yes!'*] When our soul activity is absent from the body, whiskers grow very quickly. Sleep is there to stimulate growth forces in the physical body. Absinthe, however, extends its effects even into sleep, and with absinthe-drinkers sleep does not neutralize these effects. In women who drink absinthe the red corpuscles of the blood are even ruined in sleep, and in men the white corpuscles are ruined. Something else is at work here. Since absinthe works all the way into sleep, a woman's monthly period is very strongly influenced. Irregularities then occur that become even more pronounced in her descendants. The result is that ovulation, which should occur every four weeks, takes place irregularly.

The main thing that can be said about absinthe is, therefore, that it works similarly to the ordinary alcohol in wine, beer or cognac, but in addition it even ruins sleep. Though one could go into more detail, I wish to say something concerning the other question that was asked about twins.

In identical twin births, fertilization occurs just as it does for single births. A male sperm penetrates the female egg cell, which then closes itself off; all the other processes take place within it. The number of offspring derived from this egg is determined by something quite other than the number of male sperm. Only one sperm enters the egg, whereas the whole world has an influence on the developing offspring. They are created by the forces of the entire universe.

What I have to say now sounds somewhat curious, but it is the truth. It can happen that shortly after fertilization the woman is subjected again to the same influences from the cosmos. This is what I mean: let us assume that fertilization occurs during the time of the waning moon. The woman is then exposed to certain forces in the cosmos that originate from a certain portion of the moon. Now, in the first three weeks after fertilization the initial processes are completely indefinite. Nothing can yet be distinguished. After three weeks, the human being is just a minute little fishlike thing. Before that, everything is indefinite. The three weeks run their course, always in such a way that almost anything can develop from the human germ, and if things are just right and the woman now comes under the influence of the waxing moon, then the same external influences as before are again present. Some effects have already been present from the waning moon; now the waxing moon also has an influence, and the birth of twins can come about.

It can also be possible that a woman might consciously be eager to have a child, but subconsciously she harbours a certain antipathy, perhaps a totally unconscious antipathy, towards bearing children. She need only have a certain antipathy towards the man she has married. Such antipathies also exist. Then she herself holds back the rapid development of the so-called embryo, the human germ. The influences that should have an effect once work several times from the cosmos, and thus triplets can result. Even quadruplets have been born. All this is never caused by fertilization, however, but by other influences, the outer influences of the cosmos. If identical twin births were to occur at fertilization, the twins would certainly turn out to be different from each other since they would have had to originate from different sperm. Twins can indeed also come from two eggs rather than one. But the striking feature of identical twins is that they are alike even in unusual characteristics; even what comes about at a later age, for instance, develops in the same way in identical twins. The reason is that they emerge from one egg. So you must realize that it is not fertilization which is different in the case of identical twin births, but rather the outer influences at work.

Diphtheria and influenza. Crossed eyes

A question is raised concerning why, in one family, four mute children were born along with normal children. In his youth, the father of the children tore the tongues out of birds. Could the four mute children be his punishment?

Another question: Influenza, in which people suffer from double vision, is so frequent now. What is the cause of this?

Dr Steiner: Were the children who cannot speak born one after the other in this family, or were the children who could speak born in between?

The Questioner: The mute children were born one after the other.

Dr Steiner: It is difficult to speak about such a case when one is not thoroughly familiar with it. We shall take up the question about influenza later. This first case, however, is difficult to judge when one is not familiar with the details. Much depends, for example, on whether a speaking child was born between the mute children; whether, after a certain moment in time, the speaking children were born and the mute children after, or whether the mute children were born first and the normal children after, or whether they were born alternately. Muteness in children naturally can be caused by any number of factors. If these children can hear and are only mute, not deaf-mute — something about which one can sometimes be in error of course — if they truly hear, and the problem therefore lies in the speech apparatus, then one must figure out how the father or mother could have influenced it.

Without thoroughly knowing this case, however, it is really risky to talk about it. One would have to know the age of both parents. Much depends on whether both parents were already old when they had the children or whether they were still young. Another factor is whether the mother or the father is the older. Much depends on all this.

Then, the character of both parents also plays a part. Whether or not it is important that the father tore out the tongues of birds in his youth, as you say, can be determined only after all the other questions have been answered. Such a consideration depends on whether the man was perhaps cruel in his youth. The characteristic of cruelty as such does come into consideration. To speak of a punishment, however, is out of the question here. First, punishments do not exist and second, if they did, this certainly would not be a punishment for the father! To say that the children were born mute to punish the father for his cruelty reminds me of the story of the boy whose hands froze and who said, 'This serves my father right for not buying me gloves!' When somebody is as terribly afflicted as these four children, it is not a punishment for the father; he is much less affected than the four children, although his cruelty must be considered.

Again, certain other definite matters must be considered here. In relation to children's age you can see that if a person develops a quality as a youth — let us say one develops a quality of cruelty or something similar at age 11, for example — the onset of such a tendency always recurs after about three and a half years. This individual would then express cruel tendencies again at $14\frac{1}{2}$ or 15, then again at 18, at $21\frac{1}{2}$, and so forth.

Imagine, if conception occurs during the period when such a tendency recurs, the conception itself can be a kind of cruelty and naturally can work harmfully. In this roundabout way, all such matters naturally can come under consideration. A connection can only be claimed, however, if all other factors have been excluded. I have told you what a difference there is between winter births and summer births. One would have to determine from the ages of these children whether the earlier births perhaps occurred in the summer or in the winter, and so forth.

This is why I say that to approach the problem conscientiously, one must know all the details. When you become acquainted with the whole case, we can talk about it. I would be glad to do so. You do not know, for example, whether the four mute children were the older or the younger ones. It must definitely be established whether or not this tendency to bring forth mute children was later cured or whether it appeared only after the four speaking children were born, in which case, the reason would have to be discovered somewhere after the birth of the fourth child. So, we would first have to be familiar with all the factors.

Regarding the question about the flu, it is related to all the diseases, such as bronchitis, that can afflict the human head or the organs of the upper chest, but I will refer particularly to illnesses such as diphtheria and influenza that are so widely prevalent just now. These diseases afflict the upper part of the human body, and they have a definite peculiarity. They can best be studied by examining diphtheria; here one really can learn the most.

You know well that those who study medicine in the ordinary sense today do not know much about the flu; therefore the descriptions given by doctors of the symptoms that appear with the flu are quite inexact. When I see people suffering from influenza, I must always turn my attention to something other than the symptoms that the doctors pay heed to, because the flu is actually a kind of brain illness. The flu is really an illness of the brain! I shall say more about this later.

The following points must especially be taken into consideration regarding diphtheria. First, if you look at a child suffering from diphtheria — adults can also suffer from it, you know — you can see a membrane in the throat. This membrane, this formation of tissue, is usually what can cause suffocation in diphtheria. This formation of tissue is thus the first important factor. The second thing one notices in diphtheria is that the heart of a diphtheria patient is always attacked. The heart does not function properly. The third aspect of diphtheria is that even if the patient is not strongly afflicted by the membrane in his throat, he nevertheless has a hard time swallowing because of a kind of paralysis of the throat that occurs in addition to the membrane. Finally, the same symptom that is nowadays observed in those suffering from influenza also appears in diphtheria patients: their eyes begin to cross and they see double. These are the most important symptoms of diphtheria that can be noted in the upper part of the body. A form of kidney ailment, unobserved in those who suffocate and die, appears as an after-effect in the diphtheria patients who recover.

What does diphtheria really consist of? Diphtheria can be understood only when one knows that man is actually kept alive from two directions — from the outside in and from the inside out. Man lives first from within his skin. The skin is a tremendously important organ, and man really lives within the skin, within his surroundings. It is like this [*sketching*, Fig. 25]. Here is the skin; I have already talked about it. The skin is constantly in contact with the outer air, with the external world, which causes it to become calloused. In humans it only becomes a little calloused and then sloughs off. The skin all over man's body constantly sloughs off. Man is continuously sloughing off his entire body. He is continuously exchanging his physical body because of outside influences. You can imagine what a tremendous influence the air has on the living body when you consider the following. Think of a being that lives entirely in water. The skin it forms will be quite soft. The water itself causes it

Fig. 25

to form skin that is quite soft. Particularly through the influence of sunlight, the soft skin is drawn forwards, and the being in the water becomes a fish. You can hardly see the jaw of a fish, because it is entirely covered with skin. Now imagine that this creature does not live in water but in the air. If this being lives in the air, it cannot form a soft skin. If this being who has lived in the water could not form a soft skin, his jaw would no longer be inside; the whole inner jaw would lie outside, and he would be a bird. The jaw of the fish in the water is simply covered with soft skin. By virtue of living in the air, the bird is equipped with an exposed jaw, a jaw lying completely outside. [See Fig. 26, p. 240.] Thus you see the influence exerted on a creature from outside. Man, however, can form soft skin with other organs, but this soft skin is always being sloughed off, worked off.

Aside from this life proceeding from the outside in, there is also a life passing outwards from inside, particularly from the kidneys. Both must be active in the human being.

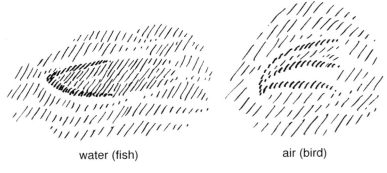

water (fish)   air (bird)

Fig. 26

Activity both from the skin inwards and from the kidneys outwards must be at work. The heart occupies a position in between and is highly sensitive to too much activity from outside or within. The heart can sense when the kidneys begin to be overactive, and it also senses when the skin's activity begins to be too strong or too weak.

Now, what happens in the case of diphtheria? In diphtheria, the skin suddenly becomes weak and subdued. The activity of the skin is too weak, so a person with diphtheria suffers from too little exchange of air through the skin. Indeed, this is the main problem. The skin, including the skin of the nose exposed to the external surroundings, does not breathe enough, and it becomes too weak. The instreaming activity, indicated in my sketch by the arrows [see Fig. 25 on page 239], no longer functions properly, and the heart senses this. The heart also senses that the kidneys' work is rising upwards. What is it that the kidneys are doing? The heart can no longer restrain the activity of the kidneys, which shoots upwards. Long before inflammation of the kidneys, that is, nephritis, sets in, the activity of the kidneys is already shooting upwards. Because the skin activity is no longer working effectively from outside, superfluous skin forms on the inside. Because the skin's activity from the outside is not working properly, a super-fluous skin is formed, filling everything out, because the kidneys' activity is too strong.

When a person becomes afflicted with shrunken kidneys, which can occur when the kidneys' activity is deficient, you can see an indentation here on the head. There is a connection between the kidneys and this section of the head. As soon as the kidneys' activity is not working properly, this indentation occurs. You can see in every person who has kidney disease this indentation in the head. Beneath it lie the optic nerves. When the indentation occurs, the optic nerves become inactive. In the case of ordinary kidney shrinkage, the patient begins to see unclearly. When shrinkage does not occur but nephritis sets in instead, the kidney activity shoots up into the head and exerts an influence on the optic nerves.

Now, you see, the optic nerves are such that when the head is viewed from above, they proceed back from the eyes. They cross in the brain, the two optic nerves, and continue on to the hindbrain [see Fig. 27]. The optic nerves must be in good condition if we are to see well, because we see with both eyes. The moment these optic nerves that cross are not working properly, we see double. The optic nerves only need to be a little numbed and the crossing not

Fig. 27

made properly for us to see double. You know how a person who enjoys drinking can tell whether or not he is still functioning when he gets home: he places his hat at the foot of the bed, gets in bed, and if he sees one hat he is still all right, but if he sees two, he is not! This is easily done. So, because the blood circulates too fast, too much alcohol numbs the optic nerves, with the result that a person who has drunk too much has double vision.

The kidneys' activity also has a stimulating effect on the optic nerves. If the optic nerves do not interact properly at the point where they cross, people see double. This is the case, for example, in diphtheria. You can see, therefore, that diphtheria is caused by a disorder in the skin's activity. Therefore, a future, more successful cure for diphtheria will consist above all of treating the patient in the right way with baths; he will have to be given baths that will immediately vigorously stimulate the skin's activity. Then the formation of membranes will cease, and the patient's skin will begin to function properly again.

Treatment with modified virus vaccine is effective in the case of diphtheria, because the body is thus given a strong impulse to become active, but it has unfavourable after-effects. Particularly if a child is treated with vaccine, it will later suffer a hardening of its organization. One must therefore strive to replace vaccines with bathing treatment, especially in the case of diphtheria, which is caused primarily by the defective activity of the skin. One can see how skin must actually receive special consideration.

It is indeed true that diphtheria is more frequent now than in former times. Of course, one must think in terms of centuries, not decades. According to all that is known of earlier ages however — though many diseases naturally existed then that were much worse; people were afflicted with bubonic plague and cholera — diphtheria was more rare. This is connected with the fact that, in general, the

European way of life increasingly leads in a direction in which the skin's activity is no longer supported. It is true that people who have money bathe a lot, but the point, however, is *what* a person bathes in. You can also see the ill-effect of civilization in the fact that bald-headed people are much more numerous today than in the past. The growth of hair is also an outer activity. Just as plants grow from the soil, so the growth of hair is affected from outside. Not enough attention is paid today to the skin's activity. Do not assume that cold baths and showers, as practised by Eng-lishmen nowadays, have such good effects. What counts is what a person bathes in. Of course, it is also wrong for a person to cause too strong an activity of the skin by excess bathing. At any rate, in the case of diphtheria, one must try above all to bring about a proper activity of the skin.

This is also connected with a factor that affects people's offspring. Take a mother or father whose skin is too slug-gish and doesn't slough off easily enough. This is most difficult to determine and takes very sensitive insight into human peculiarities and characteristics. The average lay-man cannot easily judge whether or not a person has cal-loused skin, but some people do possess a much tougher skin than others. This is difficult to determine, because the skin is actually transparent. As it sloughs off, it appears to be coloured differently because of what is underneath. Our skin is really transparent. So if a father has a skin that is much tougher than it should be, this also influences the activity of the bones. As you know from what I explained recently, the production of blood depends on the activity of the bones. If the father has such calloused skin that it reminds you of hippopotamus hide, he will produce white corpuscles that are too weak. This, in turn, influences his sperm, and his children will be weak from the beginning. So, one can say that if the father is a 'hippopotamus', it is possible for his children to be born with the English disease of rickets, for them to be born weak and to be susceptible to tuberculosis. This is how these things are related.

If the father's skin is too soft, something that can be noted particularly when anxiety and so on easily cause blushing, then his bones become too hard, but this has no serious ill-effect.

If, however, the mother's skin is too soft, alternating between blushing and paling, her bones become too hard and she does not produce red corpuscles properly. At an early age already her child will acquire tendencies to all kinds of ailments such as rheumatism, and particularly illnesses like measles, scarlet fever, and so on, diseases that are related to the metabolic system. These facts are all related.

Now, as for the flu, it really comes from a brain ailment. The lower part of the brain, located under the optic nerves, suffers a form of paralysis. The flu consists of a paralysis of that portion of the brain that lies quite near the optic nerves [*sketching*, Fig. 28]. Here I am drawing the optic nerves from a sideways angle. Since this is a very significant part of the brain, an influence is actually exerted on the entire body.

Fig. 28

Proceeding from this paralysis in the brain, something in the human being becomes ill in the case of ordinary flu. Above all, the spinal cord is affected, since this part of the brain goes right into the spine, from which the nerves extend to all the limbs. The person thus gets aches and pains in his limbs, and so on.

Recently, an interesting case of flu occurred that is most instructive. I have told you that the brain not only consists of solid substances but that it is also surrounded by cranial fluid. Particularly in the vicinity of this part here [*pointing to sketch*], which is incapacitated during flu, much cranial fluid is present. This recent case of flu was extraordinarily interesting, because the patient had one illness after another as after-effects: pneumonia with high fever, then a fall in temperature, followed by pleurisy with high fever, and then again a drop in temperature. This was followed by peritonitis with high fever that finally fell, then a kind of general paralysis, and so on. This case of flu took a different direction from that of normal flu. What happened here? You see, when studying this with the ordinary means available to medicine, it is extraordinarily difficult to figure out. The patient, a 17-year-old girl, was asked when she recovered to tell what had been going through her mind while she was ill, and the following strange thing came to light.

Her parents and the doctor freely discussed her condition in the room in which she was resting, thinking it was all right to do so since she was constantly delirious. Indeed, during her delirium she did not appear to be aware of anything, but when she became well, she could repeat everything that had been discussed in her room. She knew and could relate it. This could be confirmed. Comprehension was therefore absent while she suffered from this severe case of flu and the subsequent illnesses; the conversations, however, remained in her memory. Much is retained in the memory after all, which at the moment may not be comprehended. This shows that it was not the solid part of the brain that was affected but the surrounding fluid. This influenced the rest of the body even more than usual, because, when the solid part is partially numbed, the ensuing symptoms are brought about through the working of the solid part of the brain on the spinal cord. The fluid, however, constantly flows up and down through the spinal canal here [see Fig. 28 on p. 244]. Hence, if the fluid in the brain is afflicted, affected fluid also appears in the spinal canal, and from here it passes into all the limbs. It thereby gradually causes inflammation everywhere. Because it was the cranial fluid that was inflamed, and not the solid part of the brain, however, a more counteractive, healing force was present and — though in this case it was almost like a miracle — the girl recovered in spite of having suffered from every possible illness.

Although various remedies must also be administered, in such illnesses it is essential that the body be given adequate rest and quiet. The patient must therefore lie in bed, and care should be taken to keep the room at a constant temperature and with steady, gentle lighting, because rest is not only brought about by stretching out on a bed. One is also made restless by being hot one moment and frozen the next. But if the body is left totally to its own devices in conditions of steady warmth and light, it can itself endure even the worst attacks of pneumonia, pleurisy and peritonitis. The human being is capable of that. Even with the worst illnesses that display the symptoms mentioned, it is more a matter of proper nursing care than of remedies. In general, proper care has great value.

You can recognize the significance of proper care from the following. When a limb is inflamed or injured, the best thing to do is simply to put a ligature on it somewhere above the affected area; it must be done correctly, however. In this way, the more delicate activity of the body, the etheric activity, is brought into play, and healing begins. So when a hand or finger is ulcerated, a ligature is applied between it and the rest of the body, and then it heals quickly. The forces of healing must be summoned everywhere from within the body itself. Naturally, cases vary. One must always consider the individual and know him well if one wishes to cure him; one must have insight into what a person is like. In dealing with a patient suffering from diphtheria, for instance, it is under certain conditions best to place him in a rosemary bath so he can smell the rosemary. Repeated long rosemary baths will strengthen the activity of his skin. Sufficient rosemary must be added to the water, however, so that the patient constantly smells it during the bath. The activity of the skin is stimulated, and the patient will improve without being treated with vaccine. It really depends upon being able to use remedies in the right way to stimulate the patient's own bodily resistance.

Of course, if a remedy isn't effective on one occasion, people immediately consider it to be a bad remedy. You must realize, however, that with some people there is nothing to be done. Often the remedy is used when it is too late to do anything, or else the dose would have to be increased so much that it would be enough for a horse; the patient wouldn't be able to tolerate it and would die of the remedy.

One must remember that the flu actually has its origin in an ailment of the brain. You will have perceived that a flu patient is always in a kind of doze, because the most important areas of the brain under the optic nerve are numbed. Thus he comes to doze. Now you can also grasp that when paralysis is located in the upper sections of the brain, the point of intersection of the optic nerves is affected and the person sees double. All this shows you that double vision can come about quite naturally in influenza.

This should by no means be taken lightly. I once had a

friend who at that time was 30 years old, ten years younger than me. He was cross-eyed, but here you have the opposite problem. In flu or diphtheria a person becomes temporarily cross-eyed because something is internally out of order, but my friend was permanently cross-eyed and, of course, was unhappy about it because not everyone is totally free of vanity. There was something in his body that caused his left and right sides to work inharmoniously. This is what caused his crossed eyes; his eyes were crossed, and he also stammered. Both afflictions had the same origin. On some occasions he overcame his crossed eyes and stammer quite well, but there are those who have little compassion for such people and hold their afflictions against them. Once, for example, a person who was not the most tactful of people said to my friend, 'Tell me, Doctor, do you always stammer, or only occasionally?' The man could barely come out with, 'N-n-not always, o-o-only w-when I m-meet a p-person whom I find t-t-t-totally d-disagreeable!' This same man could recite long poems without stammering, and he didn't stammer when he was full of enthusiasm about something. The stammering is not the point, however; I only mention it because it is connected with this man's crossed eyes.

Now, my friend was a bit vain and wished to correct his condition. As you know, that requires an operation, because crossed eyes are corrected by cutting one of the eye muscles. Crossed eyes are eliminated by this operation. Since, in my friend's case, his crossed eyes were so deeply rooted in his organism that he also stammered, I was terribly concerned when he decided to be operated on. I knew that when some brain ailment occurs a person can be temporarily cross-eyed, but when a person is permanently cross-eyed, as was my friend, his brain has adjusted to this condition. If an eye muscle is cut when the problem is so deep-seated that a stammer is also present, then the opposite effect is brought about. By trying to correct the crossed eyes with an operation, a brain ailment is produced by that part of the brain being ruined where the optic nerves intersect.

Well, my friend was not to be deterred, and so he underwent the operation. If I had expressed my reservations concerning such an operation, those who imagine themselves to be real medical authorities would have been ready to call me an idiot, since one who asserts something that is not found in their books is called an idiot. As you can imagine, I naturally tried in some way to deter my friend from having this operation, but I could not come right out and say, 'If you go through with this operation, you may possibly suffer a brain ailment.' He would not have believed me since all the doctors had told him it was a simple operation. Since he knew that I was not really happy about his intention to have the operation, he told me nothing about it. One day, he visited me with a black patch on his eyes, which he removed and said, 'Now look, aren't my eyes straight now?' They were, but I remained apprehensive. Well, no more than two weeks had passed before he fell ill with a brain ailment. Naturally, this brain ailment was not diagnosed as such by the doctor; what do ordinary doctors know of these relationships! How did the brain ailment manifest itself? There was some blood in his faeces indicating that it made its appearance in the guise of an intestinal illness. The man became afflicted with an intestinal illness, but it was actually the brain ailment because, as I have explained, the intestines and the brain are connected.

When this happened, I knew it was caused by the operation, and I lost hope for him. The most famous doctor in town was called. He diagnosed typhoid. What else could he say, when the contents of the intestines showed blood and had the peculiar consistency of pea soup? If he has blood in his faeces and intestinal contents with the consistency of pea soup, he must have typhoid! It was not typhoid, however; it was an illness—really of the brain—resulting from the inappropriate operation for his crossed eyes.

So here the opposite case occurred. This man died soon afterwards. The doctor who had treated him for typhoid fever had admitted him to the hospital. I went there after his death and met his medical orderly. As such people are wont to do, he immediately greeted me with, 'The Professor wrote "typhoid" on the chart. He is supposed to have had typhoid? Well, so much for our doctors' knowledge!' After all, the other staff least of all believe what the doctors proclaim!

It really is quite upsetting to see the human organism treated in such a one-sided manner. If I were to tell a doctor what I have just told you about the appearance of an illness resembling typhoid that was a masked ailment of the brain and the result of an operation for crossed eyes, he would consider it pure nonsense. He wouldn't believe it, because he doesn't truly know the relationships within the body but is only familiar with theoretical relationships. As a result such things will happen as in this anecdote I'll tell you. It is only a tale, but it has truth in it. A person is brought to the hospital. The doctor who is chief of staff examines him, assigns him to a certain ward, and gives an order concerning treatment to his assistants, saying, 'When I return tomorrow, this patient will be dead.' He no longer concerns himself with this case until a few days later. Then he says, 'There is still a patient in Room 15; he must be dead.' 'No,' he is told, 'that patient feels better and is getting well.' The doctor replies, 'Then you've treated him the wrong way!'

Of course, this is a joke. But it is not much different when theory is put in the place of true practice. Practice means learning to judge each case on an individual basis. The moment a question is raised concerning the connection between double vision, which is always a form of crossed eyes, and the flu, attention must be drawn to how, on the one hand, a form of double vision is caused by flu, which is a kind of brain ailment and, on the other, how the brain ailment can come about when a person is cross-eyed and the problem is so deeply rooted that left and right do not fit together.

All processes in the human being proceed outwards from within and inwards from without. If a person is cross-eyed for internal reasons and this condition is externally corrected, he can become ill inwardly; in man, one never deals with a single activity but with two activities that meet in the heart. The heart is in a mediating position and is affected when one carries out an external operation to correct crossed eyes. The heart is also affected if something is not working properly inside. The heart is not a pump but a most delicate apparatus, which really perceives everything that is out of order.

Let us assume that I injure my knee externally or that by some circumstance, perhaps through drinking, I become afflicted with rheumatism. Then, internal activities are out of order, and inflammation results in that area. The processes that begin within are out of order. In such cases the heart is always influenced and doesn't work properly. Therefore, the heart's function can be influenced from within as well as from without. In all illnesses in which this is the case — that is, when something is wrong with a process so that it is prevented from running its course outwards from within or inwards from without — it will be noted that this comes to expression in the heart. One must know the correct relationship, however, between what is an outer process and what is an inner process when a person is cross-eyed or stammers, if one wishes to weigh the consequences of eliminating the condition. Operations for crossed eyes must always be weighed as to whether one should or should not do them. That is the important point.

The relationship between breathing and blood circulation. Jaundice, smallpox, rabies

Dr Steiner: Good morning, gentlemen. Have you thought of something else you would like to ask me?

A question is asked concerning the relationship between human breathing and the pulse. Wouldn't this have been completely different in earlier times?

Dr Steiner: You mean in the human being himself? Well, let's quickly review how things stand today. We have breathing on the one hand. Man is connected to the outer world through breathing, because he is constantly inhaling and exhaling air. It can thus be said that man today is constituted in such a way that he absorbs the healthy air and expels the air that would make him ill. The expelled air contains carbon dioxide. The circulation of the blood, on the other hand, is an internal process in which the blood flows through the body itself. I shall not discuss today whether it is accurate to say that the blood circulates in the body, but let us say the force of the blood circulates through the body. Now, although it varies slightly in each individual, a person takes approximately 18 breaths per minute. As for the blood, the pulse rate is 72 beats per minute. So one can say that breathing is related to blood circulation in an adult today in such a way that his pulse is four times faster than his breathing.

Now, we must be clear what is really involved in the human being when breathing is considered in relation to his blood circulation. First, we must be clear that man breathes chiefly through the lungs—the nose, mouth, and lungs—but this is only his primary way of breathing. Indeed, with the human being, functions primarily carried out by one part of his body are also actually carried out to a lesser degree by his whole body. Hence air, or particularly the oxygen in the air, is constantly absorbed through the surface of his skin. Man therefore also breathes through his skin, and along with the ordinary breathing process of his lungs one can also speak of his skin's breathing. If, for example, the holes of his skin, called pores, are clogged, the skin absorbs too little air. Something is not right with the skin's breathing. Man's skin must always be in such shape that he can breathe through it.

Now, in the case of human beings, all outer processes can, as it were, also be found to exist inwardly. Making a sketch of a human being, we can say that breathing occurs through the entire surface of the skin but most particularly through the lungs in 18 breaths per minute. All this, however, requires a counterbalance in the human being, and something quite interesting makes its appearance. Man cannot breathe properly through his lungs nor through his skin, but especially not through his skin, if this counterbalance is not present.

You know that a magnet has not only a north pole, a positive pole, but also a south pole, a negative pole. If man has his lungs and skin for breathing, then he also needs an opposite, and that opposite is located in the liver. We have already familiarized ourselves with the liver from various standpoints; now we must learn to view it as the opposite of the skin-lung activity; the liver and the skin-lung activity balance each other. One could say that the liver's constant purpose is to bring into order internally what man acquires through breathing in his relation with the outer world. That is what the liver is for.

Consider a disorder of the liver that may occur at any time, even in older people. It is quite difficult to diagnose when the liver is not in order, and frequently one is unaware of it because the liver is the organ, the single organ, that doesn't hurt when something is wrong with it. Man can suffer for a long time from a liver ailment without knowing of it. No one can diagnose it, because there is no pain. This is because the liver is related to the most outer aspects of the human being, the skin and lungs. Internally, the liver is really something like an outer world. Man does not sense it within when a chair is broken, nor does he sense it when the liver is being destroyed. It is as if the liver were a segment of the outer world. In spite of this, it is of the utmost importance to the human being.

Now imagine that the liver malfunctions. When this happens, all the activity of the lungs and skin is also thrown out of balance, and then a specific problem arises. You see, from the heart the veins reach everywhere into the lungs and the skin. Through quite delicate blood vessels, the blood circulation reaches everywhere into the skin, into the lungs, and also into the liver. The following now takes place. If the liver's function is impaired, the blood cannot flow properly in and out of the liver. If, because of a liver problem, the blood flows into it too strongly and the liver becomes overactive, too much bile is produced and the person becomes jaundiced. Jaundice occurs in man when too much bile is produced, when, therefore, the activity of the liver is too strong. Jaundice therefore results when overactivity of the liver pervades the body.

What happens, however, when the liver's activity is too weak? The blood's activity on the surface of the skin is not compensated for. The blood, which flows everywhere, wishes to be compensated, and the blood in the liver investigates, as it were, whether or not the liver is behaving properly. If the liver isn't behaving properly, the blood rushes to the surface of the body to replenish itself there. What happens? Smallpox is the result. This is the connec-

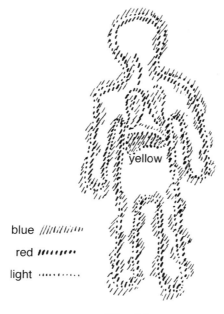

Fig. 29

tion between smallpox and a blood circulation which, due to a defective liver, has something wrong with it.

The blood reaches everywhere where I have drawn a line in blue [see Fig. 29]; there is also a red line signifying that oxygen from the air reaches everywhere. The circulation of the blood rightly makes a point of contact there with the breathing, and whether this occurs in the lungs or the skin really does not matter, because it balances itself out. If the air that enters through the breathing process does not make contact with the blood in the correct way, however, small-pox results. What is smallpox? Smallpox is really the result of the development of too much respiratory activity on the body's surface or in the lungs. A person becomes too active over his surface area, and this activity causes inflammation everywhere.

What can be done under these circumstances? Well, people already do the only thing that can be done in such cases. They vaccinate with cowpox vaccine. What does cowpox vaccine really accomplish? The vaccine inwardly permeates the body, because the blood circulates everywhere. Whereas the blood is otherwise compensated for on the body's surface, it now has to cope with the vaccine. The overactivity on the surface is thus prevented. Smallpox inoculation does indeed have a certain significance. The blood, which is not properly engaged by the liver, is now busy with the vaccine. Generally, there is good reason for all methods of inoculation. You have perhaps heard that a large part of our healing is based on injections, because an activity occurring in the wrong place can thereby be directed to another part of the human body.

Inoculation against rabies is especially interesting. Though rabies comes from something altogether different, it is basically the same response as I described in connection with smallpox. Imagine that a person is bitten by a rabid dog or wolf. Such an animal has actual poison in its saliva. This poison now enters the victim through the bite, and the person becomes involved in detoxifying the poison. He may be too weak to do it, and he might succumb to the poison, but something else is really the cause of death. You know that a man first develops rabies before he succumbs to the poison. What is the reason for this?

Let us assume that I am bitten by a rabid dog. Now I must direct all my inner activities to this spot, and I must let them flow here to use up the poison. This surge of activity is sensed by my spinal cord as though I had received a shock. This is how it affects my spinal cord. Since my body must suddenly develop such extreme activity because of the dog's bite, my spinal cord suffers a shock through which I become ill.

What must now be done to offset this shock? You know

that when a person freezes in horror he can be brought to his senses by being slapped a few times. The spinal cord also needs to be slapped, but one must first get to the spine. This can be accomplished by giving a rabbit rabies, then killing it, removing its spinal cord and drying it for approximately 20 minutes at about 20°C. This substance is then injected into the rabid person.

Now, oddly enough, all substances have a way of going to specific parts of the body. The dried spinal cord of the rabbit, which retains the rabies poison for a short time — about 15 minutes — before becoming ineffective, is quickly injected into the human being. It enters the human spinal cord, which thereby suffers a counter-shock. It is just as if you shake a person who is paralysed with fear and he snaps out of it. In the case of rabies, man's spinal cord recovers from the shock by means of an inoculation with the rabid rabbit's dehydrated spinal cord.

You see, therefore, that when an activity develops in the human being in the wrong place and he becomes ill, he can be cured if almost the same process is developed in a different place. These are some of the complicated relationships of the human organism.

Now, if you consider respiration and the activity of the blood, these two processes are related in today's adult in a ratio of one breath to four pulse beats. The bloodstream flows faster; after three pulsations man inhales, and after three more, he inhales again. This is how air goes through his body. The blood moves through the body: one, two, three, and with the fourth we inhale; one, two, three, and with the fourth we inhale again. This goes on throughout our body.

All this produces carbon dioxide. Now, most of this carbon dioxide is exhaled, but if all of it were exhaled, we would be as thick as two planks. Part of the carbon dioxide must continuously enter our nervous system, which needs carbon dioxide because it must be continuously deadened. The nervous system requires this deadening carbon dioxide. Through inhaling air, carbon dioxide therefore rises up continuously in me and supplies my nervous system.

What does this mean? Nothing other than this, that since carbon dioxide is a poison I continually require a poison in my system for my thinking. This is a most interesting point. Unless a continuous poisoning process took place in me, with which I must continuously struggle, I could not use my nervous system. I would be unable to think. Man is really in the position of having constantly to poison himself by inhaling air, and by means of the poison in the breath he thinks. Carbon dioxide constantly streams into my head, and with this poisonous air I think.

Today, man simply breathes air. The air contains oxygen and nitrogen. Man absorbs the oxygen, rejects the nitrogen.

When we study man today, the following is discovered. The human head today requires carbon dioxide. Carbon dioxide is a combination of carbon that is produced in the human body, and oxygen. Man emits the nitrogen contained in the air. If one studies the human head today, one discovers that this human head is so organized that it can think quite well because of the absorption of carbon dioxide and therefore of carbon and oxygen. Carbon dioxide, which is a poison and rises to the human head from the organs, constantly exposes the human head to damage. It is as if we were always to inhale a bit of carbon dioxide instead of oxygen. You really always inhale a bit of carbon dioxide into your head. This is of great significance, because we constantly take in something that actually destroys life. This is also the reason that we must sleep, that we require a time during which the head does not absorb this minute amount of carbon dioxide as vigorously and thereby is able to restore its organs.

Studies of the head show that in its present condition it

can make use of this poison, carbon dioxide, by repeatedly sustaining a little damage and then restoring itself through sleep, then again being damaged, again restoring itself, and so on. In very ancient times, however, man did not as yet have a head. It came about through evolution. Man would never have acquired a head if he had inhaled only carbon dioxide. The fully evolved head can tolerate carbon dioxide, but if man had always inhaled carbon dioxide, he would never have acquired a head. Therefore, he must have breathed something else long ago. Now we must ask ourselves what man used to breathe. If all human evolution is studied in detail, one discovers that during embryonic development in the womb, the human being uses something other than mere carbon dioxide. It is an interesting fact that in the mother's womb man is almost all head. The rest of the embryo, if you study it in the early stages, is minute [see Fig. 30] and is still almost all part of the head; the rest is extremely small. The whole embryo is surrounded by the walls of the womb.

You see, at this stage we are almost all head, but we must

Fig. 30

still develop, and for that we require nitrogen. We require nitrogen, and this is supplied by the mother's body. If man did not have access to nitrogen in the womb, a substance he later rejects in the air, not allowing it to enter him, it would be impossible for him to develop. We would not acquire a proper head if it were not for nitrogen. In an early stage of evolution, when his head was only beginning to develop, man must have absorbed not oxygen but nitrogen. The essential elements for man must, therefore, have been carbon and nitrogen instead of today's carbon and oxygen.

Just as man inhales oxygen today, he once must have inhaled carbon combined with nitrogen — in other words, he must have absorbed nitrogen. But what is carbon plus nitrogen? It is cyanogen, and when it is present as an acid, it is hydrocyanic acid. This means that conditions must have been such at one time that man did not absorb oxygen from the air but nitrogen, with which he internally produced cyanogen, an even stronger poison. This even stronger poison is what has enabled man to think today by making use of carbon dioxide. At that time he fashioned his organs with an even stronger poison.

Going back in time, we come to a point in ancient evolution when, unlike today, man produced cyanogen, and instead of exhaling carbon dioxide as he does today he exhaled hydrocyanic acid, a much stronger poison. Thus, from man and his present-day respiration, we go back to an ancient condition in which the air was filled with hydrocyanic acid just as it is today permeated with carbon dioxide.

In 1906, I gave lectures in Paris, and because of various suggestions from the listeners I was prompted to tell them that even today there are cosmic bodies that possess this ancient cyanogen atmosphere rather than that now prevalent on the earth. If the earth were viewed from the moon or particularly from Mars, one would be able to perceive traces of carbon dioxide everywhere in the earth's atmosphere by means of the spectroscope. Had the ancient earth been viewed from space when man was only beginning to acquire his head, however, one would have perceived traces of hydrocyanic acid instead of carbon dioxide. To this day there are cosmic bodies that have retained the earth's condition of former ages; these are the comets. The comets are what the earth was like when man acquired his head. Hence, they must contain cyanogen. I said in 1906 that the main characteristic of comets is that they contain cyanogen; if one were to study a comet with a spectroscope, one would see traces of cyanogen. Soon after this a comet appeared; they only appear rarely. I was in Norway at the time, and there was much talk about it—curiously enough, people actually observed lines of cyanogen.

People always say that when anthroposophy becomes aware of something that is based on spiritual insight, one should be able to prove it afterwards. There are indeed numerous things that have later been proved. When proof is provided, however, people overlook or suppress it. The truth is that, on the basis of this change in the breathing process, I stated prior to its having been observed with the spectroscope that comets contain cyanogen. This is the same substance that man needed in order to acquire his head at a time when the earth was still in a comet-like condition.

Now, imagine for a moment that I were to breathe nitrogen instead of oxygen; something other than human blood would naturally arise. As you know, the blood that has become blue combines in the lungs with oxygen and becomes red. Now, when man inhales oxygen he absorbs oxygen into his blood; when he inhales nitrogen, he absorbs the nitrogen into his blood. Blood functioning in a healthy way nowadays never contains uric acid, but if even a little nitrogen is absorbed into the blood, if something is only slightly amiss with the human being, uric acid appears in the blood.

In the age when man acquired his head, his blood consisted completely of uric acid, since nitrogen rather than oxygen continuously combined with the blood. His blood was only uric acid. As an embryo today, the human being swims in the amniotic fluid and thus has uric acid readily accessible. Uric acid is everywhere in his environment. In this early state the embryo needs uric acid for its development. In the past, when man was acquiring his head and exhaled hydrocyanic acid, he swam around in uric acid. In other words, he made use of cyanic acid, combining nitrogen and carbon and inwardly producing uric acid. Hydrocyanic acid surrounded him everywhere. The world was once in a condition in which uric and hydrocyanic acids actually played as big a role as water and air do today.

Even today, living creatures exist that can survive on something other than oxygen. There are, for example, creatures that are minute, since everything that was formerly large has become small today. The tiniest, smallest living creatures were once giants. But there are living creatures that cannot tolerate oxygen at all. They avoid oxygen and absorb sulphur instead. They are the sulphur bacteria that live by means of sulphur. This shows that oxygen is not the only necessity for life. Likewise, man didn't need oxygen to stay alive in earlier ages but instead required nitrogen, and was formed by means of it. Man was fashioned during a comet-like stage of the earth, and the relationship between breathing and the blood was completely different in those earlier ages.

Let's now consider what we have learned in connection with the world itself. If we focus on the fact that we take one breath to four pulse beats — one, two, three, breath of air; one, two, three, breath of air — the same rhythm can also be found in nature: spring, summer, autumn, *winter*. One, spring; two, summer; three, autumn; four, *winter*. Here we have the correlation between what's outside in the universe and what you have within man. So we can say, if we behold the entire earth, that our inner rhythm can be found outside on earth as well. People pay no heed at all to this kind of connection between ourselves and the earth.

You see, there is snow outside now. In summer there is no snow. What does that really mean? What is outside as snow now you find at other times as water. Water is completely dependent on the earth, and man must certainly sense that. The water around here in the Jura mountains contains calcium. Everything within the earth is also in the water. People who are specially sensitive to this develop goitres from what is contained in the water in the Jura region. The water is dependent on the earth. In spring, it begins to become dependent, it is most dependent in summer, and it ceases somewhat to be dependent in the autumn. In winter — well, gentlemen, the earth does not form the snow! The snow, consisting of myriads of delicate crystals, is formed by the universe, from out of the cosmos. Unlike in summer, the earth in winter doesn't abandon itself to the warmth of the world but rather to the formative forces. The water turns away from the earth in winter and receives the coldness of universal space. So we have discovered an interesting rhythm in the universe: one, spring; two, summer; three, autum; four, *winter*, and the water no longer directs itself to the earth but to the universe. Again, one, two three — spring, summer, autumn; then four, the water follows the universe, no longer the earth.

Now compare this rhythm with the blood and the breathing process. One, two, three pulse beats, the blood is directed to the body's interior; *four*, breath of air, the blood is directed to what is outside. Here you have the same activity in the human being as on the earth outside. If you compare the blood with the earth's water, the blood directs itself accordingly. The first three pulse beats are inwardly a little like spring, summer, and autumn; *four*, now comes earthly winter, and aha, we breathe, now comes the breath, just as with the earth itself. Inwardly, man is attuned completely to the earth's breathing process. It can therefore be said that what runs its course in one year in the earth takes place quickly, 18 times in one minute, in man. What takes a year for the earth takes place 18 times in one minute in man. Man is actually always filled with this rhythm, but it is much faster than with the earth. When we consider the earth in the light of our discussion today, we realize that the condition of the earth was formerly quite different, had a certain similarity to the comets. Now, when a comet disintegrates, the pieces, which contain iron, fall to earth as meteors. An entire comet, which falls to earth when it splinters, therefore contains iron.

This is also something that we still contain within ourselves. When our corpses disintegrate, the iron from our blood is left behind. Here we have retained something of our ancient comet nature, and we actually act as comets do. We have iron in our blood through developing the ancient cyanogen activity in ourselves — that is, our external bodies, the blood of which it may no longer enter, though it was once allowed to. This means nothing more than that today we withdraw our inner spring, summer, autumn and winter from the outer spring, summer, autumn and winter. Our dependency on the outer seasons has become minimal.

You need not go terribly far back into the past, however, to find that things had a totally different character then. Although things are changing now, if one grew up in a country village as I did, one knows that there used to be people who were very dependent on spring, summer, autumn and winter; there are fewer now because everything is becoming more uniform in the world. One could even notice this quality in their whole life of soul. They were in a totally different mood in summer than in winter. When they met you in winter they were always a little outside themselves; they were much more like apparitions than people. They came into their own only in summer and then were really themselves. This means that they were dependent upon the outer spring, summer, autumn and winter.

This demonstrates to us what man was like in earlier ages. When he breathed nitrogen instead of oxygen, he was completely dependent on his outer surroundings; he participated in the pulse beat and breathing of his comet body, which in my book *An Outline of Occult Science* I called the ancient Moon. The ancient Moon was a sort of comet-like body, and, as a participant in it, man was part of a large organism that also breathed. It was as if man today were suddenly to have one pulse beat in spring, one in summer, one in the autumn, and would then take a breath in winter, and so on. This is the way man was when he breathed nitrogen; he was a member of the entire earthly organism.

So, you see, we come from a completely different direction and again reach the point we arrived at earlier when we considered the megatherians, saurians, and so forth. We arrive at the same point by a different path.

This is the remarkable thing about spiritual science. Ordinary present-day scientific activity begins at some point and proceeds step by step, trotting along in a straight line without knowing where it is going. That is not the case with anthroposophical science. It can proceed in one or another direction from various points of departure, but just as a hiker always reaches the same summit regardless of where he starts at the foot of a mountain, so anthroposophy always arrives at the same goal. This is what is so remarkable. The more one honestly examines the world, the more individual considerations fit together into a unity.

We have an example of this in exploring your question

today. We proceeded from matters quite different from the earlier subjects, yet once again we arrived at the conclusion that man had his rhythm within the entire earthly organism when it was still comet-like; only now has he made this rhythm his own. Man existed as part of the earth just as he does today when he is still a germ within his mother. There he also takes part in her pulse and breathing activity.

Can it be proven that man today takes part in his mother's pulse and breathing activity? This is proven by what I said before, that smallpox develops from the blood's activity coming into connection with the breathing activity. This is interesting. If one does share the maternal blood and breathing activities while in the womb, a child in the womb should contract smallpox if the mother has it, and it does. When a pregnant woman contracts smallpox, her unborn child already has smallpox in the womb, because the child takes part in everything.

In the same way, when the earth was still the mother of the human being — although the earth was then a kind of comet — he participated in all that the earth underwent. His pulse beat and breathing were that of the earth's pulse beat and breathing. It is most remarkable that if we go back into ancient times when human beings knew things instinctively, and were not clever as they are today, they always called the earth 'mother' — Mother Earth and so forth. They spoke of Uranus, meaning the universe, and Gaia, the earth, and they viewed Uranus as the father in the universe outside and the earth as the mother [Fig. 31].

So one can say that the part of the human organism in which the child develops, the womb, is really like a miniature earth that has remained behind and is still in an ancient comet-like state.

In that ancient comet-like state, man's breathing and that of the earth were together a breathing in the great universe. Not only did man absorb nitrogen, but the whole comet-

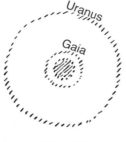

Fig. 31

earth received the nitrogen from the universe. Breathing at that stage was also a form of fertilization. This is only retained today in the process of fertilization in humans and animals. In fertilization, therefore, something of the nitrogen breathing process still takes place, because the most important element in the human sperm is nitrogen. This is transmitted to the female organism and, as a nitrogen stimulus, brings about what oxygen could never accomplish, that is, the formation of the organs that must be present later when man is exposed to oxygen. So you see that we actually receive our breathing from the universe.

Now, let's try exploring something else. You see, the year's course is to some extent reflected in the course of the day: 18 breaths per minute, and 60 times that much per hour = 1,080; in 24 hours, one day, we have 24 times that much = 25,920. Hence, we take 25,920 breaths per day.

Now let me work out something else for you — the number of days in an average human life. As you know, the year has about 360 days. The average number of years a man lives is between 71 and 72; 72 times 360 makes 25,920. We take as many breaths per day as we have days in our human life. But a day, too, is in a certain sense a breathing. One day is also a breath. When I go to sleep, I exhale my soul, and I draw it back in again when I awake: exhalation, inhalation. I exhale the spiritual and inhale it again. This rhythm in my breathing I therefore have throughout my life on earth in sleeping and waking. This is most interesting: 25,920 breaths per day, 25,920 days in the average human life.

Now we turn and look at the sun. When you observe the sun in spring today, it rises in the sign of Pisces, but it does not rise every year in spring in exactly the same spot. On 21 March in the spring of next year the sun will have moved a fraction. Year by year it moves a little. The point where it rises moves constantly and eventually comes full circle. Therefore, if the sun rises in the constellation of Pisces today — the astronomers think it is still in Aries where it was formerly, because they have not yet caught up with their notations — then it must have risen in primordial times in Pisces, too! When the number of years that it takes the sun to come full circle is calculated, the result is 25,920 years. It is the same ratio. Even the cosmic rhythm harmonizes with the faster rhythms of breathing and blood circulation. Just imagine how man stands within the cosmos! He is really a child of the universe. The cosmos is his original father and mother.

One thus arrives at a completely different way of viewing man in relation to the universe than when one simply says that God created the world and man — a concept that doesn't require much thinking. But anthroposophy wishes to begin to think something in every instance. This is held against it. Why? Well, it takes no effort to say words that don't require thinking. In anthroposophy, however, one must exert oneself, and this makes people angry. One needn't strain oneself in today's science. All of a sudden here comes this upstart, anthroposophy, and one cannot sit as if in the cinema thoughtlessly watching a film. People would even like to introduce films into schools so that children wouldn't have to make an effort to learn. I am surprised that arithmetic has not yet been made into films! Then along comes anthroposophy demanding that you don't sit around so idly but put your confounded skulls to use! And no one wants to do that!

The effect of absinthe. Haemophilia. The Ice Age. On bees

Dr Steiner: Good morning, gentlemen! Have you thought of something to ask me since last time?

More detailed questions are raised concerning the effect of absinthe and also concerning bees and wasps.

Dr Steiner: Well, we have already discussed the question of the effect of absinthe, which, as I told you, is similar to the general effect of alcohol. If we are to go further into these questions, I would like to say something about some other influences on the human body. We must be clear that we cannot speak only about the solid components of the human organism, of the human body, since they amount to at most 10 to 12 per cent of the whole. When we find the human body sketched in a book, the sketch can, of course, only be made by outlining the solid components. So it is believed that man consists only of his brain, lungs, heart, and so on, that is, that he is really composed only of such solid components. As I have told you, however, the human body is approximately 85 per cent fluid, a watery fluid.

It is therefore only partially correct to say that we drink water, for example, and the water, along with a number of dissolved substances, enters the stomach and from there the intestines, and so forth. This is only partly true. When a small glass of water is drunk, we can picture what I just said to be the case. With the second glass of water, however, what is in the water is absorbed by the body's fluid elements and does not pass first through all the organs in the way I described.

Now, it is a fact that the solid components in man are

least exposed to the outer environment. Naturally, when the heart, for example, is observed, it expands and contracts with the pulse beats, but as a whole it retains the same size and remains as it is. If we consider that we are filled with fluids, we recognize that these fluids are open to any number of influences from the outside world. Even a small amount of fluid assumes the shape of a drop, since the world is round and affects each individual drop. Because we are fluid, the whole world affects us, and because modern science no longer takes into consideration the fact that man is really a column of fluid, it has simply forgotten that the whole world with all its stars has this influence on the human being.

When one recognizes that man is a mixture of fluids, one is not too far from realizing that he is air as well. I constantly draw in the air and then exhale it again; hence, I am also air. Owing to the constant motion of air within myself, I am truly a human being. It is only due to the fact that we are composed in this way that it is possible for us really to be soul-spiritual beings. If we were only solid, we really could not be soul-spiritual beings at all.

Now, everything exerts a specific influence on the human being. We have already mentioned various poisons, and you will no doubt have heard of so-called lead poisoning. When too much lead is introduced into a person's body — such an overdose need only be a small amount, which, however, may be proportionately too much for the body — he becomes too solid. Then these solid components become calcareous, as it were. When man introduces a minute amount of lead into the body — and in lead poisoning it only takes a minute amount — the body becomes too solid. If one sees that a person is beginning to become too solid — man even ages due to lead poisoning, hence signs of ageing are noted — then silver in some form must be given as a remedy. That will make man more fluid again so that he can become

sensitive again to outer influences. Lead poisoning, therefore, can be counteracted by silver compounds, which must
be chosen to fit the specific case. All manner of things thus
have an effect on the human being.

As you know, feminine and masculine natures differ
greatly from one another. The feminine nature contains
more of the fluid element, as it were, so one can say that the
feminine nature is more susceptible to outer influences,
because it is more fluid. The masculine nature is less open to
outer influences, because it places more weight on man's
solid element. One can therefore say that certain illnesses,
like lead poisoning, can be more readily controlled in the
feminine nature with the administration of less silver,
whereas more silver must be prescribed for the masculine
nature, because that constitution is not readily made fluid.
You see, one must pay great attention to every detail in the
human being, because only in this way can we truly
understand him. Every substance has a profound influence
on the human being.

All this is connected in turn with that relationship of the
masculine and feminine that is expressed in hereditary
conditions. These hereditary conditions are extraordinarily
complicated. You can see how complicated such hereditary
conditions are in haemophilia; the blood in people afflicted
with this illness doesn't coagulate immediately. In a normal
person, the blood within the body coagulates immediately,
as soon as it is exposed on the surface. The blood is liquid
within the body; as soon as it reaches the surface it becomes
compact, solid, it coagulates. In haemophiliacs the blood
does not coagulate immediately. It flows readily even from
a small wound and sometimes even ruptures the skin. It is
difficult to perform operations on haemophiliacs. Whereas
in normal people the blood immediately begins to coagulate
as soon as an incision is made, with haemophiliacs it pours
out. It remains fluid so that they can easily bleed to death

during an operation, making such an undertaking extraordinarily difficult. Haemophiliacs are forever subject to
haemorrhage.

Now, it is very strange that a man who is a haemophiliac
can marry a woman who is not, and they will have healthy
children without haemophilia. If they have sons, the hereditary conditions will not produce any detrimental effects
in them. Should they have a daughter, however, she herself
will not be a haemophiliac, but if she should marry even a
perfectly healthy man they might have children who would
be haemophiliacs. The odd thing about this affliction is that
it doesn't surface in the feminine sex; the daughters don't
get haemophilia, but the children of these daughters do,
even if their fathers are completely healthy. Hence, haemophilia passes to the descendants by way of the woman,
without the woman getting it herself.

Here we see the complicated ways in which conditions in
the human body are affected by hereditary conditions. It is
therefore very risky for the daughter of a haemophiliac to
marry, because haemophilia will then pass on to some of
her children even if she is completely healthy. This shows
you how important it is to take such conditions into consideration.

Now, such problems could be coped with if medicine
were placed on a sound footing. What measures would it be
proper to take with the daughter of a haemophiliac? Before
she has any children, some remedy containing lead* can be
given prophylactically, as it is called in medicine. The
husband should also receive this lead-containing medication. Then the children will be protected from getting haemophilia.

Naturally, if medical thinking is so muddled that it is

---

*This presumably refers to a 'potentized' homoeopathic remedy — editor's
note.

thought best to wait until a person exhibits the symptoms of illness before beginning a cure, then this will do no good. Medicine must develop a social conscience. It must change so that steps are taken to *prevent* threatening illnesses from occurring. This cannot be done, of course, as long as today's conceptions prevail. Naturally, people do not seek a cure for an illness that they do not as yet have but could contract due to hereditary conditions. It is especially important in pregnancy to administer a lead remedy if there is any possibility at all of haemophilia.

All this cannot be understood if one does not know that only the solid body of man is really physical and material. Only that portion is material. As soon as one comes to the fluid element, one finds a much more delicate substance at work. Since time immemorial this delicate substance has been called 'ether'. Ether is present everywhere. It is more delicate than all other substances — more delicate than water, air, and even warmth. As little as ether can penetrate the solid components of the human being, however, the more active it is in his fluid element. Just as man possesses the ether in his fluid element, so his soul is borne upon the element of air. His soul permeates the air he carries within him. When this is understood, that in the air one has the soul element, it becomes clear that man exhales the soul with each breath, and with each inhalation he takes it into himself again. He really lives with the universe by means of this soul element, but because no consideration is given by modern science to the fact that he also possesses an air organism, people lose sight altogether of the soul element and even believe it doesn't exist.

The soul element must be considered quite separately. Then, the effects of fluid substances, such as absinthe, can be discerned. You see, when I take a drink of absinthe, it is of course liquid at first and then it merges with the large quantity of the body's fluids. How does absinthe deal with these fluids, however? It makes these fluids rebel against absorbing the air element in the right way. So when I take absinthe into my body, the air can no longer penetrate all of me in the right way. At the same time, something else happens. When I prevent the air element from penetrating all parts of my body, this element reacts in a most peculiar way. I will make clear to you how this air element works by making a comparison.

Imagine, for example, a person who is employed in an office and works hard from morning till night. He goes in in the morning and he goes home in the evening. His colleagues say of him that he is simply somebody who comes and goes at the same time that they do. Now imagine another person who also works in the office, but this fellow is a clown. He doesn't work much but plays around with everybody from morning till night. He is quite popular with all the employees, who think of him as one of them and are always glad to see him. Of course, his superiors are not so overjoyed with him because his work suffers, but his colleagues enjoy his clowning.

This is similar to what happens when we block out the air with absinthe. The air then rolls around the organs instead of properly penetrating them and filling the body. It remains distinct, stopping here, there and everywhere. It is just like the funny fellow in the office. It spreads pleasant feelings everywhere because it needn't do too much work. If the air is to penetrate the body's fluids correctly, it has work to do; otherwise it doesn't supply the body correctly. When absinthe blocks out the air, however, the air swirls about everywhere and the person gradually comes to feel as content as a pig. A peculiarity of pigs is that they constantly fill themselves with air that is not properly absorbed. The pig easily becomes short of breath.

Just as the ether is present everywhere in the bodily fluids, so the soul element is present everywhere in the air;

we also call it the astral element, because it is called forth by the influence of the stars. Man absorbs the soul element everywhere and feels a pleasant warmth or coolness at different places within himself. Now when the air is swirling about in him, he feels good through and through. The soul element in the body is not there, however, merely for the purpose of serving man's pleasure. It is supposed to work on the organs in the right way so that the heart and all the other organs are correctly cared for. If instead, however, man blocks the soul element so that it titillates his body, then, although he feels 'piggishly well', his organs are not cared for in the right way. In particular, those organs are short-changed that contribute most to his having healthy offspring. Here we have a strange phenomenon. People who imbibe absinthe really want to feel 'piggishly well', to have this feeling of sensual pleasure inside, but in doing so, they do not provide humanity with healthy descendants. This is the objection to absinthe.

Now you can also ask why the desire to drink absinthe actually arises in people in the first place. If you study the history of humanity, you will note that such vices occur most often in those whose development is declining and who are no longer in the full prime of life, that is, those whose bodies are inwardly already somewhat disintegrated. Then people let the soul element titillate them inwardly.

This is also the case in instances in which these vices get out of hand, when people want to introduce all possible substances into the body. People even seek these effects with cocaine, as I told you recently. With cocaine, the soul element has the effect of squeezing the body out, and I have described how such addicts experience something like snakes emerging everywhere from their bodies. The reason a person uses these poisons in this way is because the whole human being is no longer healthy, and he would like to enjoy the soul element as much as possible. Those people who have the least to do will seek out this sensual experience of the body. This is connected with all the historical processes at work in the human race.

It is strange how, if we look to western regions, people permit themselves to be enslaved, as it were, by proclaiming all kinds of laws against alcohol, absinthe and the like. Even so, people try in any number of ways to get their hands on these substances. This demonstrates that today we are faced with the greatest confusion in human life. On the one hand, human beings want to live indulgently; on the other, as nations, they do not want to deteriorate completely. This lack of insight is the cause of the really insane muddle created by the craving of individuals to subject their bodies to all kinds of substances and then again the laws created to prohibit them from doing so. People need to gain some insight again.

I have explained before that the feminine is connected more with the influences of the universe, whereas the masculine closes itself off from these influences. When men become addicted to absinthe, therefore, they ruin those organs that normally produce offspring who would become people of inwardly firm and strong character. Absinthe will cause people to become weaklings. So, if absinthe is increasingly drunk by men, their children will turn out to be weaklings; they will become a weak race, they will have weak descendants. The males will become effeminate. If women become addicted to absinthe, things will reach a point where children are born extremely susceptible to all kinds of disease.

Such matters must be viewed in relation to the whole world. I would like to tell you something extraordinarily interesting. You can ask where much of what we know today really comes from. No attention is ordinarily paid to how much wisdom humanity possesses in the most simple, everyday aspects of life. As you know, we name the days of the week: Sunday after the sun; Monday after the moon; Tuesday after Mars—*mardi* in French is definitely named after Mars. While in German Wednesday* is *Mittwoch*, or mid-week, you only have to take the French *mercredi* and you have Mercury Day, after the planet Mercury. Thursday is after Thor, the thunderer, in German *Donnerstag* from Donor, but Donor (Thor) is none other than Jupiter. In French we still have *jeudi*, Jupiter Day. Friday is named after the German goddess Freia, who is the same as Venus; this is *vendredi* in French.† Hence, the days of the week are named after the planets. Why is that? Because these names originated at a time when people still knew that man is dependent on the universe. Through the very fact of being alive, all the planets have an influence on us. The days of the week were named accordingly. Today this is called superstition, but calling it superstition is nothing but ignorance. Actually, tremendous wisdom is contained in the naming of the days of the week. Yes, gentlemen, in all these matters there lies a tremendous wisdom!

Now, if we ask where this naming of the days of the week came from, we go to Asia and find that two or three thousand years before the birth of Christ extraordinarily clever people lived there. Among the Babylonians and Assyrians were very clever people who were able to observe the influence of the stars; they were the first to name the days of the week. Others then translated them into their own languages. We owe the names of the days of the week to the East, to the Babylonians and the Assyrians, where people were already clever, extremely clever, at a time

---

*Note by translator: The English Wednesday is derived from Wotan's Day; Wotan is the Germanic name for the being called Mercury in Latin.
†Mention of Saturday was omitted by Rudolf Steiner. It is especially obvious in English that the day is named after Saturn.

when Europe looked entirely different. Let us ask what Europe was like around four thousand years ago when, in Asia, in Assyria and Babylonia, when there were people who really were much cleverer than we are. They were cleverer because they possessed a much greater wealth of knowledge. It is not true that humanity merely progresses smoothly forward. From time to time, humanity also takes steps backward.

Now, these people had a great wealth of knowledge. If people simply abandon their souls to such knowledge, however, it does not agree with them any more than money does. As funny as this comparison might sound, it is true. Too much money does people no good; neither does too much knowledge, if it is not counterbalanced by correctly employing it in the service of humanity and the world. The Asians had gradually accumulated a tremendous knowledge, but they didn't know what to do with it.

What Europe was like at that time, when the Asians still possessed such great knowledge, can best be seen here in these regions of Switzerland, for example. If you look at the rocks that have been brought down into the valleys by glaciers, you can tell from the appearance of these rocks that the glaciers have worked on them. These are glacial rocks. We can tell from their appearance that they have come down from the heights and that the flowing ice of the glaciers has affected them. From the way all the rocks around here look, we know that this whole region was once covered with ice. Indeed, the very ground we walk and feel most comfortable on was once covered with glaciers.

Again, if we go further north, to Prussia and large parts of Germany, one can tell by the forms of certain rocks that all those areas were covered with glacial ice that flowed down from the far north. Just as the glaciers descend today to a certain level, so the glaciers moved from the far northern regions all the way into Germany, covering everything with ice. Not so long ago, people had a special preference for large numbers, and so they said, 'Oh, certainly Europe was once covered with glaciers, but that was 20 or 30 million years ago.' This is nonsense, and came about through a calculation that I shall illustrate for you with the following example.

Imagine that I observe a human heart today. This human heart constantly undergoes minute changes. If I observe it a year hence, it will have become a little less resilient, still less in two years, and I can now calculate how much less resilient it has become. Now, by adding it all up, I can calculate how much less resilient the heart will be in a hundred years and from this know also what it was like a century ago. I can certainly figure that out. I can take, say, a seven-year-old person; three hundred years ago his heart was in such and such a shape. There is only the one small matter of his not having been alive then. Similarly, if I figure out how his heart will have changed three hundred years hence, there again is that small matter of his not being alive then.

Similar calculations have been made in order to work out how it looked here in Europe, for example, 20 to 30 thousand years ago. The glacial period has thus been pushed far back, but one cannot calculate like that. We need a science that, in regard to the earth, can show what one already knows regarding the human being, that in three hundred years he will no longer be living as a physical, earthly being.

In recent years learned scientists have become more reasonable, and those with some sense have realized that it was not so long ago that everything here was covered with glaciers; in fact, all of Europe was still iced over when people in Asia were as clever as I have described, when the Babylonian and Assyrian cultures flourished. We need only go back a few thousand years—four or five thousand—to find that in Europe everything was still iced over. Only gradually, as the ice diminished, did human beings migrate here.

Well, these people did not have it as easy as people today. It was much harder on them, since they came from warmer regions where they were not constantly subjected to the cold and where they really fared better. Nevertheless, these people did move into regions that only recently had been covered with ice. Through this they were prevented from experiencing the sensual pleasure of wisdom that would gradually have been theirs in Asia. Because an influence was exerted on Europe from the universe, causing it to be covered with ice when the Asian culture enjoyed a warm climate, a better, more energetic culture developed in Europe than could have evolved in Asia. You see, entire civilizations depend on influences from the cosmos.

Moreover, when one thinks of a glass of ocean water, one sees it simply as water to which a little salt has been added: sea water is salty, so when I add salt to plain water I get sea water. It is not as simple as that, however. If you look at the ocean, the Atlantic, for instance, if you could look at it from beneath the surface—here's the surface [*sketching*] and here's the water—then this is not merely salt water; a curious phenomenon would be observed. When summer comes, something reminiscent of falling snow would pass through the sea. Looking at this gigantic expanse of the ocean from below the surface, one would not say that it was just filled with sea water; indeed, one would see it snowing, as it were. What causes this? The sea contains countless minute creatures, all possessing tiny calcareous shells. These creatures are called foraminifera. As long as these creatures are alive, they swim around in the water fairly close to the surface. Now, when the time of year approaches in which they can no longer live, these creatures die, and their shells begin to sink. These shells are constantly falling, and it is truly like a snow storm. It is really like snow in the air. The entire ocean experiences a snowfall made by these foraminifera. When these foraminifera shells are finally deposited here on the bottom [*sketching*], their substance is altered and they turn into red clay. This is the ocean floor. These little creatures receive their life from the universe and then build up the ocean floor. It is exactly the same with us in this part of the world. We don't live in the ocean, we live in the air. And when it snows in winter, what is in the snow is what makes our ground as it is, for if there weren't the right snowfall the plants couldn't grow. The ground is made by what is in the snow.

Gentlemen, it is not the solid components nor even the fluid components in our bodies that absorb the right influences, but only the airy components. This influence is absorbed by our breathing when it snows in winter. What the world of the stars sends down to us when it snows in winter we absorb into ourselves and mould in the right way. To do this, however, our souls need to work in the right way on our organs; otherwise our organs atrophy. Now, when we burden our bodies with absinthe, we close ourselves off from the starry world. We can no longer absorb the influences of the starry world. The result is that we ruin our bodies by thus exposing them only to the earth's influence. You can see how tremendously important it is, if we are to bring about the right kind of human evolution, for us not to ruin our bodies with absinthe. We must realize that!

Now, you can easily picture how civilization progressed. In Asia there existed tremendously clever people who possessed strong soul natures. Gradually, however, they wanted to experience the soul element only as an inner colouring, an inner sensual feeling. Some of them migrated into the regions that earlier had been covered with ice. There they weaned themselves away from this inner sensual feeling and again strengthened their bodies. This is how the civilization of the Occident was added to that of the Orient. Even today, you can see from the glacial formations here on the mountain tops that the earth was once thoroughly frozen in this region, enabling the people who moved here to strengthen their bodies.

You also find reasons for the decline of the Roman Empire in these things. This dates back to the age when Christianity was first beginning to spread. Yes, gentlemen, if Christianity had spread only among the Romans, the result would have been pretty bad! The Romans, who possessed only the remnants of Oriental, Asian culture, had become so weakened that they could not accomplish anything. Then the peoples of the northern, ice-covered regions arrived with their more sturdy bodies, and the Roman Empire consequently perished. These northern people with their more sturdy bodies took over cultural and spiritual life.

History describes this as the barbarian invasions in which the Romans perished when the Germanic tribes arrived. These are really today's Europeans — the Germans, French, and English — because they are all basically Germanic peoples. The French have only absorbed a little more of the Roman element than the Germans, for example. All this is based on the fact that these people came from regions where they could absorb the influences of the universe, whereas the other people with their wisdom lived only on the earth. These people that came from the north renewed the whole civilization. So you see, this is how nature is related to everything that takes place in history.

You also know, however, what a strong influence the Roman element still retained. Remember, for example, that not a word of German could be spoken in the universities of Central Europe until the sixteenth and seventeenth centuries. The professors lectured in Latin. Of course, it had gradually become an odd form of Latin, but everybody knew and understood Latin. Lecturing in one's native language came about only slowly, but this tendency to hold on to what was declining because one felt more comfortable with it, even with its language, continued for a long time.

Just think how long people who wished to give themselves airs chattered in French in all the German regions. This was for no other reason than that they wished to perpetuate the old Latin-Roman element, at least in the language they spoke. It is true that what continued on in the language was also perpetuated in other vices. The Romans began this craving to experience a sensual feeling within the body, to enjoy the soul element rather than to make use of it for building up the body. The legacy of this is still present in the craving to drink absinthe, indeed, even to enjoy cocaine and so on. These things will produce a weak race, weak descendants, and will gradually lead those who succumb to such vices to decline. You can enact all the social reforms you like; nothing will result from these social reforms if true insight into such things is not achieved. Such insight can come about only when the materialism in science and religion is replaced by beginning to grasp something spiritual. When human beings begin to grasp the spiritual, they will perceive much of what is not only quite clear outwardly but that can then be penetrated by the right kind of spiritual perception.

The question put by one of you gentlemen, who is an expert on bees, pointed to the distinction between the lives of bees and the lives of wasps. There is much that is similar. I recently described to you the life of wasps, and it is quite similar to that of the bees. The life of the beehive, however, is a remarkably strange one. What is its basis? You see, you cannot explain this if you don't have the possibility of looking into it spiritually. The life in a beehive is extraordinarily wise in its arrangement. Anybody who has observed the bees' life would agree with that. Naturally, one cannot say that bees have a science such as humans have, because they have nothing approaching the brain apparatus that man has. Bees thus cannot assimilate universal wisdom into their bodies as human beings do, but the influences from the universal surroundings of the earth work powerfully on beehives. If all that lives in the surroundings of the earth, which has a very strong influence on the beehive, were taken into consideration, one could arrive at a correct comprehension of what the life of the bees is really like. Much more so than among ants and wasps, life in the beehive is based on the bees' cooperating with each other and accomplishing their tasks harmoniously. To figure out what causes this, one must conclude that bees have a life in which the element that expresses itself in other animals in their sexual life is suppressed to an extraordinary degree. In bees this impulse is extraordinarily suppressed.

You see, reproduction is actually taken care of among bees by a few select females, the queen bees. The sexual life of the others is really more or less suppressed. In sexual life, however, love is also present. The life of love is an element of the soul. Only because certain organs in the body are affected by this soul element do they reveal and become expressions of this love life. Inasmuch as this love is suppressed in bees and concentrated in only one queen bee, what would otherwise be sexual life in the beehive is transferred to the other activities that the bees develop. This is why the wise men of old, who knew of these matters in a way differing from that of today, associated this whole wondrous bustle of the beehive with the amorousness that is connected with the planet Venus.

So we can say that when one describes the wasps or the ants, they are creatures that withhold themselves from the influence of the planet Venus. The bees are completely given up to the influence of the planet Venus, developing a love life throughout their entire hive. It therefore becomes a wise life, and you can imagine how wise that must be. I have described something of the way successive generations of bees are produced. It contains an unconscious wisdom. The bees develop this unconscious wisdom in their outer activity. Therefore, the element that arises in us only when our hearts love is actually active throughout the beehive, is tangibly present. The entire beehive is actually permeated by a life of love. In most instances the individual bees renounce love and develop love in the entire beehive. One can begin to understand their life when one becomes clear that the bees live as if in an atmosphere that is pervaded through and through with love.

It is most beneficial to the bee that it sustains itself by those parts of the plant that are completely permeated by the plant's love life. The bee sucks its nourishment, which it then turns into honey, out of those parts of the plant that are integral aspects of its love life. The bee thus carries the love life of the flowers into the hive. This is why the life of the bee must be studied from the standpoint of the soul.

This is much less necessary with ants and wasps. When their lives are traced, one will see that they tend to have more of a sexual life than bees. With the exception of the queen bee, the bee is really the one being that, in a manner of speaking, says, 'We shall renounce an individual sex life and instead become bearers of the life of love.' They have indeed carried into the hive what lives in flowers. If you really begin to think this through, you uncover the entire mystery of the beehive. The life of this sprouting, thriving love that is spread out over the flowers is then also contained in the honey.

You can investigate this further and ask what effect honey has on you when you eat it. What does honey do? Well, absinthe unites with the fluidity of man, pushing out the air and with it the soul element, so that man experiences sensual pleasure. Honey generates sensual pleasure on the tongue at most. The moment honey is eaten, it furthers the right relationship between the air element and the fluid element in man. Nothing is better for the human being than to add the right amount of honey to his food. In a marvellous way, the bee really sees to it that man learns to use his soul to work on his bodily organs. By means of honey, the beehive gives back to man what he needs for his soul to work industriously upon his body. When man drinks quantities of absinthe, he wishes to enjoy his soul. When man adds honey to his meal, he prepares his soul element in such a way that it works and breathes properly in his body. Beekeeping is therefore something that really contributes significantly to civilization, because it makes man strong, whereas to indulge in absinthe is something that will gradually drive the human race to extinction.

When you consider that bees receive the greatest influence from the world of the stars, you realize that through the bees the right element can enter the human being. All living things work together in the right way when they are combined in the right way. When a person looks at a beehive, he should say to himself with something akin to exaltation that, by way of the beehive, the whole universe enters human beings and makes them capable people. Drinking absinthe, however, produces incapable human beings. By looking at things in this way, knowledge of man can thus become knowledge of the universe.

The relationship between the planets and the metals and their healing effects

Dr Steiner: Do any of you gentlemen have a question you would like to have discussed?

Question: I would like to ask what the world was like in primeval times. Had the planets Venus, Mercury, and so on deposited various metallic substances?

Dr Steiner: If this is considered simply in the way it is frequently stated in old books — in the new ones nothing is said about it, except in our anthroposophical books — that the planet Venus has something to do with the copper deposited in the earth, for example, then this is merely a matter of belief. People gain nothing but a mental image of it by being told that it was once known by men of old, but nothing is really known about it today. When something like this is to be discussed, one must really go into it in detail. I would like to call your attention to the fact that modern medicine also no longer knows much about these things. Only a few centuries ago the great majority of remedies and medicines for particular symptoms were based on the use of a metal or a plant substance.

The only remnant of this knowledge is that for certain symptoms, which appear particularly in syphilis, quicksilver (or mercury) must be employed as a remedy. One therefore makes use of mercury. Please note that nobody in medicine today can really explain why mercury is effective; it is used simply because it has been seen to be effective. Regarding this effect of mercury on syphilitic diseases, one must also mention that in recent times a number of other medications have replaced mercury. It has already been recognized that these new remedies are not entirely effective, and medicine will soon return to the mercuric remedies.

You can prove in a remarkable way that the instinct for healing—not today's science but the instinct for healing— can use mercury in a very effective way. There are certain regions in which people who were not doctors, but acted out of their instinct for healing, treated a syphilitic illness in the following way (today this rarely happens, but three or four decades ago it still occurred). They took animals that live partly underground and that therefore take in some dirt along with their food, animals such as salamanders, toads, and similar creatures. People took these animals, dehy-drated and pulverized them, and then gave this preparation to syphilitic patients. This was a kind of remedy.

Now, on the face of it, this is completely incomprehen-sible. It becomes comprehensible only when one knows that in some regions these toad remedies do not help syphilitics while in other regions they are most effective. One finds that there are mercury mines in those regions where it is effective. It is curious that in regions where mercury is present, the animals absorb it with their food, and it is the mercury that effects the cure. It is not the toad but the mercury that the toad has consumed and assimilated into its body that has the healing effect.

This can tell us two things: first, that a remarkable instinct for healing is present in people who are not as yet spoiled by ordinary science; second, that if a living creature absorbs something—and a toad is indeed a living creature—it permeates its whole body, it spreads through its whole body. This is true to an even greater extent in the case of humans. Since we used the example of mercury-based remedies, I would like to mention the following.

Only in the last few decades has medicine gone downhill to such an extent. It was better when I was a little boy. In

Vienna, there lived a splendid professor of anatomy, Joseph Hyrtl, who still knew a little—not very much, but still a little—about more ancient medicine. When, in his clinic, he had the corpses of people who at one time had undergone mercury treatments, he would break their bones open and show his students that little drops of mercury were deposited in them. This is how a substance that a person absorbs spreads throughout his body. It is the same in other living creatures, and so toads that had assimilated mercury into their whole bodies could be pulverized and used as a remedy against syphilis.

Now I will tell you how people hit on the idea of using mercury for such illnesses in earlier times when science had a totally different character. When you observe the planetary system the way we know it from school, the sun is here in the centre; near to the sun, the planet Mercury, a somewhat small planet, circles the sun. A little farther out, Venus circles the sun. Mercury is a small planet, and its orbit around the sun takes place in a short time, about 90 days. Then comes Venus, and it circles the sun more slowly. The next planet circling the sun is the earth. Beyond the earth is Mars. Then come a great number of tiny, miniature planets, or asteroids, in orbit beyond Mars. There are hundreds and hundreds of these tiny little planets; they are in orbit. I would have to sketch a lot of planets, but they are not that important and lack the great significance of the larger planets. After these planets come Jupiter, circling the sun, and still farther out, Saturn. Then come Uranus and Neptune, but these two planets were discovered most recently. I need not sketch them, since they circle much farther out and their orbits exhibit such irregularities that in reality they cannot be counted among the planets even today. This is how the planets circle the sun, just as our moon circles the earth. It circles the earth just as the other planets circle the sun. [Fig. 32.]

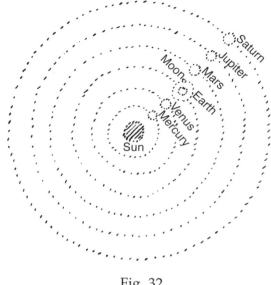

Fig. 32

Now, astronomy today looks at such a planetary system without paying much attention to the influences that these planets have on the beings living upon earth. One calculates the position of a planet for a given time so that a telescope can be turned towards it. This can be calculated. One can also work out how fast a planet moves. One can calculate all this. It is with these calculations that people are concerned today.

You see, however, that in the evolution of an entire universal system, a few millennia are not a long time, and it was only 25 to 35 hundred years ago that people looked upon the planets in a completely different scientific way. At that time the following was done. Illnesses, for example, appeared in which, due to thickened blood — I shall tell you why directly — people were afflicted with problems of the intestines. I can't go into detail concerning these critical illnesses now, because when these observations were made in ancient times they were not as extensive as they are today. But in an illness observed in Babylonia, Assyria, Nineveh, and so on, even in Egypt, people became afflicted with an intestinal disorder that was due to thickened blood, to abnormal processes in the blood. Blood was present in the stools; typhoid-like diseases were after all much more common in ancient times than they are nowadays. Let's assume that the ancient doctors, who were also philosophers, had to study such diseases. They didn't wait until the patient was dead, because they knew that once a person had died a cure was not very effective! So they did not examine those who had died of typhoid but proceeded differently. They noticed that patients suffering from cholera, typhoid, dysentery or suchlike felt better at certain times, and at others their overall condition took a turn for the worse. So they concluded that typhoid sometimes takes a good and sometimes a fatal course. There are some people who, when they fall ill with typhoid or cholera, occasionally undergo terrible attacks of dizziness almost to the point of losing consciousness; then events take a most critical turn. Some patients retain consciousness, however, and their heads remain clear. These patients can be helped.

Now, the ancient doctors maintained that man not only lives and depends on the earth but is also dependent on the entire universe. They therefore made the following observations. We can use here the planetary system taught us in school. Here is the earth with the sun's rays shining on it. The sun's rays fall on the earth. As you know, man depends a great deal on sunlight, and we have always used this as a basis of our studies here. Now, these ancient doctors didn't put such great emphasis on the sun, because they felt that its effects were quite obvious, but they observed people who had severe diarrhoea, for example, and they noted that some of them suffered attacks of dizziness at certain times;

their heads became foggy. The heads of others who suffered from severe diarrhoea remained clear, and they only became a little dizzy. These doctors realized that this difference was related to the time the illness occurred. At certain times, nothing could really be done for these patients; without fail, they became very dizzy and then died. At other times, the diarrhoea took a lighter course.

So these doctors began to observe the stars and found that at those times when patients recovered from these typhoid-like illnesses, the planet Venus always stood in such a position that it was blocked by the earth. If the earth is there [see Fig. 33, left], Venus can be located here. If a person is located there on the far side of the earth, no rays from Venus reach him. Since the light of Venus can't pass through the earth, the earth blocks out Venus for him. The ancients, of course, recognized this, since they could not see Venus, as it was blocked by the earth. Now, they continued their observations and discovered that the prognosis was good for a person ill with typhoid in the times when Venus was blocked by the earth. When Venus was not blocked, however, the typhoid patient was subject to Venus's light in addition to sunlight [see Fig. 33, right]. Then the prognosis

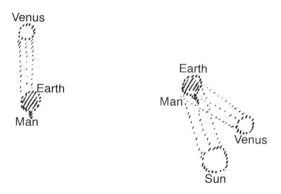

Fig. 33

was bad; the head became dizzy, and the typhoid could not be cured.

Having learned this, these doctors said that since Venus' shining rays pass through the earth, something must be contained in the earth that alters Venus' rays. Now they began to experiment, not with dead people but with patients who were still alive. Nothing happened to those ill with typhoid when lead was given. Regardless of Venus' position, remedies of iron also made no difference. When a typhoid patient was given copper, however, it had a remarkable effect. It offset the dizziness, and the patient began to recover. Aha, said these ancient doctors, copper must be contained within the earth somehow. This copper works within the earth and influences the course of typhoid in a way opposite to that of the detrimental influence of Venus' rays. When these rays hit a typhoid patient directly, they aggravate the effects of the disease, but when copper is given to them, it impedes the progress of typhoid. They now concluded that Venus is in a certain way connected with copper. It was not as if they had held seances and a medium had told them to use copper in cases of typhoid. Instead, they made observations of a kind no longer made today, which were based on an ancient instinct and functioned just as scientifically. So they concluded that in the earth there is copper. This copper is related to the force emanating from Venus. This is seen in the special effect it has on this illness.

They made other observations as well. Take, for example, the case of a patient with problems of vision, a disturbance in the eyes. People can get ailments of the eyes in which vision can become blurred; the pupils can contract. One can have any number of eye ailments. Now, the ancients again experimented and discovered that when the earth blocks Jupiter, eye problems improve more than if Jupiter shines directly on the earth. They explored further and asked what it is in the earth that counteracts Jupiter, and they found that it was tin, particularly when tin was extracted from plants.

Gradually, based on effects upon the human being, they discovered the correspondence between the planets and the metals contained in the earth. They found that Venus is connected with copper, Jupiter with tin, and Saturn with lead. They found that cases of bone diseases, which can also appear in lead poisoning, have something to do with the rays from Saturn; so, for Saturn, they discovered the effects of lead.

For Mars, which has something to do with ailments of the blood, it was easier to find the corresponding metal, iron. Therefore, Mars = iron. For the moon, which stands in a completely different relation since it orbits the earth, they discovered something similar, namely silver. Thus moon = silver.

Now this way of looking at things was completely abandoned later on. Do not assume, however, that it was abandoned in the long-distant past; it was only three or four hundred years ago that these observations stopped being made. In the thirteenth and fourteenth centuries such observations were still made. What was the conclusion? People told themselves that everything that is now separated out into the different planets was once contained within a kind of primordial soup, one universal mist. This concept is quite accurate; it is only wrong to picture that everything can develop out of such a universal mist without spiritual influences. Otherwise one imagines the great universal schoolmaster who controls everything, as I have told you previously! No, but it was once known that everything was at one time dissolved in a kind of primordial soup. There was no sun, moon, or earth; they were all dissolved in the primordial soup and separated only later.

Through the copper contained within the earth, the

planet Venus still exerts an influence. When Venus was still dissolved in the primordial 'mash', it had a special affinity with copper. It was at that time that this bond between them arose. When the moon was still dissolved in everything, silver stood in a special relation to the moon. This knowledge was not a divine revelation, however, nor was it based on arbitrary, authoritarian decree. Rather, it was founded on ancient observations.

It was due to particular circumstances that syphilitic illnesses came into being; in modern centuries, the so-called civilized peoples came into contact with primitive peoples, and there was an interbreeding, a sexual interbreeding of the civilized with the primitive peoples. These syphilitic illnesses were less prevalent when the peoples of the earth were more segregated into races. The way illnesses have arisen, as with syphilitic illnesses, is that something first causes them, but then they reproduce themselves. They become contagious. Something originally must have caused them to arise. The syphilitic illnesses arose through individuals of different races interbreeding sexually with one another. A syphilitic infection cannot occur, for example, except through a small, concealed lesion or worn tissue through which the contagious substance may enter the bloodstream. The contagious syphilitic substance can be smeared on the skin, but if the skin is completely impermeable an infection can't occur. An infection can arise only when the skin is so worn or broken in some spot that the infectious substance can enter through it. You can understand that the infectious substance of syphilis must first have originated where contrasting foreign bloods intermingled. After that, the poison naturally reproduced, but it arose originally when interbreeding increasingly occurred among different peoples. It would probably be interesting to explore the statistics of case histories of this illness in a certain part of Europe that employs various exotic peoples, since the occurrences of sexual excesses cannot always be prevented.

You see, isolated cases of syphilis also occurred in the past, but more numerous incidents date from recent times. They also occurred, however, in that age when something was still known of ancient science. Observations then showed that syphilitic patients improve when Mercury is blocked by the earth. So it was discovered that quicksilver, or mercury, is related to the planet Mercury. In this way the metals were gradually assigned to the planets:

Mercury	—	quicksilver, or mercury
Venus	—	copper
Jupiter	—	tin
Saturn	—	lead
Mars	—	iron
Moon	—	silver

People told themselves that when everything was dissolved in the primordial soup, it was the Venus substance that caused copper to be deposited in the earth, and it was the moon that caused silver to be deposited in the earth.

You see, such observations can be extended. It is remarkable how, at a certain time, it became fashionable in particular circles to make a secret of this ancient science. To this day there are books that a person without knowledge of anthroposophy cannot really read, because he wouldn't be able to make anything of them. All kinds of things are written in them, but people no longer know how to read them today. A Swedish scientist, for example, obtained such a book by Basilius Valentinus, which is rather old, and, in writing about it from the standpoint of today's chemistry, he said that what Valentinus had stated was the purest nonsense. He is right to say this, of course, because chemists today use the terms mercury, iron, and so forth without any reference at all to the human being. A chemist, therefore, though he may be a genius, cannot make anything of what is written in books such as those by Basilius Valentinus. He cannot help thinking himself quite right in saying that it is complete nonsense.

This is not really so, however, because Valentinus still wrote in an age when, for example, it was known that a woman's period occurs every 28 days, as does the full moon. The ancients were certainly clever enough not to attribute a woman's flow of blood to the moon's influence. They told themselves, however, that its rhythm was the same, so there must have been a connection somehow in earlier times, but that man had now freed himself from this connection. They realized that a woman had a similar rhythm to that which the universe has in the waxing and waning moon.

They also knew that when a woman who is having difficulty giving birth and has been in labour for a long time is given a medication containing silver, the labour pains become less severe. This was known. It was also known that when the moon was blocked or hidden by the earth a woman who might have a difficult time giving birth would not have such a painful labour. The influence of silver thus was seen to be connected with the moon.

In Basilius Valentinus' books, 'moon' is often written in the place of 'silver', and 'silver' instead of 'moon'. When this Swedish scientist reads that, he obviously can make nothing of it, regardless of how well informed he is about silver and how it works in a chemical process. It is a complicated matter. You see, the person who wrote the works of Basilius Valentinus was a Benedictine monk. This kind of science was nurtured to a significant degree in Benedictine monasteries in past times, and Benedictine monks were extraordinarily clever in such things.

Today, a Father Mager, who is also a Benedictine monk, travels from one German city to another giving the same lecture against anthroposophy everywhere. In cities all over Germany this Father Mager harangues against anthroposophy. Just recently he was in Cologne. The enemies of anthroposophy differ greatly from one another. When the Jesuits speak against anthroposophy, it differs from what the Benedictine monks say against anthroposophy.

Nowadays the Church suppresses a science that reaches beyond the earth. Gentlemen, do you know what began at a particular time? At a certain point the Church authorities began to conceal and gradually suppress this science that had flourished in the monasteries. Such a science requires a great deal of time, but the monks had this time; they cultivated this science and so were quite useful to humanity in the past. Gradually this was suppressed, however. This suppression of spiritual science often came about in this way.

Today's secular scientists now condemn such ancient science without realizing that a direct line leads from such monks of the Church to them. When monists stand up against anthroposophy, they naturally also object to the Church, but they do not realize that they are its proper pupils. Today's scientists are, in a certain sense, truly Benedictine or Jesuit pupils. They never attended Jesuitical seminars, because such thinking really can be absorbed in the outside world. This is naturally something that must also be taken into consideration.

From what has been said, you can see that the earth on which we live and that yields its various metals to us crystallized out of the primordial soup. What we behold outwardly as the planets, however, has remained behind as metals in the earth. What the earth once did together with Venus has remained in the metal copper. To heal with copper—this is what is accomplished specifically through Venus.

Metals extracted from plants today are especially effective in healing. A metal deposited in the earth has hardened and has lost some of its potency, although it is still effective against head ailments. But copper from the leaves of a plant known to contain quite a bit of it — the amounts are always small, but one can say 'quite a bit' — is especially effective. There are such plants, in the leaves of which copper is dissolved. If remedies are then made from such plants, they are particularly useful in intestinal disturbances due to a thickening of the blood, which lead to typhoid, dysentery, and the like.

This is how healing is related to what can be known about plants. You can see that today things are no longer in order when even the thickest book on botany, although containing all kinds of information, nevertheless lacks the most important instruction medical men should have. There is no mention in these books of the metals that are dissolved in blossoms or roots. If at all, they are noted only in passing. This is a most important point, however, because it shows us that a plant that still contains copper today, for example, is related in its growth process to the planet Venus; it actually opposes the force of Venus and develops its own Venus force by absorbing copper into itself.

We can thus say that once there was a connection between the earth and all the planets that circle the sun today, and this influence has remained behind in the metals. This is what can be said first in reference to this question.

From the foregoing, you can see how important it is to refer back to observations of this kind that existed in the past. We are no longer in the same position, however, that they were in then, because we no longer possess the instincts for healing they once had. Only oxen, cows, sheep and other animals, not human beings, have really retained a marvellous healing instinct, and they avoid eating harmful things and leave anything that wouldn't be good for them.

This is no longer possible for a human being, since he no longer has the healing instinct. Today, by the roundabout way of a spiritual science, we must once again learn to recognize how everything in the planetary system and in the universe is connected with the earthly plane. To do this one must begin at the beginning, one must truly begin at the very beginning.

One must realize the following, for example. One must start with illnesses that affect the human abdomen. If one has such an abdominal illness, one comes to know that the substances present in the blossoms or the highest leaves of plants are especially helpful. Good remedies can be produced for illnesses of the abdominal organs by extracting certain substances from the blossoms and leaves of plants.

Substances taken from the roots of plants, however, provide especially beneficial remedies for everything connected with the human head. Plants are in a reverse relationship to the human being. With plants, the roots are at the bottom and the blossoms are at the top. Man, however, is an upside-down plant. What is root element in the plant is actually in the head of the human being, and the blossom element is more in his abdominal region. You can see this even in their external forms. Man has his head at the top, and his reproductive organs are below. The plant has its roots below, while the blossoms, containing the organs of reproduction, are above. This drawing will help you to understand this [Fig. 34, p. 302]. Here is the human being. Here at the head I draw the root of a correspondingly large plant; here are the stems and leaves. Then, with the blossoms, I come to the abdominal organs. An entire plant is contained within man. The only difference is that it grows from above downwards in him. In a certain sense, man is also a plant. Isn't this apparent? It really is so obvious that everyone must see it. The animal, however, is between the two; in the animal, the plant is in a horizontal position.

Fig. 34

This is really not just a picture; the plant is truly contained within man. Of course, it develops in accordance
with the human form. But imagine that I were to draw this
plant in detail, sketching a real bulbous root and the various
branches — in other words, a real tree. It would be inverted,
however. Here it would have its branches, and the outermost tips would wither a little here and there; there you
have the nervous system! The nervous system is truly an
inverted plant within man that is continuously dying a
little.

Now, we know that plants grow out of the earth. First,
there is winter, then come spring and summer that coax the
plants from the earth. Within the earth is the winter's force.
Through this the plant forms its bulbous root and has its
root force. Then comes the summer's force, and the plant is
coaxed upwards; it is from the earth's circumference that

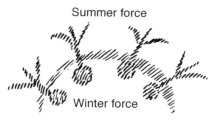

Fig. 35

the plants are drawn forth. Within are the metals — copper, let us say. The sun cannot do anything but coax forth a plant from the earth. Then, once the plant has emerged, it defends itself against the Venus forces. The force of winter from the earth and the summer's force from the universe together make the plant grow.

The human being, however, must have this winter force within his head in order that this root of the nervous system should grow downwards throughout the year. Since a baby, for example, can be born at any time of year, this force must be present in man's head in summer as well as winter. He can no longer receive the winter force in his head from outside himself in summer. This really implies that in primeval times, when the earth was still one with the other planets in the primordial soup, the human being must have absorbed this winter force, which has been handed down to this day. Man owes the winter force in his head to those most ancient times. The head of man was really made in ancient times and today remains the same. So we again find that man's head must be related to what arose on earth in ancient times and today has become completely solidified.

Go out into the mountains of central Switzerland and you will find granite and gneiss to be especially prevalent. The most active substance in granite and gneiss is silicic acid, which is present in quartz in pure form as silicic acid, or silica. It is also the oldest substance on the earth and must be related to the human head forces. This is why illnesses of the head can be most readily cured with remedies made of silica. In the age when silica still played a particular role on earth within the primordial soup and was not as hard as it is today in granite and gneiss, but flowing like a liquid, the force present in the human head was formed — the winter force — and it has been preserved ever since.

So information about the human being must really take into consideration the natural history of the whole earth. This is still connected with the question you asked, gentlemen, and with what I wanted to tell you about it. Goodbye!